"These guys are funky a
on the side. Now that's *J*

"Man, I haven't heard nothing like that since Duck Dunn! You've been my musical director. You've been my friend. You've been my brother. You've been all that stuff. I love you and the band."
– Sam Moore, Sam & Dave
Rock & Roll Hall of Famer

"Ivan is one of the best bass players I've ever worked with. We groove. I'll always admire and cherish the time that we played together."
– Martha Reeves, The Vandellas
Rock & Roll Hall of Famer

"Ivan Bodley, that fabulous bass player, he's fantastic. I love him. Anytime anyone needs a good bass player, I suggest that they call Ivan because he's the best."
– Shirley Alston Reeves, Original Lead Singer of the World-
Famous Shirelles, Rock & Roll Hall of Famer

"Ivan is not only an astounding bass guitarist and the new hardest working man in show business. He's also a very soulful and entertaining writer. I love his new book."
– Chris Frantz, Talking Heads, Tom Tom Club
Rock & Roll Hall of Famer

"It has been my pleasure to have you on board. Your talent and professionalism have been a wonderful and welcome addition to my show, to say nothing of your exuberant personality."
– Gloria Gaynor

"Aside from his bass playing, which is flawless (most of the time), he has a terrific disposition. Ivan is one of the most consummate musicians that I've ever played with. He's a good guy, and I really love him."
– Jay Siegel, The Tokens

"Ivan is the baddest. There's nobody any better, bass player and conductor. At 6 ft. 5 in. you can't miss him. There's really no one better that I'd rather have Music Directing than Ivan Bodley. Real easy going, easy to work with, nice guy."

– Dee Dee Kenniebrew, The Crystals

"Ivan is a true inspiration. He's a student of musical styles, a scientist of sound, a master of groove and a teacher of truth. Super generous of spirit. All with a discerning wink of the eye, with a healthy helping of humor. I love the man!"

– Will Lee

"When you're talking to somebody about Ivan, you're tempted to talk about what a nice guy he is, what a great player he is, how smart and funny he is. But that's really just the surface. At heart, Ivan is a writer. And he's a really good writer. I'm not talking about this book – I mean music. Ivan has a remarkable melodic sense, an understanding of groove and deep knowledge of almost every style that has ever existed. F**k being nice."

– Don Dixon, Producer

"Ivan Bodley, great bass player, excellent conductor. He hears everything! But most importantly, he stays super cool under pressure. The best!" **– Charlie Giordano**

"The guy is a great bass player. We've played all over the world together. Ivan is also a great conductor and a really great acoustic bass player. Not many people know that. He's going to be playing with me, and I with him, for a long time to come. This is the kind of guy you want on bass. You want him onstage with you. This cat is aces all the way around in his presence on the bottom end."

– Crispin Cioe, The Uptown Horns

"I really like writing with Ivan. He's a natural and one of the nicest people I know. His touring skills are mind boggling ... how many nights he's out on the road with as many groups. I'm very impressed and always have a smile for him."

– Lady Miss Kier, Deee-Lite

Am I Famous Yet?

Memoir of a Working-Class Rock Star

By Ivan "Funkboy" Bodley

Foreword by **Stanley Clarke**

CONTENTS

FOREWORD

I first met Ivan in the 1980s when he was a DJ at his college radio station. He was just a kid, a fan, but he was playing my records and he interviewed me on the air. When he graduated, he went on to get an industry job at my record label. He ended up writing the liner notes for my album *If This Bass Could Only Talk* (Portrait Records, 1988) and my bio for my website. I've always told him that he was gifted with the pen. He even studied bass privately with me for a short time in Los Angeles. I still introduce him to people as my student.

I gave him a bass years ago as a thank-you for his help on a publicity campaign for one of my albums. I signed the back of the bass with this inscription:

"Thanks for the press! This is to assure that you don't forget your duties as a member of the Inter-Galactic Bass Scouts. Stanley Clarke, Founder." I even wrote "Ivan the Terrible" on the front of the bass so people would remember him when they saw him playing it. It turns out he didn't really need my help for people to remember him. As you'll read, he remembered his Bass Scout duties as well.

I watched him make the agonizing decision to come out from behind his desk at the record company, go back to music school, and do what he needed to do to become an actual bass player. He has become an accomplished musician who has worked with dozens of well-known artists, most notably in the world of classic soul music and on Broadway.

He's a wild-looking cat, too. I remember when he did a photo shoot for his first appearance in *Bass Player* magazine. The editors asked him for some tamer photos. He was too much for them!

I tease him all the time because he's constantly worried that he'll never work again. Yet he's the workingest cat I know. He needs to learn to relax!

This book is a chronicle of Ivan's journey through the world as a bass player, a hard-working musician. It's about his search for what fame is, versus what's really important in life. I think you'll enjoy reading it as much as I did.

– **Stanley Clarke**

Stanley and Ivan, Los Angeles, 1988

1 INTRODUCTION

D ude, you've got to write a book!" I can't tell you how many times people have said that to me after I've shared some anecdote from the three-ring circus that is my alleged musical career. But I always have the same thought to myself: Who cares? Who would want to read such a thing? Why is my experience different or more interesting than anyone else's?

Well, my experience isn't special. It probably won't seem particularly unique to anyone who has been a musician or a freelance artist for any period of time. All I can say about it is that my specific combination of road stories is something that only happened to me.

I have a quote that I printed out and tacked to the wall of my practice room from a commencement address by the great pianist Oscar Peterson delivered at the Berklee College of Music: "Remember that each of you has something to give that no one else has." I keep it there to remind myself that although there is always someone who can play faster than me, sing higher, or write better compositions than I do, that I need to keep going anyway.

I remember being a student in the dorms at Berklee and really just keeping to myself, studying what I needed to fill in my particular gaps in my knowledge. I couldn't compete and try to be the fastest or the loudest or the most intricate. There was always someone who could do that particular thing way better than I could. Somehow I've been employed as a full-time professional musician for over 26 years. I must be doing something right. Either that or I just don't have any sense.

Having averaged 228 gigs a year in the past dozen years, for which I've been keeping meticulous records (I find strange comfort in statistics), I'm approaching 3,000 career shows. I have traveled to 29 countries, backed 50 inductees to the Rock & Roll Hall of Fame, and played for audiences of over 80,000 people. I have performed in everything from jazz duos up to full symphony orchestras, in venues ranging from dive bars to Carnegie Hall.

I recently added another snapshot to my celebrity photo album on my website: www.funkboy.net. I played and was photographed with former teen idol and star of *American Bandstand*, Fabian. If you were a teenage girl in 1959 you absolutely know who Fabian is the way any tween knows who Justin Bieber is today. If you're not of a certain age, chances are you may never even have heard of Fabian. Now in his 70s, he seems delighted with the reactions of his fans to this day and grateful for a long career in show business.

The celebrities' gallery on my Facebook page has a sub-caption: "Me standing next to famous people for 1/500th of a second before they caught me and complained." I have worked with at least 95 percent of the people pictured. I don't collect photos of random celebrities just because they're famous, although there are a couple of those in there.

I have a photo of Bono from U2 strangling me, for example. I never actually worked with him. It's just a great shot. I did end up playing his musical compositions when I subbed in the pit of *Spider-Man, Turn Off the Dark* over to the Broad Way. Also, his co-writer of that musical and his bandmate, The Edge, once played with the Sam Moore band when I was music director. So I have a picture onstage with The Edge. I feel like I have enough "near-Bono" experiences to justify including the photo.

As I was adding the Fabian photo to the gallery, I noticed that there were over nearly 300 pictures in there. I think my photo album may have officially Jumped the Shark at this point. It probably did that a long time ago. I'm not sure what this says about me or my career. Perhaps I truly am the gig-whore that I jokingly claim that I am. Perhaps I can't keep a job.

Mostly the photo gallery is a testament to the fact that having low self-esteem makes me think I can't be interesting on my own. Without the celebrity in the photo, internally I doubt that anyone would give a rat's ass about me or what I do for a living. As this theory pertains to any random stranger, that's probably true. And why should they?

Maybe all that a career in music ultimately gets you is a bunch of cool snapshots and some road stories. Maybe I put all of those photos in there in the hopes that however you define fame, there will be at least someone in one of those photos that you've heard of. Maybe I'm the most famous musician you've never heard of.

I have had to put a lot of thought over the years into exactly what constitutes fame, rock stardom, and career success. I've been around a bunch of fame in my travels, mostly for short intervals at a time. Mostly I'm just working for a living. Sure, there are stories to tell. They run the gamut from inspiring to horrifying. Mostly I have to laugh to keep from crying. It's been a long drive past an infinite freak show of roadside attractions.

I'm also constantly reminded what a solitary career choice this is. Even though all of my work is done in ensembles, they are ever changing ensembles. Out of thousands of gigs, at most a hundred or so were ever done with the same group of people. The nature of my particular journey is to have been a substitute musician in so many situations. I'm usually the new guy. Even when I have glimpses into being on the inside, I still feel as though I'm on the outside.

I had this thought recently at an exclusive invite-only Tony Awards after-party for yet another show where I was a substitute player. Though I knew most of the people there I still had the distinct feeling that I was somehow crashing the party. This is not an appeal for sympathy. I'm just not a very social person. I would probably feel the same way at the office holiday party if I were a banker. It speaks as much as to my personality type as to anything else, though it is a peculiar line of work that I'm in.

I have to apologize for most of these stories in advance. I don't like sounding like an operatic diva warming up, "Me, me, me, me!" But these things mostly happened to me. Sometimes the narrative voice will shift to "we," not meaning a royal we, just times when things happened collectively to the group I was traveling with at the time.

At the center of it all is just me playing the role of the circus freak, the clown, the fool, the *bouffon*. I've long said of musicians that we are mere curios in the parlors of the rich and famous. Regardless of any artistic aspirations I may have, my bread and butter is responding to the call: "Dance, monkey, dance!"

I've also long maintained that a trained monkey could do what I do. It's not that terribly difficult to play a musical instrument, especially the bass. It's only four strings. It's one note at a time. How hard could it be? But apparently if anyone could do it, everyone would. Yet they don't.

After looking at the business end of a Fender bass for more than 38 years, I now know a thing or two. I've been a place or two. I've seen a train wreck or three. I'll try to pass some of it along to you in words as best I can. Too many of these stories start verbally with: "Y'all ain't gonna believe this." It's been a long road, a hard road, an insane road, a rewarding, hilarious, and heartbreaking road.

Join me, won't you?

A cat on the road ...

2 WHEN IT ALL GOES RIGHT

Most anecdotes are about when something goes haywire. When things go normally there's nothing to talk about. There's no intrigue in the everyday. Since this collection of stories from a now-lengthy career is mostly about the less-than-predictable moments it begs the question: Why pursue a livelihood fraught with constant frustration? That's a fair question.

There are some pat answers to this question, like the potential for fame and fortune. It should appear to even the most stubborn of us that after a few years (or decades?) that the aspirations for wealth and accolades just aren't likely to be realized. Any pragmatic person should understand that the odds against becoming a rich and famous rock star are staggering. Nevertheless, we persist.

What then is the payoff?

There are as many answers to this question as there are different personality types in the world. For me it comes down to the fact that I just like playing my stupid bass. I would rather be doing that than almost anything else in the world. I would rather be playing a four-hour gig starting at midnight for $40 than sitting on the couch watching movies. It's just that simple.

That being said, there are some gigs that are much better than others. What happens when it all goes right?

As an example, I will cite a Sam Moore gig at the Tokyo Jazz Festival in 2008. I had been Sam's music director and bass player for about six years by that point. He had just released a major-label album a couple of years earlier. He was in his 70s and was enjoying a bit of a career resurgence.

We had been flying to Japan about once a year to play primarily at the Blue Note club in Tokyo. It was probably our third trip to Japan when Sam was booked to play the Tokyo Jazz Festival. The bill for the day was Robben Ford, Sam Moore, and Sly & The Family Stone. The venue held about 5,000 people and was sold out. The concert was to be broadcast live nationally on television as well. It was a big gig that we were really looking forward to.

We had a 14-piece band, Sam plus four horns, four background singers, and a five-piece rhythm section with yours truly at the helm. We had done enough shows by this point to know what we were doing. Though the band wasn't performing together more than about six times per year on average, we were still in the zone that particular day.

When we hit the stage the roar from 5,000 of our closest friends blasted us in the face like the exhaust of a jet engine. Until you've stood in front of that kind of mass energy from a huge crowd of people, it's an almost impossible feeling to explain.

The room was electric. The Japanese are a reserved and orderly society. They seem to really like rules, regimen, and dignity. Five thousand screaming Japanese already carry a much bigger punch than 5,000 yelling Americans because you know they really mean it. They're going for it. When a group of people who pride themselves on holding back decide to cut loose, you had better be able to surf the wave or know how to swim really well.

Now add to this mixture one of the great soul music voices of this or any age. Sam is a true first tenor and actually sings four songs in his catalog in higher keys than when he recorded them 50 years ago. Higher keys. Think about that for a second. Every other singer in the world eventually lowers their live keys a couple of tones just for self-preservation as they age.

Very few septuagenarians can sing with the same range they had as teenagers. That's just a fact of nature. Beyond his age there were some dark years in the 1970s when Sam wasn't taking as good care of his personal health as he might have. You can interpret that to mean whatever you choose. And you would probably be right. That's all well documented in his own oral history book. I'll let him tell you those stories directly if you're interested.

Yet the current live keys are higher. Sam is just a freak of nature in that way. His voice is astounding. Not a rock star on the planet comes up to him with anything less than pure reverence for his instrument and what he's accomplished. I have met some of the biggest music celebrities in the world standing next to Sam. Whatever giant egos they might be reported to have, none are in evidence when they're talking to Sam.

One of the many things that also makes Sam great is that he is a master showman. He knows how to work a crowd. Given the right circumstances in which he doesn't have to worry about the band playing the wrong notes, or the monitors not allowing him to hear himself, nor any other distractions, he is a force of nature onstage.

The Tokyo Jazz Festival of 2008 was just such an evening. We brought Sam on with his monster hit "Hold On, I'm Comin'." The crowd was rocking. We were off to the races. The band was firing on all cylinders. Sam was in amazing voice and humor. The audience was eating right out of his hand. Toward the end of the show was when we got deeper into the '60s Stax hits that first made Sam famous. One of these is a beautiful 12/8 ballad called "When Something Is Wrong with My Baby" written, as most of the Stax hits were, by Isaac Hayes and David Porter. I always loved playing that song with Sam because he sang the crap out of it every night. It's a gut-wrenching song about true devotion to a loved one. The main message being that any problem that my true love is experiencing is also a problem for me.

The otherwise reserved Japanese audience members were openly sobbing during this song, full-on ugly crying from a people not known for being effusive. It was unbelievably moving to witness, much less to be an integral part in having created this moment.

Then we tore into my absolute favorite groove to play in all of Sam's catalog: "I Thank You." The bubbly and unbelievably funky eighth-note octave bass line on that song created at Stax by the legendary Duck Dunn is a blast to play when I'm alone at the house, but especially fun to play on a giant concert stage with the artist who made the song famous. The top of that song is an open, occasionally lengthy, ad-lib section. What I would tell musicians joining our band for the first time—like occasional local pickup horn sections—was this: The start of every chart is an open vamp, meaning a section that repeats until there's a cue to continue on from the conductor (who is me in these situations). When that cue is received, the chart reads down exactly as written until, that is, we get to the end. Then we're in another vamp until I cue the ending.

It is precisely in these vamp sections, the non-written ones, that the magic would happen with Sam. He would go into these call-and-response sections with the audience, or say what was on his mind, or go wherever his creativity would take him.

To digress for a moment, there was another gig where Sam was to do a duet with a gentleman nicknamed "Sting." They were going to sing a Grover Washington, Jr./Bill Withers tune, "Just the Two of Us." I'm sorry for that name I just dropped. I'll pick it up and explain more about that later.

Anyway, Sam's buddy Sting likes to rehearse and likes to know exactly what he's doing onstage. Fair enough. Most performers prefer that, evidenced that day by the fact that Mr. Sting had brought his own teleprompter complete with operator for the occasion. At the sound check Sam clearly didn't intimately know the melody or the phrasing of the song. The words were on Sting's teleprompter. But Sam was pretty loose on everything to say the least.

Backstage after the sound check Sting came up to me and asked about Sam: "Is he going to be all right out there?" I attempted to explain to Sting what little I understood about the internal machinations and improvisatory performance style of Sam. I told Sting, "I don't know what he's going to do on the show. You don't know what he's going to do. And more importantly, HE doesn't know what he's going to do."

Based on Sting's concerns I went back to Sam's dressing room and asked him if he wanted to go over the song before the show.

He said, "Nope."

True to my prediction, during the show Sam started the song very shakily. By the end of the tune, by improvising call-and-response lines with Sting, Sam had leveled the building. I've seen him do it countless times. It's never less than amazing.

This is all to preface that by the time we got into the "I Thank You" intro in Tokyo, Sam was in his sweet spot to begin to take the already enthusiastic audience on an emotional musical journey the likes of which they had never witnessed. He did just that. The call-and-response built and built to an amazing crescendo before the main body of the tune even started. You could almost feel the entire building bouncing to the funky beat. When the song finally landed in its full proper form, the shock wave of energy in the room increased just that much more.

At the end of "I Thank You" Sam would wave the band out and have the audience sing the song's hook back to him. It's difficult to describe the feeling generated by the sound of 5,000 people screaming at you in unison in a language that isn't their native one, "I Thank You!" After the audience would do this three times, we would launch into the intro of Sam's most famous hit, the Grammy Award-winning "Soul Man." On any regular night this would push an audience from enthusiastic to ecstatic. On this particular night it almost blew us through the back wall of the theatre.

It was one of the greatest live performance moments I have ever seen, never mind actually been a part of. We left the stage sweaty, spent, exhausted, and knowing that we had played our asses off because Sam had given us a very special opportunity to do so.

That's why we do it. That's why we suffer the dues of this business, for fleeting moments like that one. I've seen video footage from that show. I wasn't just imagining how great it was. Sam really did knock them all dead. I was proud to be standing behind him that night as I always am.

We didn't get rich that day. We didn't get famous. But we did participate in an enormous confluence of human energy and adulation that we were all instrumental in. The love in that room transcended language barriers, international borders, and all cultural differences. Soul music by the Soul Man carried the day. It was truly a beautiful thing to behold.

3 BUT THEN SLY ...

After Sam Moore's triumphant performance at the Tokyo Jazz Festival, Sly & The Family Stone took the stage. We were all thrilled to be able to see Sly, who had been a notorious recluse in recent years. He had just begun to make public appearances again in what turned out to be a fairly brief window of performing.

The concert hall, fresh off of Sam's set, was still electrified and eagerly anticipating the emergence of the legendary Sly Stone on his first-ever visit to the country of Japan. He had never played there even back in his heyday.

Onstage that night were Cynthia Robinson, Jerry Martini, Sister Rose Stone, and Sly, four of the original seven members of The Family Stone. It was a historic night. We in the Sam Moore band were watching from the wings like the eager young fans we were.

The formula for that era of gigs was that The Family Stone would take the stage initially without Sly and play their up-tempo hits like "Thank You (Falettinme Be Mice Elf Agin)," "Everyday People," and "Dance to the Music." Then whenever Sly was ready, he would join the band for as long as he felt like it. He would then leave and let the band finish the show in the same fashion as it began.

A brief word is necessary about both Sly's state of physical health at the time and his relationship to the government of the country of Japan. While I have no direct knowledge of his personal appetites, it is well documented that Sly has been arrested multiple times for drug-related offenses. As such, the law-and-order loving government of Japan had worked out a deal with the promoters of the concert to have Sly's whereabouts known at all times. I don't know if this included something like an ankle bracelet or a personal chaperone. But the word backstage was that some sort of deal had been struck.

Furthermore, while The Family Stone was obliged to perform for 75-90 minutes, as is standard for concert appearances, Sly Stone himself was under no specific time constraint as long as he appeared for some portion of the set.

Again, I have no personal knowledge of his use of intoxicants, legal or illegal, at the time. What I witnessed was a gaunt and hunched over Sly Stone approaching the stage. Let's just say that it was unlikely that he had just come from the gym or the health food store looking the way he did. He shuffled slowly past about 3 feet from me in the wings of the theatre, and headed out onstage to join the concert already in progress.

The Family Stone had been tearing the roof off of the place. They were fantastic. When Sly finally showed up onstage, the place went ballistic. The ovation was staggering.

Sly sat at his keyboard and adjusted the microphone to meet his stooped posture and launched into his opening song. He is famous for being an artistic architect, constructing his band from mixed-race and mixed-gender musicians. He is one of the great social commentators of the 1960s, as legendary for his politics as for his music. No opportunity is lost on Sly in terms of significance or importance.

For his first selection upon the occasion of his first-ever appearance in Japan and in front of a nationally televised audience, Sly chose to sing, yes, that's right: "Don't Call Me Nigger, Whitey." As we were standing in the wings witnessing this, our jaws collectively hit the floor.

He continued on with several mellower tempo songs like "If You Want Me to Stay" and "Family Affair." After exactly 22 minutes (we know this because the Japanese time these things), Sly stood up as abruptly as he had appeared and shuffled back off into the wings. He was done for the night. The Family Stone continued without him, rocking the hall into a frenzy until curfew.

The following night we were told that Sly & The Family Stone did two shows at the Blue Note club in Tokyo. Sly was on for 12 minutes during the first show and only 9 minutes for the second show. He fulfilled his contract. The audience got a glimpse of a true legend. And everybody was in some sense satisfied.

For us it was a sight both beautiful and terrible to behold. He was still Sly. He had created so much music that shaped an entire generation. Seeing him and hearing him play and sing gave us a glimpse of all that excellence in person, in the flesh. Hearing him scream a high note, even if only just the one note, was thrilling to no end.

I'm told by people who knew him back in the day that he was never one for doing long shows. They were all notoriously under half an hour. The 22 minutes he spent onstage at the Tokyo Jazz Festival was unprecedented in his modern history and only slightly less than he might have done in his heyday.

But it was also evident that time hadn't been kind to his body for whatever reason. Most likely he's been the source of his own physical abuse according to many accounts that I have read. That he's still alive after all of that is amazing enough. It's hard to think about all of the music that he might have created in the past 50 years had he kept his wits about him. The world will never know.

4 THE KING OF ROCK & SOUL

I figure that I can lull you into this book with a description of one of the more colorful characters I've worked with before beginning to bore you with the necessary but difficult to digest biographical background information that is inherent in all memoirs. So here goes.

Solomon Burke was the self-proclaimed "King of Rock & Soul." To say that he was a character of epic proportions is an understatement. When I met him, he was already 425 pounds, an impressive number that continued to increase all the way until the end of his life when he eventually got closer to 500 pounds.

Dr. Burke started his R&B career when he was still a teenager in the mid-1950s billed as "The Boy Preacher." Fifty-five years, 38 albums selling 17 million copies, 26 charting singles, a Rock & Roll Hall of Fame induction, and a Grammy Award later, his life ended in an airport while he was on tour at age 70.

He fathered 21 children, 14 daughters and 7 sons, and was a licensed undertaker in addition to being a performer. His exploits are legendary and well-documented, including stories about him selling sandwiches to his own band on overnight bus rides between concerts and asking for permission to sell concessions at the Apollo Theatre. When the theatre agreed to this, Dr. Burke sold popcorn to the patrons rather than albums and T-shirts as the venue had expected. He was forever entrepreneurial to say the least.

Instead of going into the historical record, which I was not present for, I will concentrate on only the things I saw while performing with him about eight times over a period of about 10 years. Even in that brief amount of time there was a lot to talk about.

Starting in the mid-1990s, every time Solomon came through New York City he would hire The Uptown Horns to be his backing band. The Uptown Horns have a great story about Solomon signing a cocktail napkin in lieu of a contract in case a gig they played with him in the '80s that got recorded ever got released as an album. It did.

It became a best-selling album on Rounder records at the time. Saxophonist Arno Hecht kept and found the napkin. They presented it to the record company and ended up getting paid royalties, which helped mitigate the indignity of not even being paid for the gig itself in the first place. Solomon had skipped out. But you'll have to ask the Horns to give you the details. I wasn't there.

I first met Dr. Burke at an outdoor summertime gig we did in Central Park for about 10,000 of our closest friends. It was near 100 degrees that day. Because of the extreme weather, the band was outfitted in matching Solomon Burke black T-shirts. But Dr. Burke performed the entire 90-minute show wearing a full gold lamé suit. He did shed the ermine cape right after he came onstage. But the suit remained. I can only hope that the shiny nature of his gold lamé suit somehow reflected heat rather than absorbed it. It couldn't have been comfortable for him.

Also notable about that performance was the fact that our band was eight pieces, four rhythm section players and four horns. Dr. Burke had arranged for an additional six horn players to join us, giving us a *10*-piece horn section. Sonically this extended well beyond the timbre of Count Basie and started to get into USC marching band territory. It was a lot of brass.

Most of these extra horn players were from Los Angeles, where Dr. Burke lived. He arranged to have the musicians meet him at LAX airport to travel to New York City to perform with him in Central Park. It was a big gig that any cat would have jumped at. Once at the airport Dr. Burke informed the horn players that their passenger van was waiting for them by the curb and that he would meet them in New York.

Yes, that's right. He flew.

They drove 41 hours straight to get to the gig without having been told they were to be traveling via interstate highway or given the opportunity to pack for such an adventure. The first time we met them they were just arriving at the venue, rolling out of the epic van ride, and looking all the worse for wear and tear.

I don't remember if we had a rehearsal for this gig or not. I don't think so. We had some recordings to study including the aforementioned live album with The Uptown Horns on it. I made a four-page cheat sheet for myself of his hits that would typically occur during his shows.

There was no set list at a Solomon Burke concert. This was slightly problematic for my personality, which preferred to know what the heck I was going to be expected to do ahead of time so that I could prepare myself. This was even slightly more troublesome since I was the bass player.

More so than any other member of the band, the bass player is expected to play the correct root note of every chord on the first beat of every measure of the music. Keyboard players can listen to the bass note and then make an internal decision whether they agree or disagree with the choice. They can fill in a chord voicing later in the bar on beat two or three and still sound like they know what they're doing.

Guitarists and horn players can ostensibly noodle around anywhere in the key of the song and sound like they're not polluting the air. Drummers can get away with murder. They can jam through almost anything in common 4/4 time by playing a standard beat pattern and sound like a genius. But the bass player, not so much.

To further complicate the situation, Solomon didn't even call a particular song nor, did he have a music director count the band in. Solomon just took off singing a melody a cappella. It was your job in his backing band to figure out what song he was singing, what the chord changes were, what the rhythm was. Then you had to catch up. He was already into the second or third bar of the song before the band could process the information and fall into line behind him.

All you knew for sure is that it was in the key of G. Every song he did was in the key of G. I have seen innumerable bands deliberate endlessly about their set lists not wanting to put songs adjacent that are in the same feel or the same key. Not so for Dr. Burke. Everything was in G. And it was never boring for a second.

As songs would get started, Dr. Burke would also very often medley songs in a similar feel together. When he was finished with one song, he would launch immediately into the next, which required some keen listening skills. As I heard a new song starting, I would play it if I knew it. If I didn't know it, I would look at the keyboard player or the guitar player to see if either one of them knew it well enough to offer some assistance with chord changes. This system worked well for us for many shows. Until that one night.

We were playing a 12/8 ballad medley onstage at Lincoln Center's Avery Fisher Hall for the JVC Jazz Festival, opening for

Wilson Pickett, and being reviewed by the *New York Times*. My grandparents were even in the audience. You know, no pressure. Dr. Burke started singing the lyrics to Ray Charles's "Drown in My Own Tears." I didn't really know the chord changes. I looked at the keyboard player. The keyboard player looked at the guitar player. The guitar player looked at me. No one really had it confidently.

I could feel the blood draining from my face as we tried in vain to play some generic chord pattern that would allow Solomon to do his thing for the duration of the tune. He knew instantly that we weren't with him. So he sang just a couple of lines of it and moved on to something else. We were only twisting in the wind for about 20 to 30 seconds at most. But it felt like an eternity. It didn't stop or even slow down the show. I'm quite sure most of the audience had no idea of the panic we felt for that brief moment.

The show was a tremendous success received by a thundering ovation. We bounded offstage feeling like superheroes that night for pulling off a minor miracle. As I got to the wings the master of ceremonies for the evening, who was the great DJ and record producer, Bob Porter, looked at me and said dryly, " 'Drown in My Own Tears' huh?" Busted. I think he was the only one who knew. But I was amused that he had caught it so adeptly and commented on it.

That was the one dodgy moment in that show.

There was a dodgier moment at the sound check that same day, however. That was one of the few times when Solomon actually showed up for sound check. There was no real reason for him to be there. As long as his microphone was on and loud enough in the monitors, he was good to go. That day he had a young(er) lady with him whom he wanted to have sing the Gershwin standard "Summertime" as part of the show. In previous concerts he would occasionally have one of his children sing a song to give him a little break. So the fact that he wanted someone else to sing wasn't alarming.

What was the beginning of the concern was the fact that she called the song key as "re minor," which in Europe, in a fixed-do musical system, means the key of D minor. But in America with very trained and seasoned musicians onstage at Lincoln Center this meant absolutely nothing and was met with blank stares. After I made her repeat her request, not sure I had understood it the first time, I realized what was going on and called out "D minor!" to the band.

As we started to rehearse the song, it was instantly and abundantly clear that she had absolutely no experience performing or any musical sensibility at all as far as we could tell. While her pitch was fairly good, not great, she started each vocal phrase in a completely random spot. This meant that we had to redefine where the downbeat of each bar was every couple of measures just to make the chord changes sound correct under her melody. The panic started to set in. This would not be an acceptable performance in a nightclub much less onstage at Lincoln Center. But who were we to contradict the boss?

Fortunately, our drummer that day, the late-great Tyrone "Crusher" Green, had known Solomon for many years. He pulled Solomon aside after the rehearsal and had a little confidential man-to-man talk with him. I don't know what Crusher said to him. All I know is that the young(er) lady made no appearance onstage at the concert that evening, much to our relief.

Since Dr. Burke was over 400 pounds, he wasn't what you would call an active dancer onstage. On his technical rider his list of requirements included a throne to be placed center stage, where he would hold court during his performances while remaining seated. He also required two dozen long-stemmed roses that he would hand out to ladies in the audience. Oh, he was a charmer.

One of his sons would be standing beside him for the entire show as Dr. Burke performed as a valet or aide-de-camp, ever ready to mop the master's brow as the emotions of the evening poured forth. I have never before nor since witnessed a man able to enchant and beguile an entire arena full of 15,000 souls using nothing more than the power of his voice. It was a powerful voice, to be sure. But it was also the instrument of one of the greatest master showmen of all time. He knew how to work a room into a frenzy.

One of his classic moves came as a song was building to an emotional, rhythmic, and dynamic peak. At the pinnacle he would take the cowboy hat off of his head and hurl it to the back of the stage in dramatic fashion. This never failed to get less than a wave of cheers forceful enough to remind one of a grand-slam homer in the bottom of the ninth inning at a crucial baseball game.

The biggest climax of the evening was reserved for later in the show when at just the right moment Solomon would stand up from the throne as he hit the high note at the end of the song. In contrast to his remaining seated the entire length of the show, this move would turn the room upside down every time. It sounded like everyone's team had just won the Superbowl every time he did it. It was astounding.

It was well known that as a person of such buoyant entrepreneurial spirit, Dr. Burke was not to be treated lightly in matters of business, specifically monetary exchange. To wit, it became one of our bandleader's jobs to follow Solomon offstage at the end of every show. As we would play his chaser music to walk him off, waving to the crowd and blowing kisses to the audience, our bandleader, Crispin, would be in lockstep right behind him.

Crispin's task at that point was to follow Solomon into the dressing room and just sit with him. Whatever after-show wardrobe changes were necessary and whatever backstage meet-and-greet were incidental, Crispin's focus was to make sure that Solomon didn't leave the building before paying the band in cash. While this seemed a bit overcautious, there had been unfortunate precedent for this in years past.

Solomon had come up on the Chitlin' Circuit. He was a true "C.C. Rider." You might not have known the origin of that song title. Well, there it is. The ethos of the Circuit was to try to get yours before someone else absconded with it. Tales of misappropriation of funds are legion. Artists routinely got screwed and might be forced to pass the savings on to the next person in line. It usually wasn't personal. Business was business.

Payola was also the way things got done back in the day when it came to paying money for getting records played on the radio. It was the business model for the entire industry before, during, and after it was made officially illegal by federal law in 1960.

At one concert in the 1990s in Brooklyn, the master of ceremonies announcing the show was the dean of New York broadcasting, the late Hal Jackson. Mr. Jackson had been a DJ since

1939 in Washington, D.C., and was on the air in New York City from 1954 until his death in 2012 at age 96. He was a legend, an institution.

Mr. Jackson went way back with Solomon Burke to the start of his recording career in 1955. They knew each other for close to 50 years and respected each other. After Mr. Jackson announced Solomon, with the band playing the overture, Dr. Burke took the stage. As he sat on his throne, he whispered something to his son/valet who was at his side. Then he told the band to break it down.

As we were playing at an underscore volume, Solomon made a lengthy speech to the audience about how great Mr. Jackson was and how he had been crucial in the development of Solomon's career. Without the airplay that Mr. Jackson had given him in New York, none of this would ever have happened, etc.

We weren't listening that closely to what Solomon was saying because we were distracted by the actions of his son at that moment. After Solomon whispered in his ear, his son turned around with his back to the audience but in full view of us in the band. Out of his white tuxedo jacket pocket he pulled a bank envelope. Out of the envelope he counted one, two, three, four, five crisp new $100 bills. The Benjamins, if you will.

He returned the envelope to his jacket pocket, ostensibly with less of our band salary in it than it had just seconds ago, which was only of mild concern at this point. He folded the $500 and placed the money into his dad's hand out of sight of the audience. As Solomon was making his heartfelt speech about Mr. Jackson, he shook hands with Mr. Jackson with the cash in his palm the way you would tip a maître d' to get a good table at a fancy restaurant. This is a move we call the "happy handshake."

Mind you, this was onstage in front of thousands of people. Mr. Jackson felt the paper in his hand, looked down to see what it was, and literally did a double take. A klaxon sound effect "ah-OOO-gah" would have been well placed here.

He instantly started saying, "Oh, no, no" off microphone where no one was able to hear him over the band playing and Solomon giving his speech over the PA. He tried valiantly to hand the money back to Solomon who was having none of it. Without creating a scene or public embarrassment, his only course of action was to wave at the crowd and walk offstage. All of us in the band were watching this happen with our mouths open. Now that's old school.

We played with Solomon many times and loved it every time. Once we played as a surprise at Ahmet and Mica Ertegun's 40th wedding anniversary party in the penthouse ballroom of the swanky Pierre Hotel in midtown Manhattan. The all-star guest list included Mick Jagger, Peter Jennings, Bette Midler, other stars, wealthy socialites, and people generally in vogue. Ahmet was the founder of Atlantic Records and had signed Solomon to the label in 1961. Almost all of Solomon's charting hits were on Atlantic between 1961 and 1969 when he left for Bell Records.

Do you have any idea how difficult it is to sneak a 425-pound man and an eight-piece R&B band into anything? It's not easy. I can assure you. One tends to make quite an entrance with that much hardware in one's arsenal. Even with the slow reveal, it was still a surprise performance to a small but well-heeled crowd.

Though never known as a performer of any sort, Ahmet ended up sitting in with us and trading lines of a blues with Solomon. That's why I feel comfortable putting Ahmet's name on my résumé. I actually played with him.

The last time I saw Solomon was in London in 2007. I hadn't played with him in about six years. We were both at a gig that was the after-party to the Ahmet Ertegun tribute concert at the O2 arena after Ahmet passed away. This concert was famous for reuniting Led Zeppelin for the first time in 20 years. They released a live concert film and album from this gig called *Celebration Day*. It was star-studded beyond star-studded. People had paid the highest scalped ticket prices in history and traveled from around the world to see this legendary gig.

So instead of the 20,000-seat arena, we were playing the after-party in an adjacent theatre called the Indigo that seated a measly 2,350 people. The bill for this concert was Solomon Burke, Percy Sledge, Ben E. King, and Sam Moore, all former Atlantic Records artists. That night turned out to be the last time I saw Percy Sledge as well.

I was there music directing for Sam Moore. The house band was Bill Wyman's Rhythm Kings featuring Albert Lee on guitar and on keyboards Chris Stainton, who played at Woodstock with Joe Cocker's Grease Band. I had to kick Bill Wyman of the Rolling Stones off the bass so I could conduct the band. No, I was not worthy. Yeah, it was a heavy night.

As such, the credentials one needed to travel freely backstage at the arena were very specific and highly sought after. Security was extremely tight. For instance, Paul Rodgers from Bad Company was scheduled to sing a song with Sam Moore on his set. But as showtime was nearing, he was nowhere to be found. It turned out that initially he didn't have the right laminated pass to get backstage to where we were. Here was one of the most famous rock stars in England unable to get backstage to do his own gig. He eventually made it in time for the set. But it was that nuts.

Earlier in the evening I decided to see if my laminated pass would get me into the main arena to see part of Led Zeppelin's set, not really believing that it would. After all, I was the hired help for the after-party, not even part of the main event. Yet off I went to find out. I passed checkpoint after checkpoint with my laminate hanging around my neck. I didn't ask anyone's permission. I just walked purposefully by a number of different security guards who were all eyeing my pass.

I passed yet another guard and went through a set of double doors. To my complete astonishment I found myself inside the main arena standing in a walkway about 25 feet from John Paul Jones's butt as he sat at the organ onstage playing with the almighty Led Zeppelin. It was shock and awe. There's no other way to describe it. I didn't know how I had managed to get where I was. But I knew one thing. However, I did manage it, I wasn't going to move from that spot because I didn't think I could repeat that entry.

After only a few minutes of enjoying the show, I felt a tap on my shoulder. "Oh, boy," I thought to myself. "The jig is up." I knew I wasn't supposed to be there. And now someone else seemed to know it too. I tried to play innocent and inquire over the concert volume what the problem was.

The security guard said, "You can't stand here." He proceeded to push me through a barricade out of the walkway. He pushed me about 10 ft. closer to the stage. I was then only about 15 ft. from John Paul Jones's butt. I apologized to the security guard and was left to watch the show undisturbed from very close to the stage.

There was yet one more layer of security. There was a mountain of a human being standing on the side of the stage facing outward. I assume if your name wasn't Robert Plant, Jimmy Page, John Paul Jones, or Jason Bonham, you weren't going to get past that guy.

The after-party started about 1 a.m. and went quite late. But it was a packed house until the very end. Backstage I was able to speak to Solomon Burke. We reminisced about a few of our exploits. I wasn't playing with him that evening. I explained to him that I was there conducting for Sam Moore.

Solomon said to me a few times in succession, "Thank you for being there for Sam. Thank you. Thank you."

It was touching and also a little disturbing at the same time. It was disturbing because of the intensity of his inflection and the number of times he kept repeating the same thing. It was touching because I think he was giving voice to the gratitude he felt for having people help him musically throughout his career.

But then it was disturbing again because he wasn't thanking me for playing for him. And Sam wasn't thanking me for playing with him, although he has many other times. Solomon was thanking me on behalf of Sam using the words that he probably felt needed to be said yet weren't being said.

It was an odd yet touching exchange, somehow fitting for our last meeting. He passed away three years later on a flight to Amsterdam, where he was scheduled to perform. He rode the Chitlin' Circuit right up to the very end.

Bill Wyman

Solomon Burke live in Central Park with 10 horns

5 LOOSE ASPIRATIONS

So how did I get here? Every memoir I've ever read starts with a long biographical chapter that invariably leaves me thinking, "So what? Get to the good stuff."

But now as I sit to write my own it seems like some version of my origin story is pertinent. I'll try to keep this as mercifully brief as I can.

I was raised in Chattanooga , Tennessee, population 125,000, the son of a secular Jew and a devout atheist. My parents must have had a sense of humor naming me Ivan in the predominantly Christian Deep South in the middle of the cold war. In fact, my mom knew it was a screwed-up thing to do because she told me that she wanted to give me a "normal" middle name (Peter) in case the whole Ivan thing proved too difficult. It was difficult. But I guess not ever difficult enough for them to start calling me Petey.

My parents separated when I was seven years old, reunited briefly, and eventually divorced when I was nine. I ended up choosing to live with my father when I was 12 to escape my narcissistic mother. My dad, though infinitely preferable in my pre-teen brain as a parent, also had his own issues that centered around being focused on his sexual relationships and new wives.

There's absolutely nothing wrong with this from an adult standpoint. But a child of a divorced household with self-esteem issues probably would have benefited from a little more personalized attention. Eventually my dad went on to marry three more wives, all of whom I referred to as "future former evil stepmonster number one, two, or three." What started as a 12-year-old's humorous moniker actually ended up being quite precociously prophetic. But that's a story for another time.

Suffice to say that if there is ever a need to do some forensic psychology on my life because people on the news are saying, "He was always such a quiet fellow. I never imagined that he had this in him," look no further than my preteen period. This was when most of the trouble started.

Let me be clear: I dearly loved both of my parents. My relationship with both of them matured wonderfully as I grew up. There were just a few tumultuous years in my formative period.

My parents and my stepparents all worked for a federal government utility, an FDR New Deal program called the Tennessee Valley Authority. This made us firmly middle class and suburban. I went to public school for elementary and junior high and to a private all-boys preparatory school for grades eight through twelve in an attempt to escape the struggling Chattanooga public school system.

My mother was president of the local chapter of the ACLU, NOW, and engaged in other leftist activist pursuits. As such she was involved in a federal court case in Chattanooga seeking to prohibit the teaching of Bible studies in the public schools. They didn't win the case per se, though now the teachers must be certified, must avoid denominational controversy, and are no longer allowed to proselytize to the students. Baby steps, people.

What they were required to do during my days at Rivermont Elementary school was to send a permission slip home with each student for bible study. Unsurprisingly mine came back stamped with a resounding "no."

Each week when the Bible teacher came into the classroom, little Ivan was made to stand up and march out of the room. Incomprehensibly this did little to increase my popularity with or acceptance by my classmates. Who could have predicted?

The only good thing that came out of this situation was that they had to teach me something else in lieu of the Good Book. They taught me how to read maps instead. This is a skill that ended up serving me well in my travels. Thanks, Chattanooga public schools.

To escape this situation, off to a private school I went, a former military academy with heavy Christian leanings called the Baylor School for Boys. They dropped the military idea when it proved unprofitable during the Vietnam era. They eventually dropped the "for Boys" idea about four years after I graduated, just after the time when it might have been advantageous in my life for me to learn how to talk to girls in my adolescence. Thanks, Baylor.

If you saw the movie *Dead Poets Society*, that could have been a documentary about my high school. Except I would have been the kid who ended up killing himself at the end of the movie. In real life it was nothing so dramatic. I was threatened with physical violence constantly, though very little of it ever manifested into fisticuffs. I got punched in the nose one time at summer camp when I was seven.

A kid at my high school pulled a gun on me once. He got a slap on the wrist for it and managed to produce a fake gun for them to confiscate. I never saw the fake. They wouldn't show it to me. I have no idea whether it was the same thing he pointed at me. Whatever I was looking down the barrel of sure looked awfully real that night in that parking lot.

The football team at this prestigious high school also threatened to physically cut off my long hair, a threat that became so well known on campus that the headmaster got wind of it. His response was that if it happened, he just didn't want it to be on campus and didn't want to know about it. Can you imagine that? It was a warm and nurturing environment, to say the least. But it was a far better school than any of the public schools in town. I remained there until I graduated ranked 67th in my class of 100 kids, certainly not the smartest, but not the dumbest either.

Decades later both the headmaster and the kid who pulled the gun on me requested me as friends on social media. I didn't accept either of their requests. But I didn't block them either. I decided that the very purpose of social media is to demonstrate to all of the miserable kids I went to high school with that my life is better than theirs. It doesn't matter if this is true or not. The important thing is the appearance that my life is better.

Of the 100 kids in my class, I would estimate that approximately 5 percent thought that I was a decent guy; another 15 percent probably had no particular feeling about me at all; maybe 40 percent ranged from neutral to just disliking me. The remaining 40 percent actively wanted to participate in or to see physical harm done to me. It was not a comfortable situation.

Recently a classmate of mine told me that he appreciated the fact that I was always a good friend to him all those years ago. I found this comment a little jarring since I don't remember really having very many friends in school at all. Plus I didn't remember doing anything for anyone that could be considered being a friend during those years. I was in no position to bestow friendship on anyone. I was just trying not to get my ass kicked.

I think what my classmate was saying was that I wasn't a dick to him. That fact alone equaled being a "good friend" to him. This says much more about the general atmosphere of that school than anything specific about my personal actions.

While in high school I was editor of the literary magazine one semester and the yearbook another year. I ended up winning the drama award my senior year mostly because I had been in every school play put on during the course of my matriculation, though not due to my unflagging interest in the performing arts.

My involvement in theatre was a vehicle to get me out of the school's athletic requirement, which would have necessitated me changing clothes and being naked in the locker room at the gym. As a late bloomer, this was a perilous situation to be avoided at all costs. I had athletic interests like kayaking and long-distance cycling, all solitary pursuits. But let's just say that I wasn't much of a joiner or team player.

Because of that drama award, somewhere in a dusty hallway in the basement of one of the administration buildings at that school my name appears engraved onto a two-inch-long strip of corroded brass that is nailed to a larger plaque commemorating all of the winners of that same award over the decades. It is the identical plaque repeated innumerable times at country clubs throughout the land chronicling annual putting champions.

While in high school I also became more interested in music. I became an avid record collector. The first LP I ever got, *The Jackson 5's Greatest Hits*, came out when I was seven years old. The first 45 rpm single I bought with my own money, "If You Want Me to Stay," by Sly & The Family Stone, came out when I was nine.

I was hugely influenced by my mom's record collection, which contained Gladys Knight & The Pips, Ike & Tina Turner, Stevie Wonder, etc. She also had some Beatles, Stones, and some Broadway show cast albums. But the rock and theatre records didn't have the same immediate resonance with me that the soul records had.

Somewhere in my mid-teens I was visiting my mom's family in New York City, where she was born and where I now live. My aunt's friend was a former record label publicist who had thousands of LPs in her apartment. She told me that they were all sent to her free of charge as a professional courtesy by other record label employees. Furthermore, she had duplicate copies of several titles and offered them to me for free since I seemed interested.

My mind was officially blown. I returned to Chattanooga with albums by Elvis Costello & The Attractions, Devo, Patti Smith, Public Image Ltd., The Buggles, and others. I now had a quest: to find more free records.

I started cold calling radio stations in Chattanooga and telling them that I knew they received more records than they played. I was offering them the *service* of taking some of their surplus off their hands.

Through some combination of audacity and complete ignorance on my part this scheme actually worked. I would make runs to the stations, pick up several boxes of their castoffs, and return to my teen lair to obsess over the spoils. I developed an amateur program director's ear by having to audition hundreds of LPs. It was glorious and taking solace in the music gave me an escape from teen angst.

I had an artistic vision around this time, which was to be photographed in an aggressive pose holding two flaming drumsticks while Bad Company sang "Rock & Roll Fantasy." It would be a surefire hit. It couldn't miss. Fame would be mine.

The only drawback was that I didn't play drums or any other musical instrument. My prestigious preparatory school incredibly had no music program at all. This was going to be up to me somehow.

I got a job during the summer when I was 16 washing dishes at a dude ranch in the Colorado Rockies. I maintain to this day that this is my only truly marketable skill. The ranch gave me my first experiences with alcohol, with cleaning 100 people's silverware three times a day, and with being forced to kill the bats that had found their way into the lodge building. Were this a biography of a serial killer, that last sentence would have indicated the first signs of trouble.

Musically, however, it was a ghost town up there. The cabin girls had an 8-track player with only about three tapes: Lynyrd Skynyrd *Gold & Platinum*, I think maybe a Rush album, which I didn't yet understand, and Joan Armatrading's *Me Myself I*, which they played incessantly for three months. While I think Joan is a wonderful singer and songwriter, I can't listen to her to this day as a result.

The spoils of the summer's campaign yielded enough money to spend $425 on a used Fender Precision bass that I bought from my pal Riq who was a year ahead of me at school. Riq and his brother had a band called Alfredo Garcia and The Mellow Tones, so they were cool by default.

I began my senior year of high school enjoying the birthday present that I requested from my dad: bass lessons. For $15 per lesson, Riq got me started learning songs by ear on that Fender bass, which I still own all these years later.

I was off to the races. By the following spring I played bass in the high school talent show. We played songs like "Message in a Bottle" by the Police and "Limelight" by Rush, whom I understood a little better now. But most significantly I was playing to a gymnasium full of kids who actively hated me, yet were screaming in adoration.

They weren't cheering for me personally. It was just something that I was a part of. Also since nobody had bothered to actually organize the talent show that year, it ended up falling to me to make all of the arrangements. I charged $1 admission at the door and even took home a profit after I paid Riq the $100 for his sound system rental. Wealth and fame all in the same night? I was hooked.

So it was all set. My eventual goals were to play on the Johnny Carson show, David Letterman, *Saturday Night Live*, and at Madison Square Garden. Forty years later, I have done exactly none of those things, though I did a bunch of other stuff. As the expression goes, "Life is what happens to you while you're busy making other plans."

I did make my mom cry once, however.

Senior in high school with long hair, requisite school uniform of shirt and tie, and my first Fender Precision bass. I still have it.

6 HERSHEY HAPPY

L et's get back to the road chronicles for a moment. Here is a story about Bowzer, the lovable bass singer from the band Sha Na Na. Let me be clear about this. I absolutely adore Jon Bauman aka Bowzer. He's a great guy and a lot of fun to work with. But he will confirm that the first time we met we had a little incident.

We were playing a multi-act oldies show at Hershey Park in Hershey, Pennsylvania, "The Sweetest Place on Earth." There is an amphitheater in the middle of the amusement park that is identical to the one portrayed in the movie *This Is Spinal Tap* in the puppet show/jazz odyssey scene.

The show we were playing was billed as "Bowzer's Rock 'n' Roll Party" and featured three or four acts playing their hits for 20-30 minutes each. This is a very common setup for oldies shows.

Bowzer also likes to have the show look as much like the 1950s as possible to complete the nostalgia trip. He has all of his band guys dress in matching greaser costumes with rolled-up T-shirts, rolled-up jeans, and baseball caps.

Since I have long hair and tattoos, Bowzer calls me a "hippie." I love this. With all of the many genres of music and styles of dress that have been popular since 1959, many of them involving long hair, the one he seizes upon to describe me is "hippie." Peace and love, baby.

For these gigs often there is a house band that will back up all the acts for the day. Bowzer does these shows all over the country. He has a great road-tested format that plays really well with the crowds. He prefers to have his own guys be the backing musicians for all the singers. It keeps the changeover time between acts to an absolute minimum and keeps the show running at a good pace. He's right about this. It works well.

That day I was performing with Rock & Roll Hall of Fame inductee Shirley Alston Reeves, Original Lead Singer of The World-Famous Shirelles. That's her full legal marquee billing. I'll discuss this more later on.

Shirley is more comfortable having her own band playing behind her so she doesn't have to worry about the pickup musicians giving her anything other than what she's used to hearing. She shouldn't have to be distracted by them making mistakes playing her arrangements or songs that may be unfamiliar to them. She is also right. This works well for her.

Because both of these positions were correctly held, there was a tiny bit of tension in the air that day at the Sweetest Place on Earth. Bowzer wanted to keep his show running smoothly. So maybe, just maybe, he introduced Shirley a tiny bit quicker than he might have introduced the other acts to prove a point or more likely to realize his fears that the band changeover would be uncomfortably long.

Since it was going to take time for us to physically change guitar cables and reseat a different drummer and keyboard player, he worried that there would be dead air between his introduction and the start of the first song. This would not be good in terms of a tight show business presentation.

We knew about this fear and were ready for him. As soon as he said, maybe a little too quickly, "Ladiesandgentlemen-MsShirleyAlstonReeeeeeeeves!" Boom! We came in with the downbeat of the first song. It had to be a land speed record for a band changeover. Shirley is a lovely performer who has had a lot of hit records, all of them fabulous songs. As always with her, the show went over great with the audience.

That gig was a two-show day outdoors in the heat of summer. I'm pretty sure that was one of the same days our diabetic drummer got dehydrated and needed some medical attention to get his electrolytes back to normal. As such we understandably had our shirtsleeves rolled up, no tuxedo jackets on, and were trying to get away with wearing as little as possible.

Backstage between shows Bowzer poked his head into the band dressing room and said to me, "You'll have to roll down your sleeves because you're not Hershey Happy." Then he kind of giggled and left the room.

The whole band were scratching their heads. Hershey Happy? What the hell is that? Was he serious? Was that an actual thing? I went to talk to Shirley to find out if that was a real concern and if there was anything I truly needed to do about this.

She confirmed that, yes, the park management had told Bowzer that I was indeed not Hershey Happy. Apparently, this was a corporate motto they used around employees of the park. Although

I wasn't a park employee, we were still appearing on their property and being paid by them. By displaying my tattoos, I was decidedly not Hershey Happy, even though all of their patrons were walking around with wife beaters on and tattoos a-blazin'. I had to make a couple of adjustments.

I rolled down my sleeves to cover up my ink. I also pulled back my long hair into a pony tail. The problem was apparently solved. The second show went off without a hitch. We heard no more about it.

The following winter I got a call from a drummer friend, Gary Weiss, who was hiring a band to back up Bowzer at a private Christmas party at a house in New Jersey.

Most people who know Bowzer from the movie *Grease* or from the hit Sha Na Na variety show on network television don't realize that he is a Juilliard-trained classical pianist as well as a lovable greaser.

His knowledge of music is extensive. His ears are extremely sharp. The charts in his book are very specifically written out note-for-note. When one is playing a Bowzer show, one must be a fairly adept sight reader (which I am not particularly) since he doesn't advance copies of his book to allow practice ahead of time. You have to really be on point, or he's going to fuss at you. And he will be right to do so. You will have had it coming.

I was intrigued about having the chance to play Bowzer's book. But I also had the recent Hershey Park incident freshly in mind. I told Gary that I would love to do the gig. But I had one request: "Don't tell Bowzer it's me."

I had no idea if he actually knew my name or remembered me at that point. But I didn't want to take the chance that he had a "no hippie" policy for hiring musicians.

We met at Gary's house in Staten Island a couple of hours before the gig in order to rehearse. Then we were going to caravan over to the gig not far away in north Jersey.

When I arrived for the rehearsal, I knocked on Gary's front door. For some reason Bowzer himself answered. He saw me and exclaimed without missing a beat: "Oh, it's you!" It was looking like it might be a long night.

We rehearsed in Gary's basement. I was sight-reading Bowzer's book with every fiber of concentration I could muster. I was already behind the eight ball with him from Hershey Park. I knew that he was a perfectionist with bat-like ears. I really had to nail his book as best as I could if I wanted to survive the gig. I also knew that it was just hours before the show. So he didn't have time to fire me and get someone else to play the bass. This was all part of my nefarious plan.

As it turned out, my sight-reading ability coupled with my familiarity of 1950s doo-wop music was sufficient to make Bowzer remark after the rehearsal, "Well, we can't fire you because you played the book so well." Whew! A happy boss makes for a happy gig.

Off we went into the crisp winter's night out into the ritzy suburbs of northern New Jersey. Christmas lights were out in full force as we passed lawn after lawn bedazzled with myriad Santae and Rudolphs. Finally, we pulled up to the most garish display of holiday lights I have ever seen. The house was a gigantic McMansion on perhaps an acre of property that seemed to have every square inch covered with tiny twinkling lights.

As soon as we stepped toe into the driveway of the house, we were met with a couple of sides of beef who were apparently event security. They wanted to confirm that we were indeed the band, as if carrying our instruments wasn't enough of an indication. We were then beefily escorted around the home to a separate pool house out back. This amazing scene appeared to be an exact replica of the "cement pond" set from *The Beverly Hillbillies* show, complete with faux Greek columns and statuary.

The pool house was adjacent to a multicar garage that seemed to house several very large and very aggravated dogs. We could hear them barking and scratching on the other side of the wall and were pretty glad that we were out of their range. I'm quite sure that garage door was routinely opened with the command, "Release the hounds!"

Also notable in the pool house were mountains of food and a couple of the waitstaff hired for the evening. This didn't seem unusual since there are often staging areas for the caterers outside of the main party for the waitstaff to pick up trays of food, return empty plates, and whatnot.

This wasn't a staging area at all as it turned out. This food and these waitstaff were there for the exclusive use of the bands performing that night. There was more than just Bowzer on the bill. This is almost unheard of. As musicians we are routinely reminded that we are the hired help. We don't get provided with people hired to serve us. The wheels started turning in our heads.

McMansion, garish lights, cement pond, bodyguards, attack dogs, mountains of food: "Dude, I think we may be working for a mobster! Um, I mean, legitimate businessman."

Keep in mind, this was years before *The Sopranos* was on television. We never did confirm the name of our host. Nor did we want to. In those situations, the less you know, the better.

When showtime arrived, we were escorted by security into the main house. The place was mobbed, um, I mean, really crowded. Scantily clad women seemed to be everywhere, all but falling out of their dresses. I kept saying to myself: "Don't make eye contact with them. Don't look at anyone." It just felt like my continuing good health depended on it.

They walked us down into the low-ceilinged basement where the main action was. There was a gigantic rumpus room down there with people packed in like sardines. There was a full concert rig set up as part of the house. The gear wasn't brought in just for the party. Stage lights were screwed to the ceiling. There was a full PA system, backline, amps, drums, keyboards, everything. It was like a rock & roll man cave down there.

To further set the scene, our host was on the microphone in the process of introducing Bowzer as the next performer. That's when we noticed that, apparently, he had decided that a Christmas party was also fair game to be used as a costume party, though he seemed to be the only one in fancy dress.

What was his costume, you ask? He was dressed as a 1920s Prohibition-era zoot-suited gangster. Yes, I know zoot suits were from the 1940s. But that didn't seem to matter to this dude. It was a subtle statement he was making. Whatever his occupation, he seemed to relish the aura of being perceived as a mobster.

As we mounted the stage, I noticed another phenomenon that would become a challenge for me during the gig. The stage was only about a foot high. But with the low ceilings in the basement and me being 6 ft. 5 in. tall, it was impossible for me to stand fully upright on the stage. I had to bend my head sideways a little and eventually settled into a spread-legged stance that allowed me to keep my eyes level for reading the sheet music. Reading was crucial for a Bowzer gig.

It was a sweaty mess down in that basement. Everybody was feeling everyone else's hot drunken breath. As the show got underway a visibly intoxicated young lady was dancing right in front of me. (Don't make eye contact.) At one point she bumped into my music stand, nearly knocking it over and jostling the sheets, making them much harder to read. I just shook my head and turned the music stand back to where I could see it. I knew that any chance I had to remain in Bowzer's good graces depended upon my duplicating or bettering my performance in rehearsal.

A moment later she drunkenly bumped into the music stand again. And again. My blood pressure was starting to ratchet up. I saw her coming toward the stand yet again. At that moment everything suddenly went into slow motion. I saw my hand ... reach out ... and physically push her shoulder ... away from the stand ... while simultaneously my mind was saying, "Noooooo, dooooooon't toooooouuuch heeeeer!"

But it was too late. Reflexively I had just shoved some mobster's girlfriend. Though it did seem to prevent her from knocking into my stand for the remainder of the show, my internal voice was saying, "Well, this is it. This is how it ends. This is where I will die. This is the place where I will be outfitted with cement shoes and thrown into the lake. It's been a good life. I wish I could have seen a little more of it though."

After the set, as we were winding our way back through the mob, I mean, the crowd to exit the premises forthwith, the same girl was blocking my path. "Oh, boy, here it comes," I thought.

She said, "I just wanted to say that I'm so sorry I bumped into your music."

"Oh, no worries at all," I said. "I'm so sorry that I put my hand on your shoulder."

And that was it. Instead of getting whacked I got an apology. That did NOT go the way I expected it to. We beat a hasty retreat out into the Springsteenian winter.

Bowzer and I have been friends ever since then. I always enjoy performing on his shows.

"Grease for Peace!"

7 THAT'S NOT A THREAT. THAT'S A PROMISE, JACK!

So where was I? Oh, yes, at 17 years old off I went to Tulane University in New Orleans to major in Biomedical Engineering. I went to that school sight unseen. I hadn't even visited the town. I knew one important thing, however.

New Orleans had the highest population of any of the cities where schools had accepted me. I needed a more cosmopolitan environment than Chattanooga if I had any hope of finding my way in the world. New Orleans won by default.

At that age I was too nascent a musician to have had academic aspirations yet in the field. But I did have the need to once again find a new source of free promotional records to feed my jones.

Since I had so much luck with radio stations back home, I went down to the campus radio station, WTUL, to see if there was a possible vinyl hookup there. With the benefit of my high school drama experience, I started reading the news on the station within a week. I was subbing on overnight DJ shifts within a month, and had my own regular show shortly after that. By that winter I had become the station's music director. You know, the guy who auditions all of the promo records and gets to take some of the duplicates home as a perk of the job.

I had found my new home. I remained music director of the station until I graduated. After a couple of years of engineering school, I noticed that all of my classmates were military ROTC. Once again it was a crowd into which I did not fit. So I transferred to the Psychology department where I got my undergraduate degree. I tell people that I mainly majored in college radio because right after school I started working in the music industry.

While in New Orleans I also majored in the local music scene, studying at the unfortunately nonaccredited Meters and Neville Brothers' University, Mardi Gras College, and Jazz Fest Academy. I got my first professional experience playing with local bands on and off campus at clubs including Tipitina's, Jimmy's, and even the Saenger Theatre and the New Orleans Jazz & Heritage Festival.

I played on my first recording sessions down there for the alt./country/punk band Dash Rip Rock and the late unfortunately obscure soul music legend "Mighty Sam" McClain. "Mighty" was an accurate and well-deserved moniker. He was really something to see and hear. He was also a great friend.

I was also starting to learn about the dark side of the music business and human nature in general. New Orleans was a dangerous place in those days. I had a couple of friends die from being shot.

One of them, my pal Ben, was an especially pointless tragedy. We had just started a band together called The Radical Shiite God Squad that was great. You could name a band that in the '80s without worry of scrutiny by Homeland Security. Everyone in the band was young, eager, and exceptionally talented, bass player excepted. We did a couple of initial gigs where the band was firing on all cylinders. It felt important. It felt great. It felt right. It felt like we were really onto something.

One day Ben got into an argument with his brother at their house. His brother grabbed a hunting rifle and shot Ben dead on the spot. Game over. End of Ben. End of band. End of hopes and aspirations. End of a very talented singer, guitar player, and songwriter. And over what? Nothing.

We probably only did about two or three gigs total, decades ago. But I still think about him every once in a while. I wonder what we could have become as a group. Mostly I wonder what Ben would have been able to contribute to the world in the 50 or 60 additional years he might have lived. We'll never know.

During this same period at WTUL radio, I started doing an overnight punk-rock radio show with a couple of buddies we uninspiringly called *The Hardcore Show*. From 2 to 6 a.m. we would play punk and thrash records that weren't getting spun anywhere else on the air in New Orleans.

I still hear from people to this day who listened to that show when they were in high school and were hugely influenced by it. We probably had tens of regular listeners. I don't know, maybe hundreds. But it was a tight-knit community, a fraternity of like-minded DIY punks and skaters that somehow felt like an extended family when we gathered at live shows of bands touring through town.

Part of my gig at the radio station was to help promote these shows, play the records, and where possible, get the artists to come down to the station for on-air interviews. I have souvenir autographed LPs from many of these interviews during this time from The Ramones, The Circle Jerks, The Butthole Surfers, The Dead Kennedys (oy, what a combative interview!), Red Hot Chili Peppers (they were punk/funk initially), and even a band from L.A. called Tex & The Horseheads.

Not quite what I would call punk, Tex & The Horseheads were more of a trashy, loud rock band with a punk sensibility. Texacala Jones was their female lead singer, kind of a Madonna on meth type character with smeared mascara and in a torn crinoline dress. I liked them.

I called their record label, Enigma Records, which was also the Chili Peppers' label at the time, to ask for an interview. I was told that since they were on tour without transportation other than their equipment van, which was already parked at the venue, the only way this interview could happen was if I drove downtown to pick up the band myself and brought them to the radio station. For some reason I agreed to this.

When I got downtown and found the band, the guitar player, Mike Martt, said jokingly that they would only do the interview if I would buy them beer. I just laughed and said something sarcastic like, "Yeah, right, come on. Let's go." I drove them to the station.

When we got there, one of the band dudes went directly to the campus bar. The legal drinking age was 18 in New Orleans at the time. But the practical drinking age in New Orleans was: old enough to see over the bar. What major university with any self-respect wouldn't have a full-service bar right there in the student center?

Band dude came back with a six pack of opened beer bottles for the group to enjoy during their interview. They were rowdy. They were loud. They were punks. But we got it done and had some fun. They even signed my souvenir Horseheads LP.

As we finished up and were preparing to leave, Mike Martt said, "Hey, you owe us $21 for the beer." He was dead serious.

I told him that I never agreed to that. I was in college. I didn't have any money other than what I made working as a part-time clerk at the record store for $3.35 an hour or whatever pittance it was.

Plus, I was helping to promote and sell tickets to *their* gig by putting them on the air. I was just staring at them in disbelief.

Martt started to get belligerent, grabbed "his" album back, told me to fuck off, and stormed out of the station with the band. I was speechless. My mouth was open.

Literally 20 seconds later the whole band came back into the studio. Martt was smiling. He said, "I'm sorry, man. We still need a ride back downtown."

I said, "Just a minute," and walked out of the studio. I got in my car, and drove away without them, livid, perplexed, flummoxed. My brain could not process the audacity and nerve of what had just occurred. No good deed goes unpunished, it is said.

Then the real fun began. This was before cell phones. Somehow the band got my home number, probably from someone else at the station who couldn't imagine why I might have stranded them there. This was during the time of cassette recording answering machines. Wow, did I have a few messages waiting for me when I got home.

Texacala growling, "The more people who say I act like an animal, I have people like YOU to thank for it!" Click, buzz.

Mike Martt menacing, "The next time I see you you're going to the hospital! That's not a threat. That's a promise, Jack!" Click, buzz.

On it went in that vein. So now I was basically staying in for the night rather than risk attending the show or going anywhere else I might encounter a group of aggrieved idiots from L.A. bent on kicking my ass to the point of needing medical intervention.

Martt's local girlfriend du jour reiterated the threats to me as well, indicating that the incident had spread outside the band and into the scene. It was not the result I anticipated when taking the initiative to help promote their concert.

The Enigma Records representative called me the next day to cheerfully ask me how the interview went. She hadn't heard. I told her. The level of embarrassment over the phone was palpable.

Shortly afterward their label dropped them. I'm quite sure it was from lack of sales and interest. But I would love to imagine that my anecdote played some tiny part in it.

Three or four years later, I ended up moving to L.A. to work for Epic Records. One night I was going up the stairs at the Roxy as the one and only Mike Martt was coming down the other way. L.A. is a big town. What are the odds?

I recognized him immediately though he was now wearing some sort of hipster suit jacket with satin stripes and the sleeves rolled up instead of the Keith Richards wannabe getup he had on back in New Orleans. He saw me. We made eye contact. My guts jumped into my throat. My body tensed in anticipation of whatever confrontation was about to occur.

But there was no look of recognition in his eyes, no acknowledgment. He walked right by me and off into the Southern California night. I've never been accused of having a forgettable face. Though the Horseheads did a national van tour, they didn't play that many shows and did even fewer radio interviews. Was it the $21 worth of beer or drugs that clouded or erased his memory? I'll never know. Apparently, he's in recovery now. I wish him well.

During my New Orleans days, I also got my first chance to play with a Rock & Roll Hall of Famer, the great Bo Diddley, at a nightclub called Storyville in the French Quarter. To save money, Bo often used local pickup bands in each city in those days rather than traveling with his own musicians.

I was dating the local booking agent for Bo's show at the time. Since nepotism is the way of the world, I called in the favor: "Get me on the gig." I constantly maintain that I've slept my way to the bottom during my career.

Even though I had next to zero real-world playing experience, I managed to get myself an audition with Charlie Brent, a great New Orleans guitarist who had been hired to be the local bandleader.

I would find out many years later that Charlie Brent used to be music director for Wayne Cochran & The C.C. Riders out of Miami in the early 1970s, a band that included a young kid on bass named Jaco Pastorius. Jaco credited Charlie publicly with teaching him everything he knew about arranging and orchestration, skills that Jaco elevated to genius status and great fame.

I knew who Jaco was and was a huge fan. But I didn't know anything about his connection to Charlie Brent, which was just as well. It would have served to make me nervous in my audition. I only really knew enough about music at the time to be able to play a 12-bar blues, though apparently with a decent enough feel.

One of the astounding things about Bo Diddley that most people don't realize is that most of his hits were one-chord songs. He had a couple of 12-bar blues forms in his catalog. But mostly there were absolutely no chord changes.

There was no harmonic knowledge required to play his show as a pickup musician beyond these simple, easily observable facts: Bo played with his signature cigar-box guitar tuned to an open E chord. He used a capo for some songs. If there was no capo on the guitar, he was playing in the key of E. If the capo was on the third fret, he was in G. If it was on the fifth fret, he was in A. Here endeth the lesson.

Out of these one-chord songs Bo would do a 90-minute show that was never boring except maybe to the jazz pianist who was also hired for the gig. But that's another story. Bo was amazing, a force of nature. I've never seen anything like him before or since.

The point of all this was not that Charlie Brent saw in me some budding talent along the lines of the astounding young Jaco. Certainly not. Charlie was faced with a booking agent who had probably hired him and had asked him to give me a chance. He knew full well that anyone who basically owned a bass and wasn't a total disaster on it would be able to cut Bo's gig.

I was not a total disaster. I was hired. It was an amazing experience. Bo returned to New Orleans two more times in the next year or so. And I was asked back to play with him again each time. We rehearsed for about half an hour before the first gig and then never again for the other shows.

By the third gig I felt that I wanted to have some souvenir of my playing with the great Bo Diddley. I had not yet mastered the art of the two-shot selfie back in those days. Photographs required cameras, film development, and printing. It's not like today when everybody has a camera in their pocket.

By now I had taken in the landscape of the club, befriended the sound man, and noticed that he had a cassette deck on the sound board. Since I was in radio at the time, the logical thing in my inexperienced mind was to bring a blank cassette to the gig and ask the sound man to record it for me. I would have my souvenir.

Another fascinating thing about Bo was that he had a lot of bad experiences with bootleg recordings being released for which he was not compensated. He was aware enough of this to show me a special feature that he had actually built into his custom-made guitar the first time I met him.

He had taken a bunch of usually floor-mounted effects pedals and given them to the luthier with the instruction to put them all into the guitar. Needless to say, this guitar had a lot of knobs on it. It must have weighed a ton. One knob he showed me seemed to do nothing but emit a shrill high frequency whistle. He said that was the "anti-bootleg knob." When the illegal record producers heard that sound, they would think the recording was bad and would be unable to release it. This should have been a clue to me not to ask the sound man for a souvenir board tape.

Apparently, I had forgotten about this knob by the third gig a year later and/or had been too anxious to have the souvenir recording to have taken the hint that this could be a pretty bad idea. I didn't ask anyone for permission. I just asked the sound guy to tape the show on the down low. He did. I gave him two blank cassette tapes, one for each set that night.

At the end of the show I went to the sound guy to get my tapes. He said there had been some problem with the sound board during the first show. So he had recorded the second set on the same cassette, taping over the first flawed recording. He gave me back two tapes, one still blank, and one with just the second set on it. I got paid my $100 for the gig or whatever astronomical sum they were paying me and went home, thrilled to have my own bootleg souvenir. I never had any intention to sell it or even to play it for anyone. It was like having a trophy. Or so I thought.

When I got home, quite late, probably 2 a.m., I started listening to the tape. The tape had all of the band recorded on it but somehow no vocals at all. How the idiot sound guy managed to do this was beyond me. I was listening to a bizarre 90-minute one-chord jam that made no sense at all and had no evidence of its being Bo Diddley or anyone else for that matter. I was crestfallen but resigned to my fate.

But then the phone rang. It was the club owner. He asked me if I had taped the show that night. Stunned that he knew this, I stupidly said yes. He said in a very stern tone to get into a cab right now and bring the tape back to the club because Bo knew about it and was livid. For some inexplicable reason I decided to comply with this order and took a cab ride that I could ill afford back down to the French Quarter in the middle of the night to return this bootleg and apologize.

When I got there, Bo was still with the club owner. The club was otherwise empty of patrons. Just the porters were cleaning the room since it was after hours. I returned the one tape to Bo and said I was sorry. Bo said, "Where's the other one? There were two shows." I explained what I had been told by the sound man who was no longer on the premises to back me up. Needless to say, Bo was skeptical.

It turned out that Bo had *also* given the sound man two blank cassettes that night that he wanted back, mainly to prevent the cassette deck from being used to make a bootleg recording of his show. You know, exactly as I had done. Bo was not given a recording of the show, nor was he given his blank tapes back.

How the idiot sound guy managed to A) honor my request over that of the actual artist and B) then provide me with only one tape instead of two, which contained no vocal whatsoever, remains a mystery to me as intangible as the existence of Sasquatch or the Loch Ness Monster.

At this point the club owner beckoned me to follow him into the kitchen saying, "Let me talk to you for a second." Again, for some reason I complied.

Once out of Bo's earshot, the club owner began to explain to me his position, which was basically this, "If you're lying to me about this tape, and furthermore if you don't go out there and convince Bo right this second that you're telling the truth, I will murder you. I will shoot you dead and burn this club to the ground so no one finds your body." Though no actual firearm was brandished, the setting and his tone let me know that this was a serious threat.

Shaking and pale with fear, I returned to the presence of the great but understandably disgruntled Bo Diddley whereupon I promptly burst into uncontrollable tears, heaving sobs that can only be described as a bona fide ugly cry. I once again repeated my story, which happened to be the absolute truth, about there only being one tape, I swear, I swear, in that unintelligible wail between gasping breaths and with snot streaming down my face.

It must have been quite a show because Bo accepted the story. I was allowed to depart and take a second expensive cab ride home, relieved that I had somehow escaped with my life if indeed not my dignity fully intact.

The next year my friend, James, interviewed Bo for the local New Orleans music magazine, *Wavelength*. James happened to mention to Bo that he knew me and knew that I had played with him, to which Bo replied, "I still love him."

I guess he believed my literal sob story. But my tenure in his band had come to an unceremonious end. To be fair so had everyone else's from the last three gigs. His fourth trip to New Orleans involved a completely different pickup band and nightclub.

Decades later I passed Bo in an airport somewhere. It was the type of seemingly random road encounter that happens occasionally to touring musicians. He showed no recognition of me. Why should he? I was just another in an infinite line of pickup musicians he encountered over his 60-plus-year career.

I waved to him as he passed me on the moving sidewalk. He merely addressed the obvious group of musicians I happened to be standing with that day by nodding his head and saying, not uncordially, "Fellas."

Broadcasting on WTUL, New Orleans

8 SOMETIMES YOU SMOKE THE MARIJUANA, YES?

I don't care who you are, what your lifestyle choices are, or what the level of legality of cannabis currently is in your state of residence. When you are asked that question by a jack-booted Italian carabinieri in an "interview" room at the Milano airport, the only sensible answer is an emphatic, "NO!"

But let's back up a second. I tried marijuana maybe a half dozen times total in high school and college. Unlike Bill Clinton, I did indeed inhale. Clearly, I wasn't repulsed by it, or I wouldn't have tried it more than once. But also as clearly, I wasn't particularly enchanted by it, or I would have said yes any one of the innumerable times that it has been offered to me since then.

I haven't touched the stuff in 35 years. I haven't even been tempted. It's just not for me. Other than an occasional adult beverage, I don't dabble in controlled substances at all, which is no mean feat in the rock & roll business. There's a lot of it around. A lot.

Even when drinking, one or two beers is my entire night. I'm a cheap date. I come from temperate people. My 102-year-old grandmother told me that she doesn't remember ever going to a bar in her life, much less drinking a beer. My mother, the wild child, would occasionally enjoy a piña colada once a year on vacation. What a rebel.

Of my half dozen Maryjane experiences, I remember exactly two of them. The first was when I was quite young, in high school. A joint got passed to me on a camping trip that had something else in it besides just weed. I wasn't informed of the presence of whatever chemical this was. I never found out what it was. I only know that I spent most of the night envisioning a bleached steer skull with a barbed wooden tongue raspily intoning, "Koo-tin-koo-LAIR-um" over and over again. It was an unpleasant evening, to say the least. That turned me off from even wanting to try weed again for a few years.

The only other experience I recall was also my last experience with it. Someone passed me a joint in the audience at a reggae concert. What are the odds of that happening? Ordinarily I would have politely declined or just passed it along to the next person as a courtesy. But this time my scientific curiosity got the better of me. One almost gets a contact high just breathing the air of the Rastaman vibrations. I thought I would try a couple of hits to see what the hype was all about.

Just a few minutes later, I said, "Ooooohhhhhh, I get it." It was a lightbulb moment. The "buzz" one experiences when one is upon the pot is called that because one has the sensation that one's whole body is vibrating. You literally feel like your body has become some sort of high-rise apartment door entry tone.

At a reggae concert, the bass is coming out of the PA speakers at fire hose velocity. It's loud, low, and very boomy by design. The buzz you get from the doobie feels like it is the same frequency of the sound vibrations of the bass. Suddenly the music is moving through you, with you. The bass amplifies the buzz. I finally got it. I understood it. And I never felt the need to touch the whoopee weed ever again.

I had a similar psychoacoustic musical revelation the first time I saw the band Journey play arena rock in an actual arena. The length of time between each drum strike was the length of the reverb that the sound bouncing off the back wall of a hockey rink made. If the notes came any faster than that, the resulting sound would just be mud.

Think about the giant Phil Collins tom-tom fill on "In the Air Tonight," the air drummers' anthem. That's maximum speed drumming in the acoustics of any gymnasium. I had the same reaction that night as at the reggae concert, "Ooooohhhhhh, I get it." That night didn't involve any recreational chemicals, however.

But let us return to the arrivals hall at the Milano airport in scenic and sunny northern Italy. We had just landed after a seven-hour flight from New York. This was to be our seventh or eighth van tour with a singer-songwriter I was working with at the time. She also happened to be my live-in girlfriend of four years. We knew the drill on these tours, knew our booking agent, knew many of the promoters already, and knew every curve in the autostrada between Milano and Roma.

Well, I did anyway. In addition to playing bass on those tours, I was also performing the duties of road manager, merchandise salesman, guitar tech, van driver, and, of course, the loving and supportive boyfriend. But at least I wasn't getting paid extra for any of this. So that was cool. Italy was a romantic place and a grand adventure for us, even if the autostrada started to look like the New Jersey Turnpike pretty quickly.

By that time, we knew enough rudimentary Italian to function as tourists, though certainly not enough to philosophize. We could ask where the bathroom was, how many kilometers to the next town, and, most importantly, for food and drink.

"Un bicchiere di vino rosso, per favore!" Though I know how to say that when asking for a glass of red wine, I had to Google it just now to be able to write it. We were functionally illiterate in Italian even then.

Being partially trained musicians did help us a little. Most written musical terms are in Italian. When barreling down the highway where the speed limit signs seem only to be casual recommendations rather than the law of the land, I remember seeing a sign that said in big red letters RALLENTARE. Scrolling through my dusty memories from sight-reading class, I remembered that "rallentando" written below a staff of music means that the tempo should start to decrease. So that road sign clearly meant, "Oh, shit, hit the brakes!"

As we were waiting in the long line to exit the airport in Milano through the "nothing to declare" lane at customs, we noticed the very imposing looking carabinieri coming down the row with their black shirts, boots, and hats, looking every bit as intimidating as their fascist throwback uniforms were designed to be. They even had a huge black German shepherd with them who was sniffing everyone for drugs. They didn't have bomb sniffers back in them days.

As the big old toothy black dog got up next to me, he made the faintest whimper without even slowing down on his very active olfactory tour of duty. It was an almost imperceptible gesture, not at all like a pointer at attention or a baying bloodhound. But to his handler it was like a fire alarm had gone off.

I don't remember exactly what was said. Nobody put their hands on me. But the sentiment was immediate and clear, "You! In the room!"

This was not a good position to be in. We were aspiring guests in their country hoping to put out a hat and make money as wandering troubadours with nary a work permit in sight. Plus, I don't know how well you get along with authority figures, but they don't seem to like me right away because I "fit the profile." Oh, sure, once they get to know me, they're always surprised to find out what a great guy I am and that I don't seem to act anything like what they expected from my antiestablishmentarian rock & roll regalia.

I like cops just fine. They don't seem to like me.

At this point I had no idea why I had been singled out or what was even happening. This was before the time of prominent so-called "random" searches made at airports, which I enjoy so frequently as a touring musician these days. Also, I was trying to get *out* of the airport, not into it. It wasn't a security issue.

As soon as I was in the room with all the luggage that I had packed for the six-week tour along with my bass, the officer now in charge of my fate asked me, *"Parle Italiano?"*

As I mentioned, I had absorbed enough of what I call "truck stop" Italian to get by. But I wasn't willing to chance anything being lost in translation that could impinge upon my immediate physical freedom, nor was I of any mind to assist this gentleman in the prosecution of his constabulary agenda against me.

"No," I answered, semi-truthfully.

That's when he hit me with a question from out of nowhere in heavily Italian-accented broken English, "Sometimes you smoke the marijuana, yes?"

"No!" I answered after half a beat, though completely truthfully.

Now I began to worry, though not about any potential ride on the Midnight Express. I was in possession of no questionable pharmaceuticals whatsoever. Instead I began to fret about the several hundred CDs I had secreted in my luggage to sell at the songwriter's concerts. These were salable goods potentially subject to an import duty that I was planning not to declare.

The smuggling operation I was involved in was partly to dodge paying the tax, but mostly as a protest of the Italian bootleg record sales industry, which seemed to be rampant and ubiquitous.

Case in point, the songwriter I was touring with had only a few magazine reviews and a couple of regional television appearances. And already we had found a bootleg live concert CD in one record store. It didn't inspire us to want to pay money into a system that so clearly didn't seem to be doing anything to protect artists' rights.

Yeah, that's it. We were trying to make a political statement and stick it to the man. It had nothing to do with us being too cheap to pay the duty ("duty," heh, heh).

I started to sweat a little. I'm quite sure the experienced customs agent sensed my discomfort. He asked me to open my bass bag and all of its various storage pockets.

"What's this?" he asked.

"That's a guitar tuner," I replied.

"What's this?" he asked.

"That's a package of extra strings," I replied.

Then out of the blue he said again, "Sometimes you smoke the marijuana, yes?"

"No!" I replied. But now I was confused. He had just asked me that. What was up with the repeat question? Was that the only English he knew?

Now that the bass case and all of its contents had been thoroughly molested, he continued his search of my carry-on messenger bag. In it he found my shaving kit, which I guessed wss where most people hid their contraband. He pulled out each item one by one and gave them a careful examination.

"What's this?" he asked.

"Hand lotion," I replied.

"What's this?"

"Vitamins."

"Sometimes you smoke the marijuana, yes?"

"No!"

This continued. He must have asked me that question at least half a dozen times.

"What's this? What's this? Sometimes you smoke the marijuana, yes?"

Each time I answered, "No!"

Perhaps he thought I would crack under pressure and confess, "Yes! Yes! I done it! I'm glad I done it! And I'd do it again." I don't know.

After a fair amount of time into these proceedings, I finally explained to him that I was a musician, that I worked in nightclubs, and that it was possible that other patrons in nightclubs maybe smoked the marijuana, yes. Not me, of course, never me.

This seemed to satisfy him. He allowed me to repack my carry-on and bass bags and exit the "interview" room.

Incomprehensibly, he stopped just short of opening the big duffle bag with the hundreds of contraband CDs in it.

As I exited the airport on slightly wobbly knees, I realized that my smuggling operation was complete. The cruel irony of the situation was that they weren't even my CDs. They were my girlfriend's. I was just the CD mule in the operation. "Honest, your honor, I was just holding them for someone."

Only later did it occur to me what must have happened. Three days before we flew out on that trip to Italy, I played at an outdoor street fair in New York City. On a set break, some of those naughty band boys were passing around a left-handed cigarette. I wasn't partaking. But I was near enough to them that three days and 4,000 miles later a German Shepherd had the good nose and good sense to know that I wearing the same pair of jeans and was clearly was up to no good.

At the end of that tour, we drove the promoter's van back to the airport in Milano to hand it off to another band who were arriving the same day we were leaving. These were some blues guys we knew from New York who were using the same booking agent as we were. It was amusing and also a little odd to see them in an airport in a foreign country.

When we found them, only two of the three were present. The drummer was missing. They said that the carabinieri had pulled him out of line and took him off into a side room.

"Oh, boy," I thought. "I know exactly what he's going through right now."

About 20 minutes later, we saw the drummer rambling toward us down the airport concourse, seemingly without a care in the world. I knew this guy and knew what kind of stoner I thought he was, though I had never actually witnessed him enjoying the wacky tobaccy. He just had the complete countenance and demeanor of one who frequently partook.

When we asked him what happened to him, he said, "They kept asking me if I smoke weed. I told them, 'Yeah, but I don't have any with me.'"

DUDE!! Wrong answer! He was lucky he wasn't on a one-way bus to Papillon Island. Wow.

An interesting footnote about that tour was that it also marked the simultaneous complete disintegration of my domestic situation. We had been doing these tours as a trio with two hotel rooms. The girlfriend and I would share one room. The drummer would have his own room.

Shortly before this tour, I had introduced the girl to a pal of mine whom I knew well from my record business days. He emailed me the very next day asking what her romantic "status" was, calling her a "Hebraic homegirl deluxe." He was right. She was.

She and I had an "understanding" that while out in public in business settings we were not to announce our relationship. She had the idea that as a chick singer-songwriter she needed to appear to be romantically available as a way to allow fans and businesspeople alike to fantasize about her. This idea wasn't completely far-fetched. The Beatles had to disguise their relationships at the height of their popularity to preserve their marketability as pinups. It was an arrangement that I went along with.

I wrote back to my record company pal and told him that "I think she has a boyfriend," though I didn't mention that this had been me for the past four years and that we lived together. In retrospect perhaps I should have because what I told him did nothing to deter his advances, apparently.

One evening as we were about to go to sleep, she told me that she was in love with my friend. I was stunned. I think I just sat there blinking slowly, not knowing how to react. We hadn't been having any relationship problems that I was aware of. It seemed to come from out of left field.

That six-week Italian tour was already booked with plane tickets purchased. We agreed that I should do the tour for a number of reasons, all economic apparently. See previous mention about the number of hats I was wearing on those tours without compensation.

I went from sharing a hotel room with my girlfriend on the road in romantic Italy to abruptly rooming with the drummer. Though he was a dear friend of mine, it just wasn't the same. That was a long six weeks for me. She was constantly sneaking off to find a pay phone to call back home to her new love. I was pretending not to notice.

They ended up getting married and having the exact type of wedding ceremony in the exact location she always told me that we would be married in one day. Apparently, the groom in that scenario was completely interchangeable. I don't know if the new husband knew this. They ended up having two kids, too.

That breakup caused personal and professional complications for me. The personal ones were obvious. I was gutted, devastated, crushed.

The professional hurt was that her career was just starting to take off at that time. All of the hard road miles I had done with her were just starting to pay off with some higher profile gigs and a couple of TV appearances. Some good pals of mine got to play those shows instead of me. I was sure that her star was on the rise and that I was being left in the dust.

While I take no pleasure in these facts, with the benefit of hindsight it turns out that I didn't miss much personally or professionally. Her career never really went anywhere. She managed to sabotage many of her professional connections and sour most of the opportunities she was given. That was one of her many talents. It was like she had an Uzi pointed at her own foot all the time.

She and my former pal also got divorced about 10 years later. I felt bad for the kids.

It all did remind me, however, of the ancient proverb, "If you sit by the banks of the river long enough, eventually the bodies of your enemies will come floating by."

Milano, Italy

9   THE BIG CITY

N ext stop: New York City. After college I moved up north to Gotham with the intention of gaining employment in the music industry, specifically at a major record label. This was a logical extension of my music director gig at the college radio station as well as the next step in being able to procure free vinyl for life.

I spent my first summer in town searching for an apartment and a job. By the fall I had landed a 6 ft. by 12 ft. room in a welfare hotel that was "upgrading" to "student and artist" housing. It was cheap. I'll give it that much. Sure, the shared bathroom was down the hall. But privacy and, I guess, hygiene is a matter of personal choice. Needless to say, there wasn't a unified tenants' association at the aptly named Midway Hotel. I liked to think of it as being midway between life and death.

Only a few months into my residency there, a "full-sized" studio room opened up, which was a full 12 ft. by 12 ft. So I upgraded and built myself a loft bed out of plywood and two-by-fours that I bought from the hardware store. I was living pretty high on the hog, you know, for living in a welfare hotel. I stayed there for about a year.

Eventually a gal pal of mine gave me a line on an illegal sublet on Forsyth Street on the Lower East Side bordering Chinatown. Her "uncle" (who was actually her mother's extramarital affair) used to ship out to foreign lands every so often on years-long contracts as an English teacher, which would leave his rent-controlled apartment vacant and ripe for a sublessee. He was charging me something very cheap at the time, like $375 per month, which made me certain that his rent-controlled rate was even far less than that. It's hard to resent being gouged when the price is that low.

There were a lot of rules and special circumstances around this three-room railroad flat, which was positively palatial after the Midway. Firstly, the rent had to be paid to the dude's brother so that the brother would then pay the landlord with dude's pre-signed checks to make it look like he was still living there so as not to lose the coveted control of the rent.

Secondly, I was told to never under any circumstances answer a knock at the door. I wasn't sure what havoc this dreaded visitor could potentially visit. I soon ascertained that this was largely to avoid the prying eyes of utility meter readers. The gas meter had been completely removed. There was just an unfettered connection allowing the use of all the natural gas one could inhale.

Similarly, all the electricity in the apartment could be traced through a long line of extension cords to one master supply cord that came in from outside of the apartment window. I'm pretty sure it went to the guy's apartment next door, though I never inquired fully. It's hard for me to imagine what possible threat my "landlord" held over his next-door neighbor to make the neighbor think that this electrical arrangement was a good idea.

I'm speaking about this strictly from a financial arrangement, saying nothing about the fire safety of said arrangement. I'm also quite unsure what would have stopped the neighbor from unplugging the single cord, plunging my life into darkness while dude was away in Saudi Arabia for a year or more.

There were other interesting aspects of living there, including occasionally having to step over (sleeping?) bodies to get in the front door or walking by the working girls on the corner. But especially interesting was the challenge of taking a shower.

In the old tenement buildings, the bathtub was in the kitchen in the center of the apartment. This was a tub, not a shower. Initially it was meant to be used as a laundry tub or a very small person's bathing area. Starting in 1901 when New York City passed a law requiring that cold running water be available to all tenants, bathing at home became a real possibility. And proper-size tubs were installed. When this law got amended to include hot and cold running water in 1929, the landlords ran just one hot water pipe up into the apartments to save money. The only hot water was therefore in the kitchen and tub room, not in the toilet/water closet, which was at the back of the apartment.

To take a shower it was necessary to fashion some sort of high-mounted shower nozzle as well as some sort of shower curtain to contain the spray. The easy way to do this was to construct a 360-degree shower rod hanging from the ceiling from which you could suspend two standard-size shower curtains to get the job done.

In order to avoid having a giant opaque object in the middle of the kitchen blocking all of the light from the security gated windows, the best choice was clear plastic shower curtains. In my mind I exchanged the word "shower" for the words "display case," as in, "I just got back from a run and need to take a quick display case before I go out for the evening." It was a lifestyle.

Concurrent with my housing search was my employment search. After pounding the pavement for about three months, I landed three job offers at the same time. Since they were so close together, I managed to spend a day or more at each offered position before making my decision.

Job number one was as the assistant to the president of a large indie record label called Tommy Boy, which had some major hip-hop artists. It was an interesting opportunity to work at the center of all aspects of the label. It could have been an invaluable learning experience. But the gig only paid $12,000 per year.

Even in 1980s dollars, that was not a living wage. I asked the boss how someone was supposed to live on that little amount of money. He replied without the slightest hint of irony, "You live in Brooklyn, and you temp on the weekends." Reality adequately checked. I worked there for one week.

Job number two was for TV Tunes (later TVT) records, a label that had started by putting out albums of, you guessed it, television theme songs. They sold well enough for the company to eventually sign artists and make a go of it as an actual record label. This job offer was for the princely sum of $18,000 per year.

While this was a much more manageable wage for someone having low overhead by living in welfare hotels and illegal rent-controlled sublets, there was a catch. The gig was basically seven days a week, 10- to 12-hour days. Again, without any irony, the label owner said that I wouldn't have any weekends for a while. It was a 70-hour per week job. I worked there for one day.

Job number three was as a "per diem" assistant in the publicity department of Epic Records. It also paid $18,000 per year, but for a 40-hour workweek. The only catch here was that pesky phrase "per diem." This was a loophole whereby a major corporation, CBS Records, could pay me only for the days I worked, no paid vacation, no health insurance, no benefits.

I was just out of college. This was a major label, which had been my goal all along. I was in. It was my job to answer phones, duplicate and mail out press photos and bios, run errands as needed, and very occasionally to accompany artists to press interviews.

After a year and a half, I worked my way up to the position of Manager of West Coast Publicity, a title that came with a corporate Amex card, an expense account, full benefits, and the lavish salary of $26,000 per year. It required a move to Los Angeles, of course. But I was more than happy to pursue my music business aspirations.

The slight problem was that I was completely miserable. Los Angeles just wasn't my tempo. I was lonely and having trouble adjusting to life in a new city where I knew nobody. My introversion level ratcheted up while I was trying to do a job that is by definition social.

Being a publicist requires being an expert schmoozer, a social butterfly, and a brilliant salesman. I was and am none of these. I hated the job, hated most of my coworkers, hated many of the publicity campaigns I was asked to work on, and hated most of the music I was promoting.

I did learn a couple of important things while being a major-label publicist. For example, let's say there was a horrible album on the release schedule that needed to be promoted. The first step was to write an artist biography, which I seemed to be able to do, unlike all of the other publicists on the payroll. They all farmed out their bios and press releases to freelance writers. I did some of that too so I could get my writer pals extra money. But I wrote most of my artists' stuff myself.

Writing a biography became an exercise in extolling virtue. I realized that even though it could be a huge steaming pile of doo-doo, *somebody* liked this record. It might only be the singer's mom who was proud of her son's or daughter's major-label debut. But somebody liked it. It became my job to figure out who this was and why. It became easier to write the bio from that perspective. It didn't make the record any better. But it made the press materials at least more positive and less about bullshit hype.

One of the most telling things that indicated exactly to what level of hell I had descended was when the vice president of product management, one of the big dudes at the label, told me to my face, "I don't know anything about music. I could be selling soap. It doesn't matter." This was the dude who had made Gloria Estefan a huge star, among others. Reality checked once again. The music business has nothing to do with music.

It wasn't all misery. I did get to work with some excellent bands and one particularly important campaign for Living Colour's first album, *Vivid*. Not only were they amazing musicians and writers, they were also socially relevant and just great people. I'm proud of the work I was able to do with them.

As mentioned in the foreword of this book, I also got to work with my bass hero, Stanley Clarke.

I have gold and platinum album award plaques from my Epic Records days from Living Colour, Luther Vandross, Joan Jett & The Blackhearts, Michael Jackson, and "Weird Al" Yankovic, though I fear the Luther and Michael plaques got pawned for crank somewhere in North Carolina by some former evil step-sibling or someone during a decades-long stint in storage in my dad's attic. I'll never know for sure. While I certainly did work with all those artists, the platinum records were kind of given out like interoffice bowling trophies.

That stack of awards was amassed in just a year and a half of being a publicist. I even got a raise to $30,000 per year by the end of it. But it was the end. I needed to go. I needed to see if I could work making music rather than marketing horrendous corporate product. After only three years in the biz, I was cooked.

**The Godfather of Soul, James Brown,
being escorted to a day of press interviews by a young
office assistant**

10 WAKE-UP CALL

I have a learned behavior from decades of road experience, which is this: If an alarm clock is ringing, it's time to get up.

Though this sounds like common sense, I'm not referring to the 7 a.m. alarm to get ready for school Monday through Friday. I know people who will hit the snooze button repeatedly for another hour in the morning. I'm talking about the Sunday 4 a.m. alarm in a seedy hotel room in Indianapolis when I've not gotten to bed until 2 a.m. after the show.

I know from hard-fought experience that there is some kind of plane or bus to catch that has required this rude awakening from an all too brief slumber. A missed flight could wreak havoc on the successful execution of a contracted performance. Dozens of people can be adversely affected personally and professionally. Hundreds of fans could be disappointed, not my fans, mind you, but those of the person who is employing me. Litigation is possible for broken engagements.

When an alarm goes off, I'm up. It may take some time for me to figure out what my name is, where I am, and why the hell someone is making noise at this infernal hour. But something at my core understands that I'll figure all of this out later. What needs to happen right now is that I need to get vertical and get moving.

If you spend any time looking at discount air travel websites, you will notice quickly that the 6 a.m. flight out is something like $20 cheaper than the 10 a.m. flight. Also, the early flight is more likely to have available seats. These facts are not lost on concert promoters and band managers who book groups of plane tickets for their bands. Saving $20 for an individual isn't a huge incentive for missing an extra four hours of sleep. Saving $200 when buying 10 plane tickets for an entire band starts to feel like the beginning of some actual money.

One of the main reasons we don't complain too loudly about these meager savings on the early flights is that travel always involves logistics. By this I mean that it's wise to build some padding into your travel time whenever possible.

When flying, weather delays in Seattle can be a factor for flights coming in and out of Dallas. Airlines can screw up. Connections can be missed. And very often a gig can be two- or three-hours' drive from the nearest reasonably priced major airport. You can fly to Cletus's Airfield in East Pork Lick, Tennessee. But it's going to cost you. Road traffic can be heavy. Distances can be far.

We typically take the first flight out wherever we're going. It gives some extra time for things to screw up and still be able to get solved before curtain time. The best-case scenario is a 6 a.m. flight that requires a 4 a.m. lobby call, which for me translates into a 3 a.m. wake-up call. It takes me 45 minutes to an hour to wake up, get showered, get packed, make a cup of tea in my go-mug, check out of the hotel, and get on the bus.

I'm no mathematician. But to get a full eight hours of sleep when waking by 3 a.m., one must be in the rack by 7 p.m. This isn't usually feasible for everyone in a practical sense. And it's even more difficult if the concert we're playing doesn't start until 8 p.m.

We'll play until 10 or 10:30 and come offstage full of adrenaline. It will take at least an hour or so for the star of the show to deal with the after-show meet-and-greet, autograph all the merchandise, and settle accounts with the box office. Meanwhile we band folk have to get our gear packed up, get changed back into our civvies, see if there are any hospitality leftovers backstage because we're hungry now instead of before we went on. There almost never are, by the way. They pack the food up or throw it all away while we're onstage because the caterers want to go home too.

By the time we get the band and singers back in the van or on the bus and get back to the hotel, it's well after midnight. Even if there isn't a hotel bar still open in this godforsaken one-horse town where we can unwind and do a postmortem of the show, we're not going to hit the rack until 1 a.m. at the very earliest. That's right. Enjoy your two hours of sleep before that alarm goes off.

I have a recurring malady that I call an "oldies cold." A typical oldies gig involves a 6 in the morning flight out on a Saturday (after playing some other gig late Friday night) and a 6 in the morning flight back home on the very next day with a show thrown in there in Tahlequah, Oklahoma.

"Where?" you ask.

Exactly.

Basically, you get no sleep for three days and travel for hours in an enclosed petri dish of an airplane. Monday morning you wake up with a cold almost every time.

The hotel in Tahlequah could be anything from a Bates Motel to a Four Seasons. You never know. And it really doesn't matter much. I have stayed in a whole bunch of five-star hotels for only three hours each. This business is all glamour all the time. Don't let anyone ever tell you differently.

"But surely," you protest, "once you reach a certain level of the business, the travel and accommodations must get more humane, no?"

The hotels may get nicer. But the travel stays ever as brutal. We often say that we do the gigs for free. What we get paid for is the travel.

As an illustration I will tell you about the first weekend I ever did on the road with Rock & Roll Hall of Famers Little Anthony & The Imperials. The Imperials recorded "Tears on My Pillow" in 1958 and haven't stopped moving since then. They got inducted into the Rock Hall in 2009.

After a few missed scheduling attempts years earlier, I first got to play with them in 2010. We played on a Friday night at a nice theatre in Naples, Florida, and Saturday at a casino in Niagara Falls, Ontario, Canada. I don't know what your level of familiarity is with airline hubs and common routing. But I can tell you this, "You can't get there from here."

We had a 4 a.m. lobby call to make a 6 a.m. flight to Washington, D.C., just enough time to run through the airport on a short layover, catch a flight to Buffalo, New York, grab a bus, clear Canadian customs (does anybody in show business ever have any prior arrests that slow down border crossings? Nah), make it to the sound check in Niagara Falls, and play the show. That's a full day right there.

We did have time to make it to the all-you-can-eat buffet before the show to try to caffeinate ourselves enough to perform that night. We were most amused that the tables in the cafeteria all had signs cautioning the patrons that there was a 90-minute limit on visits to the buffet. Clearly, if there's a need to make a sign, this is enough of a problem to warrant doing so.

Be warned, folks. If you're ever up in Niagara Falls, you may only have an hour and a half to strap on the old feed bag. So don't waste your time with the chitchat.

My point is that these were Hall of Fame performers who had been on the road for the past 52 years by the time I met them. They were in their 70s and highly respected artists. When a 70-year-old industry veteran tells you young whippersnappers that you need to be in the lobby at 4 a.m., the only possible respectful response is, "Yes, sir!"

Occasionally people miss their call time. This is to be avoided at all costs because you become "that guy." Nobody wants to be "that guy."

Friends of mine on long bus tours have had a policy that the bus call time was nonnegotiable. The bus left at 8 a.m. (or whatever the appointed hour) no matter what. If you missed the bus, you were "riding the dog." That meant it was your responsibility to get yourself to the next city on a Greyhound bus, aka "the dog."

As de facto road manager on many trips, I have had to make "the call" to roust someone who was late for the bus. The exchange was always some variation of this:

Riiiing. Bewildered raspy voice: "Hello?"

Road manager: "Will you be joining us today?"

Slowly dawning, newly panicked voice: "Oh, shit! I'll be right there!"

Fifteen minutes later, he drags his sorry carcass that looks like it had just been hit by a truck down the bus aisle past a dozen people who are already unhappy that they are up that early too. And, scene. It happens often enough that it isn't a huge deal. Except sometimes it is a big deal.

A band I was traveling with had a horn player miss a bus call in London once. We were staying in a bed-and-breakfast type of place that didn't have phones in the rooms. The only remedy was to go knock on the door. This time there was no answer. It was time to pound on the room door. Nothing.

Said horn player's brother was also in the band and knew from years of road experience with said horn player that there was absolutely no way to wake him up short of getting the key from the hotel manager, opening up the room, and physically dragging him out of bed.

That was above my pay grade. I decided that this should be a family activity. So I sent horn player's brother to get him up and get him on the bus. It took a little longer than it probably should have. But we made it to the next show.

I cite this example for two reasons. One, because it was an extreme version of the wake-up call. Having to forcibly enter a hotel room to get someone up is heavy stuff. And, two, because said horn player's brother ended up pulling a very similar stunt with the same band years later.

These cats are great players and great people. Anyone can miss an alarm. So two such incidents in a dozen years isn't an extraordinary failure rate.

That being said, brother number two's incident set off quite a bit of panic. This same band was in Tokyo for only two or three nights of shows. That was a 13-hour flight from New York, a 14-hour time zone difference, two nights of highly jet-lagged performing, and another 13-hour flight right back to New York. We have done that trip a bunch of times. It's beautiful there. The Japanese are amazing and lovely people. It's a cultural wonder every time we go. But the plane ride just hurts.

If we had Thursday and Friday night shows in Tokyo, for example, we would leave New York Wednesday evening. With the time difference and crossing the international dateline, we don't get to Tokyo until Thursday evening, local time. It's always a struggle to try to stay up late enough the night of arrival to justify going to bed. Ideally the later you can stay up, the easier it will be to try to get on the local time.

On one of those trips, we were taking the hour and a half bus ride into town. The people at the Blue Note club, where we were playing the next evening, offered us tickets to come see the last night of Tuck & Patti's run at their club. Five of us in the band took them up on their very kind offer. Tuck & Patti are a really wonderful husband-and-wife guitar-and-vocal jazz duo if you're not familiar with them. We really like them. The only problem is that they are extremely mellow and pretty quiet being only a duo.

The Blue Note people very sweetly wanted to treat us like VIPs. We were given a nice booth off to the side of the stage, maybe 15 ft. away from this beautiful and delicate performance. The club even treated us to free desserts as a courtesy. It was a lovely evening. Or it would have been had we not just disembarked from a 13-hour plane ride.

I am proud to have managed to keep myself awake for the entire performance. It wasn't easy. It took a lot of concentration and occasionally pinching the back of my hands with my fingernails to do it. The other four of my bandmates? Not so much. Heads back, mouths open, all but snoring right in view of these wonderful artists. It wasn't Tuck & Patti's fault. I'm not sure those people could have stayed awake for an Ozzy Osbourne concert.

But back to the missing horn brother. It was the second night of our two-night "run." In order for us to have the maximum time to ourselves during the day to rest, see sights, or do whatever we needed to do, the club scheduled a pretty tight pickup time for the second night. We would only get to the club about a half hour before showtime since the rig was already set and the mics were all checked from the night before. All we needed to do was walk up and play.

Brother number two missed the bus call. I rang up to his room but got no answer. I tried him several times. Nothing. We were kind of up against the wall. Either we had to leave right then, or we were in danger of starting the first of our two shows that evening late. Late starts are not tolerated in Japan. The trains run on time in that country.

We had to bail and leave him at the hotel not knowing where he was or whether he was dead or alive. There have been a couple of famous American bass players who have died in that town. One of them died in the very hotel where we staying. It wasn't unheard of, though as a bass player I thought I should have had more to worry about than a horn player.

Some folks in our touring party went into panic mode immediately. There were fears voiced that maybe he had ODed in an alley somewhere or had been robbed and killed by a pimp over a hooker. I thought this was a little extreme and pulling the fire alarm way too early, especially since I knew the cat well and hadn't experienced any such behavior from him at all.

Of the two brothers, the one sleeping in the London hotel room was probably the one to worry about. But there has been precedent for all these doomsday scenarios in the music business. We all knew people who had met such fates.

I certainly hoped the cat wasn't dead. But I had a couple of more immediate concerns. For one thing, I found the panic in the band room to be premature, unnecessarily upsetting, and definitely detracting from everyone's ability to stay focused and perform well that evening.

For another thing, as the music director, I was having to retool the show somewhat in my mind on the spot to steer the band away from the songs that featured this horn player. I was pretty sure we could pull it off if we had to. But it was requiring some mental math on my part to make sure it would run smoothly.

Fortunately, we had a local friend who offered to stay behind, get the hotel manager to open up the room, and get the cat to the gig if he was indeed still breathing. The band were already at the venue. None of us had cell phones that worked internationally. Plus, we were about to go onstage. I didn't know if the cat was alive or dead until he magically walked up onstage during the third song. The show was completed on schedule and the contract fulfilled.

Afterward we found out what had happened. Because of the jet lag and having the heavy curtains over the hotel windows, he woke up at 4 in the afternoon, looked at the clock, and decided it was 4 a.m. rather than 4 p.m. He did a wise thing then, which was to take a sleeping pill so that he would sleep through the night and be back closer to local time by the next day, except that he ended up taking the pill two hours before he was supposed to be in the lobby for bus call. He was OUT.

Our local friend got the hotel manager to open the room door, got the horn player up, got him dressed, and got him to the gig and onstage about 11 minutes into the show. Not bad, considering. He was very apologetic.

The worst one of these missed lobby calls I ever had was with a drummer at a gig in Pittsburgh. It was bad for a few reasons. The whole thing started out on the wrong foot and got worse as the situation wore on.

I had hired a fusion jazz drummer with an excellent reputation who had played with some pretty famous people. This guy was a monster player. I was excited to have him on the gig. But this gig was backing a classic soul singer, not fusion jazz.

What I didn't understand then but do a little better now is that fusion jazz and soul music may well have some skill sets in common in terms of what is required to play the show well. But they are by no means completely interchangeable skills. A jazz gig requires chops, a lot of chops. Backing a soul singer requires playing specific parts, nailing arranged endings, and usually reading charts verbatim.

When I hired him, I told the drummer the songs on the set list. He said, "Man, I been playing those songs since I was 12 years old."

Cool, I thought, I got the right guy. It wasn't until the sound check that I realized something was amiss. While he may have known the songs in a general sense, he didn't know any of the specific arrangements of this particular live show.

I've seen quite a few players fall into that trap. They assume that because they know a song they will be able to play it on any gig at any time with no problem. What I have found through much experience and falling on my face too many times to count is that if you have to play some rhythm & blues standard song with 12 different acts, they're going to have 12 different ways of doing it.

You have to do the homework for each act to nail those artists' shows. They have written endings, set vocal arrangements, and even choreography that go with their specific version of the song. Just knowing the song, especially if you know the famous recorded version note-for-note, isn't enough.

This drummer man wasn't cutting it at sound check at all. The rest of the band and, more importantly, our boss were looking at me as if to say, "You're going to fix this, right?" Now suddenly I had much more work to do before showtime.

I went with the drummer back to his hotel room to have a little "talk-through" about the songs. I was going to have to try to teach him all of the arrangements in about an hour. This was a daunting task that had to be done in fading light.

I got the distinct impression that although I had sent him complete charts and reference recordings for the show weeks in advance, he seemed to be looking at the charts in the hotel room that night for the very first time. I could feel my teeth beginning to grind. That type of behavior infuriates me.

In the old days we used to have to snail-mail Xeroxed copies of the charts with a cassette tape of a live show to members of a pickup band. The singers and I, as their music director, would fly out to the provinces and use a band we had probably never met before. When we got into the same-day rehearsal right before the show, if the musicians were tearing open the envelopes that I had mailed them weeks before for the very first time, I knew we were in for a hard night. It's completely disrespectful to the artists not to even pretend to prepare for their show.

Back in Pittsburgh, we finished the talk-through, drummer boy and myself. Come showtime we went up onstage. As we were plugging in our guitars and tuning up, the drummer said to me, "Oh, man, I left my charts back in the hotel room."

This guy was instantly no longer on my Christmas card list. But there was nothing I could do. It was time for the curtain to go up.

What I ended up having to do was spend the entire night facing the drummer and being his personal music director. Occasionally, I was able to send some cues out to the rest of the band. But my main focus was on this one dude. It was uncomfortable. The band felt it. They were all looking at me like, "Oh, you poor bastard."

Somehow the soul singer seemed to think the show went fine. I don't know if this was a tribute to my expert skill at personal drummer music directing or, more likely, the fact that there was so much else for him to deal with, like the audience, that he didn't notice all of the half-stepping coming from the drums. Somehow, we made it through the show without any major train wrecks.

As we began to pack up our gear, I saw the drummer, whom I was no longer speaking to at this point, holding his arm and looking pained. Remarkably he had managed to step off the back of the stage where there weren't any stairs. What was there was a road case with PA amps in it that he had tried to use as a step down to the ground.

One important thing to remember about road cases is that they are designed to be moved, you know, on the road. As such, they typically have wheels under them to facilitate this process. This case was no exception.

As the road case rolled out from under him, he grabbed for the stage railing to catch himself and completely dislocated his shoulder in the process. It took us a minute to figure out just how badly he was hurt. He left the venue that night in an ambulance. One of the promoters went with him to look after him.

At 5 a.m. the next day, we had lobby call to get the band to the airport and back to New York. Everyone was there except the drummer. We had a flight to make and had no time to fool around. As was common in these situations, by the time you realized there was a problem, the whole band was starting to be late for the flight.

I called the drummer's hotel room. No answer. I thought maybe he was knocked out on muscle relaxants and out of it. So I went to the hotel manager, explained our situation, and had him open the room with the master key. No drummer. He wasn't even in the building.

Now it was 5:15 a.m. I started making phone calls. Nobody likes to be awakened at that hour. Any office numbers that you might have are useless at that time of day. Eventually we got to someone who called someone who found out that the drummer was still in surgery at that moment having his shoulder reinstated. Apparently, they were unable to accomplish this in the ER all night. This was not good.

I spoke to the same promoter who had left with the drummer in the ambulance. He assured me that the drummer would be looked after, that all medical bills would be covered, and that he would personally get the drummer on a later flight. He told us all to go to the airport. We did that.

There were eventual lawsuits to cover his medical expenses that dragged on for years. It turned out that everything was indeed not covered. Can you imagine a concert promoter not actually keeping his word?

It's the only time I ever left a man behind. I felt badly about that.

Van rides at 5 a.m. to the airport are notoriously silent affairs because no one is really awake. This particular trip started that way until one of the horn players who remembered how difficult the show had been asked me, "So did you push him off the stage?" That woke everyone up.

I said, "Nobody could prove that it was me. Nobody saw anything. I take the Fifth."

In nearly 30 years of touring, I have never once missed a lobby call time. It's a statistic I wear with fierce pride. Well, it was, that is, until recently when it finally happened to me too.

I was in Culver, Indiana (Heard of it? I thought not), with a Motown tribute act. We had to drive six hours to Hopkinsville, Kentucky (Heard of it? I thought not) for the next show. The bandleader told me we had a 6 a.m. rollout after getting back to the hotel past 1 a.m., exhausted.

"Thank you very much," I said. I made a note in the calendar of my smart phone. "6 a.m.," I wrote. And then I set my alarm for 6 a.m. I like to be prepared.

It wasn't until 6 a.m. when my alarm went off that I realized my mistake. "Oh, no, no, no!" I thought. I started hustling faster than I have ever hustled. At 6:05 a.m. the phone rang. I didn't even ask who it was. I knew.

I answered the phone by saying, "I'm terribly sorry, sir. I'll be there as soon as I can."

"Don't worry," he said. "Take your time." This meant the opposite of what was actually said, of course.

It is always amazing to me that there are new things for me to learn, new lessons, new experiences, even after having done this for so long. What I learned that day was that it was possible for me to go from a dead sleep to a bolt-upright panic, throw all of my stuff into my luggage, throw on some clothes, and get onto a bus within six minutes. I definitely wasn't as showered as I had hoped nor were my teeth as brushed as I might have liked. But I was on the bus. And the band wasn't *too* pissed off at me. They were a little, as they should have been.

I also learned that even with a six-hour bus ride ahead and comfortable padded seats, even after only sleeping four hours in the hotel, the last thing I am able to do after that much panic and adrenaline is take a nap. I watched the sun come up over the cornfields of Indiana out of the bus window that day.

11 Pop-Star Girlfriend

Back in my record company days, I was so unhappy working behind a desk. One of the things that finally helped me quit my job and leave Los Angeles for good was the fact that I had hooked up with a pop-star girlfriend who lived in London. She wasn't a gigantic star. But she had three platinum albums and a gold one and was touring the world doing the thing that rock stars do.

She was signed to a record label owned by the company I worked for. So our romance was kind of on the down low. It was possibly the worst-kept secret in show business history. Everyone in the office seemed to know about it. I'm sure the $800-per-month phone bills on the company dime certainly got noticed by my boss.

I know I had some whopping long-distance phone bills at home in those days too. The phone company even called me at home once to make sure that everything was OK and that the charges were legit. This was before the days of free internet Skype. Hundreds of dollars a month were going to the phone company.

Because it might appear to be some business impropriety, we never acknowledged our relationship publicly. It was one of those things that everyone knew existed. But as long as nobody ever admitted the truth, public deniability was somehow maintained. It was like politics.

There was another level to the secrecy. She was 10 years older than I, actually a little long in the tooth to be a pop star. I was but a lad of 24 tender years. She was too ashamed at having a boy toy to admit it to anyone, I think. Throughout the year and a half we dated, she never wanted to be seen in public with me in anything more than an official capacity. Perhaps this should have been a red flag for me in retrospect. That and the Catholic-shame crying jags after certain intimate encounters.

The relationship was long-distance for about the first year. Because of her touring schedule and my business trips, we were able to rendezvous every few months in some city or other. It was all very cute. We were both giddy about it.

Finally, she said, "Why don't you come to London?"

I didn't need to be invited twice. This was my big rom-com moment. It was my opportunity to chuck my whole career for love and adventure. I was young, single, and hated my job. I basically had nothing to lose.

I sold everything I could of my personal possessions. I shipped the rest to my dad's house to be stored in his attic in North Carolina. A bunch of stuff stayed up there for many decades. I felt a little badly about that.

Off I went on a one-way ticket to London. I brought a bass with me because I hoped to begin my playing career in earnest in the U.K. rather than aspire to another desk job. I wanted to play as much as I could in between all the international travel she and I would inevitably end up doing.

On the same flight with me from Los Angeles to London there was a reggae band who had a bunch of guitars and gear also as checked baggage. Once we got to Heathrow, I believe that somehow my bass must have gotten "mixed in" with their stuff. I think they just took it, perhaps unwittingly. Somebody did. I would like to think that there is honor among musicians and that upon realizing their mistake they would have made efforts to return the bass. It was a nice one. Alas, I never saw it again.

The very first thing I had to do when I arrived in England was to fill out an insurance claim for my lost or stolen bass. Welcome to England.

When I got to the pop star's house, I was surprised to see that it wasn't like anything I had imagined. It was a small, humble brick home way out in the suburbs, about 45 minutes south of central London. There were no other pop stars around, no nightclubs, no culture, and no adventure. There were just lawns, clotheslines, driveways, and bad weather, which rendered the clotheslines almost comically useless. Everyone dried their laundry on their radiators.

The pop star had to go out on tour soon after my arrival, as pop stars tend to do. I was left in charge of the house and babysitting her 13-year-old son. He was a really cool kid. I liked him. But somehow, I went overnight from being a music industry insider to being an au pair, a live-in maid. There is nothing wrong with being an au pair. I just don't remember signing up for it specifically.

Concurrently with my doing laundry and cooking for the kid, all of my self-confidence and swagger exited the building. Since so much of my self-worth seems to be directly tied to my level of employment, being unemployed and being asked to babysit since I clearly didn't have anything better to do felt pretty demoralizing. It was also very isolated out there in the burbs.

She had a cousin with kids come in from out of town to visit her during the time that I lived at the house. I was told that I needed to completely clear out for the length of their visit. This was partly because there would be a lot of people in the house. But it was mostly because she was ashamed of having me around as the admitted boy toy.

I ended up finding a £15-per-night tiny bedsit in some hellhole in London for the week. It was the kind of joint with crusted carpet full of cigarette burns. It probably would have been a shooting gallery if it were in New York. But somehow the British were ever so slightly more refined about it. There were no visible junkies present. Very civilized.

This should have been another red flag for me. It was. It was clear that the pop star didn't really want me around. I had just quit my career, sold all of my possessions, and left the country of my birth to hang out with her. But, hey, no biggie.

The situation in the U.K. wasn't measuring up to my expectations. And I damn sure wasn't measuring up to hers. I'm not sure what she thought I was going to do or how I was going to act when I got there. But I was clearly not fulfilling whatever she thought that was.

Things were getting bleak pretty fast in rainy auld England. The relationship had completely run off into the ditch within six months of my arrival. I had to get myself a cold-water flat in north London and decide if I wanted to try to stay in the U.K. on my own or not.

I ended up staying another year by myself, burning through my savings while trying to make a few pence here or there as a freelance musician. In a way, it was the grand adventure I was looking for, though it didn't come in the form that I thought it would. I ended up making a couple of lifelong musical friends while I was over there. But that took a while.

One day in the winter, it had been raining for about a month straight. It doesn't really snow that much there. But it surely does drizzle. I went to get a haircut from a local tonsorial artist. As he was working on my skull, the immigrant barber said to me in heavily German-accented English, "So vat is an American doing in north London in the middle of February?"

I was hard-pressed to give him a suitable answer since I really didn't know myself.

The following summer, I eventually ended up with a regular gig playing bass nightly and being a booking agent for a new restaurant in Covent Garden. It seemed like the perfect combination of my aspirations to play coupled with whatever business acumen I had accrued while at the record company.

Yes, that is how it initially seemed.

12 WHAT IS A ROCK STAR?

Rock star is a term that gets thrown around too casually these days in my opinion. It's now possible to be a so-called "rock star businessman" or "rock star plumber." While there is certainly eminent dignity in being a plumber, being branded the rock star version of any particular vocation is not the same thing as being an actual rock star.

But what is a rock star? At its core, rock stardom implies fame and fortune acquired by a singer or musician through the medium of popular music. Beyond these basic assumptions are also implications of celebrity and adoration gained from talent, creativity, panache, artistry, and fashion sense.

Rock stardom is acquired and maintained through repeated appearances on radio, television, movies, music videos, world tours, newspapers, magazines, blogs, and social media. Along with all of this come groupies, sex, drugs, trashed hotel rooms, and never-ending world tours on luxury buses and private planes. Let us also not forget the stereotypical long hair and bad-boy reputation.

By all of these qualifications, it turns out that I am an actual rock star ... except for the pesky fame and fortune part. I have toured some of the world's most famous concert stages, appeared in all manner and nature of mass media, received adoration from rabid fans, and been paid large sums of money for my work.

I should probably qualify all of that a bit. I have indeed done all those things, but in limited quantities and at separate times. For instance, I had one or two gigs in my life that paid me $2,000 or more for a single night. If you had 200 such gigs a year, for instance, you could make $400,000 in that year, which is a lot of money. Is it rock star money? It's not cliché rock star money, but I do know more than a few actual rock stars and Hall of Famers who would be thrilled with this level of income, especially over time.

Like I said, this level of compensation has graced me only a handful of times. Each time the pay for the "single night of work" involved weeks of musical transcription, writing charts, practice, and preparation. Add to this hours and hours of often international travel to the venue, days of rehearsal, and about 90 minutes on a concert stage at the end of it all.

Occasionally I try to work out an average hourly wage based on the amount of time I put in on any given gig. Even discounting the travel time, it turns out that I am working cheap. The bass player in the old *National Lampoon* Mister Rogers sketch was right all along.

There are some gigs where afterward there is a meet-and-greet or a stage door scene. Fans will be waiting for the performers to exit the building to get autographs and take pictures. I have been photographed and have signed programs and playbills countless times. It makes me smile every time it happens, not only because it's fun to have the attention, but especially because I know that once I walk about 100 yards from the theatre, I will have sunk back into total obscurity again.

I'm a rock star only from the stage door to the corner of 44th Street and 8th Avenue. Once I turn that corner, I am back to being another schmo on the subway back to Brooklyn.

TV, movies, radio, videos, newspapers, magazines, social media? Yep, been there and done them all to one extent or another. Have you heard of me? Has your grandmother heard of me? Probably not.

Sex and drugs? More drugs than sex get offered. I always turn them down not being a user. Trashed hotel rooms? One time I stole a particularly cool do not disturb sign from a boutiquey hotel that said, "Leave me alone!" They ended up charging my credit card $10 for it.

So what does that make me? I guess I'm more of a working-class rock star, an hourly wage earner humping my own gear and slogging all over creation to try to earn a peso. Instead of coveralls with my name on a patch over the left breast, I often wear a bargain tuxedo made overseas by child slave labor to be allowed to amuse the rich folk for short periods of time.

Occasionally, I stand next to an actual rock star for an hour, making music with him or her, listening to the roar of tens of thousands of fans. There are certainly moments when rock stars and I breathe the same rarefied air and eat at the same buffet in the backstage "hostility" suite.

Mostly I spend time entertaining drunks in bars or playing four-hour functions like the Lipschitz bar mitzvah in Piscataway, New Jersey. This inevitably involves being yelled at by maître d's with cheap toupees who view me as less qualified to be in their catering halls than their dishwashers.

Then there are the irate drunken bridesmaids and groomsmen who belligerently scream at us after the end of the contracted four hours. After spending all that time feeling miserable while playing cover songs in a tux, I hear them howl, "One more song! One more song!"

You see? They treat us like rock stars.

Having passively ignored us or actively scorned us for the first three hours of the function, they imagine that they can somehow appeal to our vanity by complimenting our musicianship, however slurred their verbal delivery. Since we are but lowly unwashed musicians, unable to recognize their shrewd manipulative tactics, they assume that we will continue to entertain them long into the night, ignoring our own contract.

This doesn't even take into account the contract of the catering hall and the dozens of their employees desperately trying to clean and clear the room so that they can punch out and get home to their own miserable lives. These chants for encores take place under the watchful eye of the toupeed maître d' who is staring daggers at us and giving us the finger-across-the-throat symbol.

All of the contracts in the building at these functions contain provisions for overtime to be purchased in half-hour increments. This includes the band, the sound system, the lights, the food, the waitstaff, and the hall itself. All someone needs to do to continue a party that is proceeding amazingly is to agree to write a check. A thumbs-up from whoever is the benefactor or sponsor of the festivities can indeed extend the celebration in 30-minute blocks well into the wee hours. Money changes everything.

As you can imagine these extensions do happen, but seldom. Often this requires the band to pack our gear in the midst of an angry drunken mob with varying levels of belligerence. The good feeling of receiving the rock star adulation turns ugly very quickly.

The actual amount of time one is able to enjoy this adoration of the fans is roughly 10 to 15 seconds. That's about the amount of time it takes for the cheers and applause to turn into chants for an encore, triggering the chain of events detailed above. When the extension generally doesn't materialize, nor is there any explanation from the hosts, the cheers turn quickly to jeers, chiding the band for being party poopers.

So yes, for those fleeting seconds I am indeed a rock star.

13 WHAT'S YOUR WORST NIGHTMARE?

I would venture to guess that the majority of people very wisely choose not to participate as performing artists because they correctly fear public embarrassment. Breaking wind loudly on a crowded train car is bad enough. But imagine standing in front of a thousand people who are all pointing at you and laughing or booing. Almost everyone has had some version of that nightmare, haven't they?

As a performer, no matter how much you have rehearsed, no matter how carefully you have prepared, no matter how expert you are at that special thing you do, occasionally things are not going to go well. A lightbulb could burn out. A microphone wire could abruptly stop working. A drunk heckler could disrupt the performance. There are so many forces beyond our control that can derail the mood of an entire roomful of people.

Inevitably there will come a time when there will be public embarrassment. Occasionally it can be epic public shame. If you are the type of person for whom this is absolutely terrifying, perhaps a career in the performing arts isn't your wisest choice.

On the other hand, one of the things that makes a live performance exciting is the very possibility that something could go wrong. This is one of the attractions of watching a NASCAR race, not that someone can drive flawlessly at 200 mph for 500 miles, but the fact that one of them could crash at any moment.

This metaphor gets used verbatim in Broadway orchestra pits. If a first-time substitute player comes in and doesn't play well enough to get asked to make a return engagement, this is called a "crash and burn." I have witnessed this happening two times. Both times it was very upsetting to everyone in the room.

I have heard playing in a Broadway pit for a long run described as hours and hours of total boredom interspersed with brief flashes of white-hot panic. It's the nature of the beast. Performing the exact same songs over and over again takes a lot of skill. It also requires intense concentration, probably more so on the 100th performance than on the 10th. Your mind inevitably starts to drift.

As a substitute musician, I have played close to 500 performances of 12 different Broadway shows. I have never officially held a chair as a full-time orchestra member. But I have put in some time over to the Broad Way. I have seen performances go spectacularly well. I have also seen a few go much less spectacularly.

I was subbing in the pit of a show that I will simply call the most expensive and most infamous show in Broadway history without naming any names. This is to protect the guilty. I played about 45 performances at this superhero musical. Ah, there, I've said too much.

The beginning of the second song of the show started with just the bass (played by me) and the drums in an exposed moment. The bass was going through an effects pedalboard that was supposed to make the bass sound huge and a little cartoonish. Imagine singing in a basso profundo voice, "Boom, wow-wow-wow-wow-wow." That was how it was supposed to sound, big and menacing.

Now factor in that the show had been running for two years by that time. The equipment that was being used for eight shows every week for over 100 weeks was starting to show its age. Somehow the effects pedalboard had developed a hair trigger in all that pounding, so that the volume pedal, which the bass player had to ride the whole show, could inexplicably switch itself into a different mode function. Instead of a volume pedal, it might without warning turn into a wah-wah or pitch shifter pedal. This was what happened to me.

Instead of the basso profundo sound, the effects unit had transposed the bass up two whole octaves. It sounded like a drunk hummingbird barking in its highest register, "Bing, meow-meow-meow-meow-meow." This sound wasn't computing in my head because I had never heard a bass guitar make any noise in that register before. I didn't even know it was possible.

I just kept thinking, "I don't know who's making that ridiculous sound. But I know it can't be me!"

One by one everyone in the orchestra room turned to look at me with that head-tilted confused Scooby-Doo look until I realized that somehow it was indeed me making that awful sound at this very exposed and inopportune moment in the show.

Now the panic began to set in. I started scrambling for a setting that sounded anything like a bass and nothing like a piccolo on crack. I needed something that resembled a bass, even if it wasn't the exact tone that everyone was used to hearing in that spot. I found one soon enough and spent the rest of the performance on high alert in case the pedalboard decided to throw me any more curveballs.

Mercifully, it did not. Also, mercifully the gaff was rightly blamed on the equipment and not me as a player. All was forgiven by the conductor.

Another evening at this same theatre, a first-time sub came in on the "guitar-one" chair. There were three guitars in that pit. Guitar-one tended to do more of the exposed parts and lead lines. While all of the guitars were important chairs, guitar-one had a lot more to do out in the open. There was less opportunity to hide if something went wrong.

That evening the guitar player was just too inexperienced in general and underprepared specifically to play that particular book properly. Unfortunately, this deficit was not small on either count. It did not go well.

It was apparent to us in the orchestra almost instantly that something was amiss. It was also apparent to the guitar player, who, realizing he was screwing up, then proceeded to do what we all do and let his nerves get the better of him. Mistakes get compounded in a situation like that. A lot of stupid errors get made that would never happen when practicing the same music in the safety and comfort of your own home.

As the first act was proceeding, the tension in the room was mounting steadily. The conductor, who was also a substitute that night, kept his head down and didn't make eye contact with anyone. We all knew this kid was fired by the time we got to the intermission. But we still had act 2 to play. There was no choice. They needed someone to remain sitting in that chair, no matter how disastrously, for the last hour of the show.

I found myself looking ahead in my score to try to figure out which cues I had to play together with the unfortunate guitarist so that I could steel myself. I wanted to be prepared to play as if the dude weren't even in the room.

By intermission the stage manager had called down to the conductor in the pit to confirm that there was indeed a sub guitar player on instead of the regular dude. It had been noticed upstairs. That was extremely not good. This dude's career at that show opened and closed on the same night.

All Broadway pit subs live under a constant state of fear for our jobs. There is a long line of people waiting for those chairs. We have to play better than the person we're subbing for while at the same time trying to do our best impersonation to sound exactly like them so that the actors aren't able to notice a difference when a sub is in.

Mistakes are frowned upon in general, though it's understood that they do happen in live theatre. A mistake made by someone who holds a chair on a show will be laughed at by the other orchestra members. The same exact mistake made by a sub will prompt the other members to say, "I don't know if this guy is going to work out." It's a tough racket.

This brings me to probably my greatest moment of potential embarrassment on any stage. I was subbing on the Broadway musical *Hedwig and the Angry Inch*. It was an onstage role in full costume and makeup. There was a little choreography. The music had to be memorized along with a couple of lines and a bunch of stage business.

I was playing bass, singing background the entire show as well as two different lead-vocal spots, playing keyboard bass in a few spots, and playing acoustic guitar on one song. It was a fair amount of heavy lifting to be sure.

As a sub I got the luxury of sitting in at a put-in rehearsal for one of the actors. I had a dry run before going on in front of an audience. But this was unusual. Generally, one has to learn the book in the privacy of one's home and just show up and nail it at a performance in front of an audience who have paid a lot of money for their seats.

As I said, mistakes are frowned upon. It's very likely that the one performance opportunity you've been given as a first-time sub could potentially be your one and only performance. It can take upwards of a month just to prepare for this first show.

Add to this the fact that all the regular orchestra members are usually bored silly. They're doing crossword puzzles or checking their phones every moment that they're not playing a song. They have also been through hell to get where they are, not unlike what pledges to a fraternity have had to endure.

There is a persistent sensation that the other orchestra members actually want you to fail.

Seeing someone else fail gives them a war story to tell. And it confirms their feeling that they are somehow members of an elite class of performers. And they are. Except that they're also really not. They put on their pants one leg at a time like everybody else. It's just that they practice putting on their pants over and over again until they're really good at it.

The vibe in the theatre at *Hedwig* wasn't like this at all. Everyone was super nice and completely supportive. They all wanted you to do well because you then made them look good. This is as it should be, yet unfortunately it's not the usual situation for most Broadway shows. Even so, as a first-time sub on Broadway, you still have to basically wear a diaper. It's that tense.

My very first performance at *Hedwig* went amazingly well. I had a thousand things in my head that I was trying to remember: the bass lines, the vocal parts, the lyrics, my stage business, choreography, and on and on. It went well. I was nervous but hit all of my marks with sufficient competency.

Late in the show, there was a choreographed mosh pit scene. While wearing sunglasses on a darkened stage lit only with a strobe light, I was told to hit a tiny mark on the floor with my back facing the character Yitzhak, played by Lena Hall, who had just won a Tony Award for the role. Lena was to come barreling into my back at full speed two different times, knocking me forward and apparently off balance. I think Lena weighs about 90 pounds soaking wet. But I was in the proper position to take my beating anyway. This all happened exactly as intended. So far, so good.

At the end of the show after we played the music for the bows, my instructions were to put the bass down and join the cast and band up on a riser for a final group bow. Simple enough.

What I didn't realize was that during the mosh pit scene somehow the metal chain necklace that I was wearing had gotten wrapped around a button on my leather jacket. This entanglement took place over the top of the guitar strap, effectively physically locking the bass onto my body.

The bass was literally fastened onto my costume. It was also plugged into the stage rig. I was trapped in that spot unable to complete the final duty I had for the evening, which was to simply walk up and take a bow. The music was already over. One thousand people were on their feet giving us a standing ovation. The show, the hard part, was over. All I needed to do was bow and go home.

I started tearing at the necklace chain. It clearly wasn't going to be moved. So I tried to take the strap off the bass to release myself that way. As I began frantically pulling at the bass strap, it got tangled in the cable connected to my in-ear headphones, in the necklace chain, and even now in my long hair. The more frantically I pulled at it all, the tighter the knot it made.

The cast was looking at me. The 1,000 people in the audience were looking at me. And I was digging myself a deeper and deeper hole.

The music director, Justin, finally said to me, "Just bring the bass," which I did.

The guitar cable was fortunately long enough to reach where the cast was standing and waiting patiently for me to take their final bow.

Justin took mercy on my soul and reached over to unplug the bass. He tossed the cable aside so that I could at least exit the stage in my shame. That had never occurred to me.

I was trying to follow orders and put the bass down. The bass proved impossible to put down for what Justin later described as "an uncomfortably long period of time." It was probably only 20-30 seconds. But that's a *looong* time to be on a Broadway stage in front of that many people visibly and comically screwing up.

The cast did a post-show huddle every night. That night the star, John Cameron Mitchell, looked at me and said, "Now that's rock & roll!"

Thank god I amused them rather than pissed them off, or that might have been my one and only appearance on that stage.

After the show I was going to meet my girlfriend in front of the theatre. While she was waiting for me, she saw a friend of hers on the way out who had just seen the show. She told her friend that she was waiting to meet her boyfriend who played bass in the show. The pal told her, "Oh, my god, did you hear what happened?" My infamy preceded me all the way out of the theatre and onto West 44th Street.

Amazingly I wasn't mortified about what had happened. I found it very odd and funny. The potential embarrassment in front of a large audience didn't bother me. By that point in my career I had spent so many thousands of hours in front of people that I almost didn't care anymore.

Well, it wasn't that I didn't care. I always hope to perform well. It's just that it hardly fazed me anymore. I no longer feared being onstage at the high school assembly while somehow forgetting to wear clothes that day.

What I was nervous about instead was the acceptance of my fellow performers and particularly of the music director. If I got the thumbs-up from him, I would live to screw up another day. If I got the thumbs-down, it was curtains for me.

Thankfully they all thought it was really funny and were glad that it had happened to me instead of to one of them. They had my back for a dozen more shows over the course of the run. I loved playing that show.

I did learn, however, never to wear that necklace again onstage.

The *Hedwig* costume without the offending necklace

14 WHAT IS FAME?

Paul McCartney once told me never to drop names.
OK, I don't actually know Paul McCartney. I've never met him. But the joke doesn't work unless you use the name of someone who is really famous. I have met some other famous people in my travels. So why didn't I use one of their names instead? Well, because then a question would arise about whether that person truly said that to me, which that person didn't because it's just a joke.

How is someone supposed to know that I have met famous person X, but that I haven't met Paul McCartney? OK, listen, this is getting complicated. It was just a joke, a hackneyed old vaudevillian line that I've heard dozens of times and didn't write myself. Lighten up, will you?

My point is this. Fame is a tenuous thing. Let us imagine that you did something hugely famous and sold 10 million albums, books, concert tickets, or whatever unit of demarcation you feel comfortable with to define someone who has "made it." In this country alone that means that potentially about 320 million people don't know who you are and don't care.

It wouldn't take a trip to Appalachia searching for Amish people (who don't usually live in Appalachia) without electricity to find people who haven't heard of you. You could be massively rock star famous. Yet my family would still have no idea who you are.

Fame is relative. Recognition is fleeting. Superstars become superstars not only by having incredible talent and charisma coupled with tremendous luck and opportunities, but also by having a machinery around them designed to crush the competition and trample on any challengers to the throne.

Of all the gigs I've done, the higher up the fame food chain they are, the more this principle is noticeable. Superstars like to keep tight control on images that get released. This was especially true before social media became ubiquitous. Now everybody has a camera in his pocket.

Back in the day, there would be one photograph of the star that would be circulated to the media for each project. This press image was the result of a designated photo shoot with specific makeup, wardrobe, and photo retouching. When publishing, anything that wasn't cleared by the artist's management was asking for trouble. A media outlet could be in jeopardy of not receiving access to a star on future projects for printing unflattering unofficial photos.

I once sent a selfie I took with a superstar to an alumni magazine, which printed it. Somehow word got back to the superstar, and I got a severe reprimand and was threatened with dismissal from the position that had allowed me contact with this star.

This was before the days of Facebook or even Myspace. The selfie I had taken was with an actual camera and not with a phone. The word "selfie" hadn't even been invented back then. Releasing a photo like that without clearance that got picked up by the press (even an alumni magazine) was a big no-no.

These days, of course, you can't even take wedding photos in Central Park without having Tom Hanks crash your shoot for selfies while he's out for a jog. Look, dude, we didn't invite you to the wedding for a reason.

As musicians we are constantly reminded that we are in a "glamour profession." There is a line of people around the block just waiting to take your job and to do it for less money or no money at all just for the opportunity. There is some truth to that.

A booking agent friend of mine used to call and say, "I've got a gig on May 15th. I don't know who it's with. I don't know how far away it is. And I don't know what it pays. Do you want it or not?" He was halfway kidding, but only halfway.

My friends and I frequently quote the old joke about the dude who works for the circus walking behind the elephants and scooping up massive amounts of poop. When asked why he would endure such indignity, he says, "What, and quit show business?"

We don't tell the joke anymore. Now, anytime something messed up happens on a gig (which is all the time) we just look at each other and say, "What, and quit show business?"

Similarly, we find the classic mockumentary *This Is Spinal Tap* to be gospel truth. Innumerable times when we're hopelessly lost backstage trying to find the wings, someone will inevitably blurt out, "Hello, Cleveland!" When we find ourselves actually playing in Cleveland in the great state of Ohio, these outbursts are incessant. That movie is not a joke to us. It's a religion.

So, what is fame?

Well, for one thing, it's a recording studio and record label down South that was originally named as an acronym for Florence Alabama Music Enterprises. Arguably, this is a hubristic name for a studio on its first day of business.

Berry Gordy similarly put a sign up over the house at 2648 West Grand Boulevard in Detroit proclaiming it "Hitsville U.S.A." before they had recorded a single song at Motown Records.

But that's not what I'm talking about here. The dictionary decrees that fame is "the condition of being known or talked about by many people, especially on account of notable achievements." This is not to be confused with fortune, which is good luck and/or riches aplenty. One can be rich and not be famous at all. One can also be famous and poor. Mother Teresa would be the positive example of this.

What is it about being known or talked about by many people that seems even remotely desirable to us? That's a good question. There are certainly people who are more than happy to be out of the spotlight. But judging from the audience pan shot every day on *The Price Is Right,* I have to assume that there are a lot of people who, given the slightest chance, would gladly accept fame into their lives with or without winning ... "a new car!"

As a side note, the Sam Moore band once performed on a show that was shot at CBS Television City in Los Angeles. The main entrance to the building required us to pass through the audience waiting to be loaded into *The Price Is Right.* They were all wearing their name tags and fired up with anticipation at their imminent winnings. Let me tell you something. It is an interesting cross section of humanity, that audience. They were like the people who are more than fully prepared to trample one another to death to get a flat-screen TV that's on sale for 20 percent off at malls across America on Black Friday. The only difference was that these people had their hair and makeup all "did" for the TV cameras.

So, what is it about fame? It's not even about the money or the patio furniture. Photobombing postgame sports interviews to silently mouth the words "Hi, Mom!" is an unavoidable crowd phenomenon.

Maybe those are the two key words to unlock the entire mystery: "Hi, Mom." What makes those two words the knee-jerk reaction for anyone unexpectedly faced with a network TV camera?

Are we as a people looking for the esteem of strangers and hoping to become a topic of their conversation? Or are we just hoping that enough people will talk about us and that it will get back to our moms so that they will know we're giving them the shout-out, and are therefore lovable people?

In my case it comes largely from having a narcissistic mother and grandmother who tended to operate with great vigor the *pollice verso*, the turned thumb. This was a gladiator-style judgment upon every possible action of the child, which carried with it a binary conclusion. Thumbs-up meant you were a good child, therefore lovable, and would be allowed to live another day. Thumbs-down meant you were a bad child, unlovable, and must die. It was the polar opposite of unconditional love.

Not only did this judgment seem harsh and oppressive, it was also extremely mercurial and could completely reverse course on a dime. It was difficult to know where you stood at any moment. It turned out that it didn't really matter because it would change the very next moment due to circumstances seemingly out of your control. Whether there was something you could have done to change a given situation or not was immaterial. Somehow "you should have known better."

Over the long-term, this situation has left me with a consistent nagging voice in the back of my head that says, "You ain't shit." Nothing I do ever feels like it's good enough.

Even if I do something good, where people are applauding or praising me, the feeling is that this praise will inevitably evaporate at any moment. The reversal will somehow be due to something that I'll be blamed for even though I haven't realized I've done anything wrong. It's a tough paradox to live with and an even tougher one to try to dig out of psychologically.

To this day, when I'm supposedly in the "good kid" category, the slightest stimulus can evoke a memory in a family member that will require a retelling of a negative story from decades ago, a recounting of some failure of mine from the past.

This family folklore never allows me to be fully successful at anything in the eyes of my family or even just to be proud of my accomplishments. It never lets me feel OK just being in my own skin. These stories are always told with a smile as if recalling a funny joke from years past. The feeling that they leave is never quite funny, though.

There's a story my mother used to tell about me rolling around and throwing up on the floor in the hallway at her friend's house, a scene that caused her some embarrassment. Admittedly this wasn't one of my finest moments, and would have been especially so if I was a drunk teenager or in my 30s or something. But the incident in question took place when I was approximately one year old.

A couple of things come to mind. 1) No, Mom, I don't remember this incident, though I've heard this story many, many times, thank you. And 2) I was ONE. Many babies I've met are prone to this same antisocial behavior, not necessarily choosing their locations to vomit with good manners in mind. In fact, this is so common an occurrence there's even a cute name for it, "to spit up," which removes most of the stigma.

That's just an example. There are other stories.

"I saw a guy on TV whose hair was worse than yours," said my grandmother a few years ago. She was only 97 at the time and just out of surgery to repair her broken hip. It's possible the adjective she was searching for was "longer" or "wilder." But the word she used was "worse." I guess she had shaken off the effects of the anesthesia just fine. And so it goes.

15 IN SEARCH OF ...

L et us revisit my junior high and high school years and the painfully elaborate choreography it takes anyone to discover one's place in the social hierarchy. The need for acceptance we all feel in my case got coupled with the constant feeling of being off balance because I never knew when the next familial judgment was to befall me. This made for some difficult times.

As I've discussed, my parents made this one level more challenging by enrolling the young me in an all-boys preparatory school, thereby removing any opportunity for me to socially acclimatize to female human beings during the crucial pubescent years when these social skills are formed. To make it just a little more interesting, for some reason they enrolled me in said preparatory school in the eighth grade. All the other students had begun in the seventh grade and already had a full school year to form their various cliques.

Understand also that an engineer and a computer programmer with good solid government jobs raised a child who never went hungry or unshod a day in his life. Yet this same fortunate child seemed like a poor townie in relation to the children of wealth and status who were sent away to this boarding school.

Never mind that many of these rich kids were being parked at a boarding school in hopes that their bratty behavior would be curtailed by institutional discipline. Their families assumed that this would make up for their lousy parenting.

At this former military academy, we were expected to observe the "honor code" and gain moral character through discipline, education, and, most of all, athletics. Of the 100 students in my class, there were two Jews and, well, that was it. It was 98 percent white, male, and Christian. Needless to say, it didn't go very well for me.

It took a year or two for me to give up trying to fit in altogether. As a 6 ft. tall eighth grader, a nonathletic, non-Christian, townie pauper, I was clearly unwelcome in their midst. Rather than waste my time trying to dress in fashions from the L.L.Bean catalog, including duck boots, khaki slacks, and blue Oxford button-down collar shirts, I decided to go the opposite direction.

We were required to wear a dress shirt and a tie to school every day. There were no explicit color or fabric requirements on the shirt, however. My mother happily gave me the run of my stepfather's closet to pilfer all of the 1970s garishly printed polyester leisure shirts that I could carry.

Since these shirts were originally designed to be worn in nightclubs exposing a silver coke spoon dangling in one's ample porn-star chest hair, they were not manufactured with collar buttons. I had to cut buttonholes and sew on top buttons to comply with the letter, if not the actual spirit, of the school dress code.

To complement these woefully out-of-fashion shirts (were they ever really in fashion?), I raided the thrift store for 25 cent extra-wide loudly patterned polyester neckties. I can assure you that there were combinations I was able to come up with of leisure shirts that clashed with themselves, coupled with ties that also clashed with themselves, that were both beautiful and terrible to behold.

Did I mention that I was not a popular kid in high school?

Ostracized, ignored, hazed, bullied, and threatened, I was no longer searching for acceptance. I merely sought tolerance, peace, to be left alone. The only place I ever felt anonymous was on St. Mark's Place on visits to see the family in New York City. New-wave skinny satin fluorescent neckties purchased on St. Mark's made their way back to Chattanooga with me to be integrated into the school wardrobe.

During this period in my teen life, music became a solace. Listening to, discovering, and reading about new music was a solitary activity that provided emotional release without the need to involve other people. I admired the musicians. I identified with those who seemed to be coming from some counterculture or other.

It wasn't about idol worship with me at all. In fact, I remember being appalled at listening to a girl talk about hero worship of Pete Townshend of The Who just because he was famous and a rock god. I was a big fan of The Who. But this girl was into them for all the wrong reasons. It had nothing to do with their playing, singing or writing. The fame itself was somehow paramount to her.

It's too bad, too. This girl was 6 ft. tall. She was really cute. We have a prom picture together somewhere. We had been fixed up on a first date just for the promenade. Finally, here was a girl I could see eye to eye with. Or in reality here was a girl, any girl. It turned out to be simultaneously a first and last date.

I liked music. I liked the idea of rock stardom. The previously discussed problem that I didn't play an instrument was a minor detail that could not possibly stand in my way.

In the fall of my senior year in high school, when I finally started to learn to play the bass guitar, I found that I had some aptitude for it and apparently some natural ability. This surprised no one more than me. That aptitude, coupled with some great lessons from my pal, Riq, got me off to a promising start. Although only a year older than me, he had been playing bass for a couple of years. He was experienced.

Willie Nelson said in an interview once that he was asked to play bass for his hero, Ray Price. This was back in 1960 because Ray's bass player, Donny Young (aka the future Johnny Paycheck), wanted to quit the band. Ray called Willie and asked him, "Can you play bass?"

To which Willie replied, "Can't everybody?"

The point is that on some level, getting functional on the bass isn't that difficult. I always say that anybody can do what I do. Getting proficient is another story. I haven't read that story yet. But I have been able to keep myself occupied with a Fender bass in my hand for almost 40 years now. So that's something, I guess.

Meanwhile back in high school, almost as soon as I started playing bass I was able to find some like-minded students with similar rock star aspirations. There were just a few guitar players, drummers, and singers. But I seemed to be the only bass player in the school. This was an early fortuitous career decision that has served me well.

In the spring of my senior school year, there was an annual talent show that I had attended as an audience member in previous years. This year I was to be a performer in the show in three different bands. We set up a stage in the gymnasium, hired a sound system from my pal Riq (see above. Are you catching how small towns work here?), and performed cover songs by The Police, Rush, Rolling Stones, Pat Benatar, Tommy Tutone, The Who, and Neil Young.

The crowd went ballistic. I have a cassette recording of that night, which has survived to this day. So I can say without the cloud of misremembered, over-romanticized youth that the audience were indeed screaming like maniacs for us.

Part of this can rightfully be attributed to the sheer volume that teen males tend to exhibit when unsupervised. But that didn't account for all of the crowd's enthusiasm. They seemed to genuinely and enthusiastically love what we were playing.

Was this fame? Were the 600 kids in this school gymnasium transformed instantaneously from disgust and revulsion at my mere presence to acceptance and, dare I say it, actually liking me?

As it turned out the answer was no. The previously mentioned threat of forced removal of my long hair by the football team with the tacit acceptance of the highest levels of the school administration was yet to follow this concert. But for that evening, it felt good. It felt like this might be my ticket out of there.

Having started so relatively late in life, playing music remained a secondary pursuit for me during college and into my initial career in the record industry. It took eight years more from the time I first picked up the instrument before I decided that music was something I might pursue as a primary career. It took a full 14 years from that first time until it became my primary source of income.

I had a former high school classmate write to me on Facebook years later to say that I was the only person he knew who grew up to be what I said I would be. He clearly had misremembered my career trajectory and romanticized what he imagined my life to be. I didn't set out to be a musician at all when I was in high school. That happened much later.

The acceptance by that classmate, however skewed and factually incorrect, was the acceptance I had craved. Never mind that I didn't find out about it until 30 years later. I hoped that by playing music, the resulting inevitable fame would gain me the esteem from others that I so desperately wanted in high school.

The dictionary definition of fame doesn't specify the number of the "many" people who have to be talking about you to fulfill the requirement. It's quite possible to be famous among 100 students at a prestigious all-boys preparatory school and to go absolutely no further in life. High-school football quarterbacks and cheerleaders are prime examples of the popular kids who peak a little too early in life.

Here is a good place to illustrate this phenomenon with the story of a dude I'll call Jay. Jay and I went to elementary school together for all six of those years. During that time, we were probably of roughly equal social standing. We weren't stars of our elementary school. But we weren't outcasts either. We ended up going to separate junior high and high schools.

The next time I saw Jay was over the winter break of our freshman year in college. As I've said, I had a rough time in high school and had turned into a fairly introverted music nerd who was in all of the school plays. Whatever little self-confidence I might have gained over time as a senior in high school was completely stripped away again when I became a freshman in college.

Also, since there had been zero girls at my high school, I couldn't relate to them at all as a species. I couldn't talk to them, didn't date much in high school or college, and was pretty much a disaster when it came to making time with the fine sexy ladies I might meet back home in Chattanooga, Tennessee.

Jay, however, had gone a different way. He had undergone a remarkable transformation since elementary school.

One night during that winter break, some pals had dragged me out to a disco. Ah, maybe "disco" is too extravagant a word. It was a Ruby Tuesday chain restaurant where they pushed the tables aside after hours. Somebody was playing records. And there were colored "party" lights involved. There were at least eight people there, too. So it was clearly a "scene" by Chattanooga standards.

Keep in mind that at this age I didn't dance. I didn't socialize. I seemed to be rendered completely mute when attempting to talk to girls. I would never have been tempted to go to a "disco" or any other social gathering of this sort.

It turned out that this kid, Jay, had become the king of that scene. He had stayed in Chattanooga to attend college and had somehow transformed himself into the Jewish version of Tim Meadows's character, the Ladies Man. He even had the polyester shirt. He seemed to be holding court, lording over his loyal subjects, all eight of them.

The DJ put on a new record that had just come out that fall. It was Prince's "Little Red Corvette."

Jay jumped up and ran over to the DJ rig saying emphatically, "Give me the mic! Give me the mic!"

He then proceeded to perform a sort of karaoke sing-along with Mr. Prince. He already knew all the lyrics of this new song, which was rocketing up the charts. It wasn't actual karaoke because he was just singing along with the record. It was a sort of performance piece for his faithful minions.

That alone was odd enough. But the next move was even odder. I don't remember if it was the very next song or not. But Jay's fans started chanting, "Do the dive! Do the dive!"

Not knowing what the hell they were talking about, I just sat there in amazement witnessing the following move. In one fluid motion and to the beat of the music, Jay dropped from a standing position into a push-up position on his hands and toes. Then he arched his back and pushed himself up backwards into a kneeling position. He continued this move into a sort of kneeling limbo position, all the while doing a sexy shoulder shimmy. Hot, right?

The complete choreographed maneuver was clearly known as "the dive." It looked like a deleted scene from *Saturday Night Fever*, except that it was five years out of date and seemed completely out of place in a redneck Southern town. But it didn't matter. His eight fans were thrilled.

I drank my one Budweiser and went home. I was out of control as a youth, I tell you.

That odd scene has stayed in my mind for nearly 40 years. I don't know what part of it haunts me the most. It's partly the disconnect between what he and I became as people in such a short period of time.

More than that, I think about how futile this scene of a theme restaurant being turned into a faux nightclub really was. It was awful. Yet here was a guy I knew who had become the king of this extremely sad gathering, who had no sense of irony about it. He knew he was hot shit within this microcosm, without realizing how ridiculously puny it was.

It occurred to me decades later when I saw Jay's photo as an adult on a social media website that he had quite possibly peaked when he was 18 years old. That might have been as good as his life ever got. The person looking out at me from the photo was a chubbier old man. I say "old." We are exactly the same age.

He still lives in the same town. In the photo he seems like a pleasant enough guy wearing a generic cotton button-up dress shirt. I think he's an accountant or something. He might be quite happy. I don't know. But I do know that he no longer looks like the Ladies Man holding court at a Ruby Tuesday.

I have always heard that people who reach their pinnacle in high school have nowhere to go but down and a very long time in which to get there. I don't know what became of any of the jocks at my high school. I couldn't care less. But seeing that adult photo of Jay and remembering that bizarre scene back in the "disco" made me wonder if there wasn't some truth to the idea of peaking too early.

Prom date

16 HALF-STEPPING AT HALFTIME

I have always enjoyed playing music in my life and career. If it were only the fame I was seeking, I probably would have chosen a different path. I like the mechanics of music. I like the connection within an ensemble of musicians. I like the collective enjoyment that comes from interacting with an audience. Clearly, I enjoy it. Because if I didn't, I wouldn't put up with how hard it is to be able to do what I do.

Often, I have opined to fellow performers that there is something collectively wrong with us. The need that we seem to have in varying degrees to stand up in front of a room full of people and demand their rapt attention means there is something seriously damaged about us. For us to think that everyone else needs to shut up and listen to what we have to say because it's more important than what they have to say is clear evidence of mental disease.

Arguably bass players who stand back in the shadows of the stage are slightly less afflicted with this malady than are lead singers or lead guitar players. But we all have it to some extent. This is the longing for acceptance, esteem, and regard. It's the "They like me. They really, really like me" syndrome.

These two things exist simultaneously within me somehow, the love of the craft coupled with my hope for acceptance. Now we come to the Groucho Marx paradox: "I would never belong to any club that would have me as a member."

Clearly this is an extension of never feeling I'm good enough at anything for acceptance by the maternal line of my family. But it is also what motivates me to push forward and to try to get better at what I do. You know, on those days when I actually get motivated.

After a long week of half a dozen gigs, it's very easy to just want to stare at a screen during my one day off rather than write a book or music, or practice my instrument, or go to the gym, or do anything else to get more famous. I don't even want to better myself in any way on those days. I'm tired.

One indication of fame could be the size of the audience one performs in front of, right? So because I played at the New York Jets football stadium to a capacity crowd of 82,566 people that would surely indicate I was famous, wouldn't it? Perhaps.

Those 82,566 people didn't pay their hard-earned money to see me, however. They came to see the Jets play football. I was there with the cast of the Broadway show *Rock of Ages* performing as a part of the Thanksgiving Day halftime festivities.

And wouldn't you know it? I didn't play a single note. This was not because I was seized with stage fright or anything. As often happens with gigs like that, the music is canned (prerecorded). The only things live are the lead vocal microphones. I must say that the cast sang beautifully that day. All I did was grimace convincingly, shake my bass guitar and hope to catch a glimpse of my two-story-size head on the Jumbotron.

It shouldn't come as any surprise to anyone, yet I think it still does. Most TV gigs are either partly or completely prerecorded, including the Super Bowl halftime show. Flea from Red Hot Chili Peppers famously left his bass completely unplugged on their Super Bowl appearance just to make the point.

There are some notable exceptions to this practice. Bruce Springsteen insisted that the band play live for his appearance and rightly so. But it took a superstar's insistence to force the network to allow him to do it.

Networks and superstars don't like to leave anything to chance. Sound-checking a 15-piece band in the 10 minutes between the end of the second half of the game and the concert's airtime is almost impossible. So most of the time the music is on track, and just the lead vocals are live.

I "performed" in front of 82,566 of my closest friends. But I didn't feel particularly famous that day. My former landlord still tells his coworkers and neighbors that he had a tenant upstairs who played at the Super Bowl. I didn't. I corrected him on this repeatedly. He still never gets it right. To him the Super Bowl is fame.

I am also an inductee into the Blues Hall of Fame. The word "fame" is right there in the title. That has to be fame, right? I am certainly honored and humbled by this distinction.

But then I also notice who some of my inductee peers are from the New York blues community. Then I don't feel so special. For one thing, there are quite a few of us. For another thing, some of the inductees never played much more than tip jar gigs in bars.

I will continue to proudly display my induction certificate in a frame on my wall. But that particular hall of fame not only lacks an actual hall, it also seems to allow what they call "unsung heroes" like myself to be inducted. Somehow it doesn't quite feel like actual fame.

To revisit the discussion about my celebrity photo album, of the nearly 300 photos currently in there, I would venture to speculate that the average nonmusical person has heard of less than a third of them. A musical enthusiast may have heard of more like half of them. This is not to say that only half of them are famous. There are other factors at play here.

One of them is that fame is partly a function of a particular time period. Someone who was famous in 1959 is arguably less so today. One has to be of a certain age to know some of the celebrities pictured. My pool of employers has been traditionally skewed toward the oldies or classic rock end of the spectrum, though by no means exclusively.

Another factor is diversity of musical genre. To have heard of everyone in the photo album, one would have to be almost a musicologist with expertise in many different styles: rock, pop, rhythm & blues, soul, country, jazz, folk, New Orleans, Broadway, and classical. That's a pretty wide spread for anyone.

I'm enthusiastic about music but by no means any sort of academic expert. The only reason even I know who all these people are is that I've met them, worked with them, and done my own research into their careers.

The reason I leave all the photos up there is the same reason that I leave everyone on my résumé (see appendix), which is clearly too long. What I've discovered repeatedly is that I never know which particular credit or photo is going to resonate with someone. I can't tell you how many times someone has looked at my website, scrolled through the hundreds of names or photos up there, and come back to me with a completely random single thing that impressed them.

They'll say, "Wow, you played with Buster Poindexter?!"

"Yes. Yes, I did," I say aloud.

To myself, I think, "Dang, that was the one that connected with you? Did you lose your virginity to 'Hot Hot Hot' or something?"

As I get older, I have realized that maybe it's not all about being famous. It's certainly not all about being rich. I live fairly humbly but happily. When asked what I want for a birthday present, I always reply, "I already have everything I've ever wanted or needed."

It's true. I don't covet having a lot of stuff. I have more basses than I have time to play and more pairs of socks than I really need, although that does help stretch the time between loads of laundry.

The salary I gave up when I left my corporate record company gig in 1989 was $30,000 per year. That's equivalent to $62,000 in 2020. On average, I'm doing a little better for myself now than I was in 1989, even adjusting for inflation. This assumes, of course, that I never would have gotten a promotion at that company, just had salary raises to match cost of living increases. Some years I do quite a bit better than my old corporate salary. Some years are just a little bit better. That's the nature of being a freelancer.

What I do know is that I'm a lot happier playing music than I ever would have been as a corporate shill. Even though making money has nothing at all to do with being famous, it certainly feels like an accomplishment. As a full-time musician, I have been able to maintain continuing economic accumulation sufficient to pay my rent consistently for decades. That has to count for something.

**The New York Jets Flight Crew cheerleaders and fame-seeking
pantomiming musicians**

17 TRADE SHOW CHOPS

There are certain cats who get famous for being musicians' musicians. These are the players who are so gifted, flashy, or spectacular that other instrumentalists aspire to be like them. There is a whole circuit of players who are well known on niche recordings, in players' magazines, and at industry trade shows.

These players have developed a skill I call "trade show chops." They can sit down at a manufacturer's booth at a gear expo on a crowded convention center floor with an instrument in their hands and play unaccompanied. They will inevitably do something so fast and flashy that it makes everyone else at the show want to stop what they're doing and watch the performer. Usually this is something highly technical to execute, very flamboyant, showy, loud, and impressive to the average musician.

Once these skills have been developed over years of practice, it is possible to turn them into a full-time career making paid appearances at trade shows, demonstrating instruments in music stores, performing at clinics, appearing in specialty magazines, and writing and selling instructional books and videos.

The only drawback to having chops like these is getting an actual gig in a real band. With a few exceptions of virtuoso bands, usually led by the chops-y musicians in question, most sidemen gigs require functionality, collaboration with and support of other singers and musicians. When playing in an ensemble format, if one cat is furiously shredding away on his axe, it will cause the other players to turn to him and say, "Dude, what's up?"

It is possible to have tremendous chops and also the well-developed taste to know that mostly they're not to be used. But once that waterfall has been turned on, it's quite difficult to turn it back off again. It's also a common cop-out to claim, "I'm a groove player," meaning that the player isn't interested in the super chops because the true music is made by laying back in the pocket and playing simply.

I use this cop-out a lot. I never developed trade show chops. I enjoy ensemble playing, especially as a bass player. But I respect and admire the cats who can sit down by themselves and shred something interesting. It's even more impressive when it's on a less traditional solo instrument like a bass.

In fact, the truth lies somewhere in the middle. The best overall musicians are those who have tremendous facility and command of their instruments and the good sense to know when and where not to show off.

Imagine now a musical instrument trade show with dozens or hundreds of manufacturers showcasing their latest models. Imagine hundreds to thousands of eager music store owners, trade magazine journalists, and consumers all dying to get their hands on the newest piece of kit, the redesigned guitar, the shiniest new finished drum set, the latest synthesizer with the newest sound patches, and the latest custom-made bass.

Imagine if you can the sound of up to a thousand instruments all playing in the same room at once. Oh, no, I don't mean in the sense of a symphony orchestra where everyone is a master of an individual instrument, all of them in tune with everyone else, and all playing the same compositional masterpiece in perfect concert. Oh, no, not that.

Imagine countless perpetual adolescents slashing away at instruments that aren't even in tune with themselves, instruments over which they hold little to no mastery yet desperately hoping to appear that they do, instruments capable of making gorgeous artistic statements but equally capable of generating the most agonizing caterwaul known to man or beast.

Imagine a thousand people playing a thousand different songs on a thousand different instruments. Even if each individual performance is brilliantly executed and perfectly in tune like a thousand phonographs all with their needles playing beautifully produced vinyl, by the time all of them are going simultaneously, quite a cacophony has been generated.

Some trade shows have sound police with decibel meters in hand penalizing manufacturers who have noise coming from their booths over a certain level. This helps the overall crush of eardrums. But even a thousand cats playing quietly is a hell of a noise when it all adds up.

As I said, I never developed trade show chops. I have been asked at different times to appear in instrument manufacturers' booths to demonstrate the equipment, to talk about my experiences with the gear in real world settings, and generally to be some sort of artistic ambassador for the company for the day. These invitations also allow me to see all of the other new gear from all the exhibitors as well as to enjoy the schmooze fest that these trade shows invariably become.

There is another phenomenon I have identified that I call "trade show schmoozing," which involves a combination of asking questions like, "So what gigs are you doing now?" which is closely followed by, "Hey, who is playing (the instrument played by said questioner) on that gig?"

The answer I always want to give and occasionally do is, "Not you, apparently."

Hopefully this is done in a good-heartedly enough way to help prevent the next inevitable request from the musician, "Hey, get me on that gig."

Trade show schmoozing also involves exchanges like this:

"Dude! How's it going?" (As guy looks past dude's face over dude's right shoulder.)

"Man, I haven't seen you since that gig in Singapore." (Looks past dude, this time over dude's left shoulder.)

"We gotta play together again soon. That gig was a blast!" (Sees more famous dude over less famous dude's right shoulder.)

"Seriously, dude, send me an email. Make sure I still have your number." (Scoots off toward more famous dude to get a selfie and begin same exchange again. Repeat ad nauseam.)

It's exhausting. It's fun to see everyone and to try out all the shiny new toys. But it's also tiring, cacophonous, and very loud.

One particular trade show I attended was a bass-specific show, all basses, bass amps, bass strings, bass magazines, bass effects pedals, bass T-shirts, and lots and lots of bass players. Though it was smaller than some of the largest trade shows, there were still easily a hundred kids actively playing basses all in the same room at the same time.

Trade show chops for bass players almost always involve the slap and pop technique played with the thumb and index finger. It's percussive. It's flashy. It's rhythmic and loud. It allows a hundred kids to simultaneously imagine that they are Flea from Red Hot Chili Peppers. Flea can fill a stadium with sound all by himself pretty well. So imagine how eye-crossing a hundred kids flailing away on basses at the same time must sound.

The company I was showing gear for that day, Warrior Instruments, makes gorgeous custom-designed basses out of beautiful exotic hardwoods. They do tremendous work. Some of the basses have ornate mother-of-pearl inlays, high-fidelity onboard electronics, and even LED fret dots that illuminate the neck of the bass on dark stages.

One of the showpieces for this company's display was a hyper-extended-range nine-string bass. It was a beast. It had a very wide fingerboard necessary to accommodate all the strings and weighed a ton. While I have met people who do play such instruments, this one was designed to be as much of a conversation piece and a curiosity to get people into the booth as anything else.

A standard Fender bass guitar has four strings on it. Most players use standard four-string basses in most applications. There is a significant number of players who regularly use five-string basses that have one additional lower string than the standard Fender. This low B string can range from thunderous to just plain flatulent depending on the player and equipment. There is even a smaller yet more dedicated number of musicians who swear by six-string basses. These have one extra lower string and one extra higher string than the standard Fender.

This custom-made nine-string bass had the standard Fender four plus three higher strings that took the instrument up well into the lead guitar range. But more significantly, it had two strings lower than the standard four. Recall the potential flatulence just described of a bass having only one string below standard. The low B string on a five-string bass emits a pitch vibrating at only 30.68 hertz, or cycles per second.

The Warrior builders had added another bridge-cable-size string below that tuned to a theoretical yet arguably imperceptible low F sharp. This creates a piece of steel oscillating at a mere 17 hertz. Human hearing is said to be only practical down to 20 hertz with occasional frequencies being perceptible down to about 12 hertz in ideal laboratory conditions.

A low F sharp is somewhere down in the blue whale or earthquake range. Is it musical? There is some understandable debate about this, not to mention the fact that most consumer stereo listening equipment is incapable of recreating these tones even if you were to successfully record them. It would be of questionable business sense to write and record music that would actively destroy the playback equipment of the consumer. This would allow for very limited repeat business.

Also, at this same trade show at the very next booth to Warrior Instruments was a great and successful bass amplifier company called Gallien-Krueger (aka GK). Bob Gallien himself was there that day with his brand new 1,000-watt bass amplifier. This was probably the first year that the number 1,000 had ever been written on the front of any bass amplifier.

Keep in mind that the Marshall guitar amps Jimi Hendrix played out of were only 100 watts each. Even if he had two or three of them going, he still wasn't up to 1,000 watts. We won't get into The Who and their stadium-size walls of amps. Those stacks were still just multiples of 100 watts or so each.

Here I was standing between a nine-string bass and a 1,000-watt bass amp. Clearly all I needed was an instrument cable at this point. I asked Bob Gallien if he minded me blowing up his new amp. I meant this partly as a joke, though I am hard on amps and have blown up a lot of them. I also meant it as a friendly challenge to the ego and reputation of a well-known design engineer with a successful line of products.

Bob said, "You won't blow it up," not meaning that he knew for a fact I was not a miscreant bent on destroying his product, but rather implying that he was confident in the performance of his new earth-shattering drummer-crushing doomsday device.

Challenge accepted.

I plugged the nine-string bass into the 1,000-watt amp. I turned up the volume all the way. I hit one single low F sharp note that sent a standing wave of rumbling sound through the building like a sustained clap of thunder. For a few brief seconds, over 100 kids who were furiously flailing away like little jackhammers on as many basses stopped what they were doing and turned their heads in unison like groundhogs to look at the source of this rumble.

For one brief instant, the hall was silenced as though Billy the Kid had just walked into the Dry Gulch Saloon. While I don't have and will probably never develop trade show chops, for a fleeting moment in time I was the dude who played the low F sharp that stopped the world.

At a trade show with Warrior Instruments co-endorsee, Rick Derringer

18 YOU'VE MADE IT

After practicing for years, after taking every crap gig that comes your way, after crawling and clawing and begging your way through the music world, eventually, if you're really lucky, you might actually "make it," whatever that means.

I remember several different times in my career when I felt like I had accomplished something, tasted the holy wine, and could possibly be on my way toward something bigger.

The first time this happened was at those previously mentioned Bo Diddley gigs when I was in college in New Orleans, even if I did get threatened with murder in the process. Bo was a star. He was famous. Little did I know that it would be nearly a decade before I would once again play with a Rock & Roll Hall of Famer.

That next Hall of Famer I played with was Ms. Shirley Alston Reeves, Original Lead Singer of The World-Famous Shirelles. In fact, that is her full legal billing for trademark reasons that I'll describe in depth later.

I had recently graduated from Berklee College of Music in Boston and relocated to New York City to make myself available to fame. In an instance of networking well before the days of social media, an old college pal of mine, Cynthia, who still lived in New Orleans, told her cousin, who lived in New York, that I had just graduated music school and was new in town. I didn't even meet the cousin until later.

With that one random recommendation of a stranger to a stranger, Cynthia inadvertently started most of my entire career in New York City. I don't think I ever told her that. So thanks, Cynthia.

The cousin told a dude she was seeing, we'll call him Kevin, about me. Kevin was a guitar player, bass player, drummer, keyboard player, and singer. Talk about a utility guy. He was also the music director for Ms. Shirley Alston Reeves. On the cousin's recommendation, he called me to ask if I was available to cover a Shirley gig he needed to sub out.

Never having heard me play before, he said there was one caveat. He asked if he could come to see me do a gig. I happened to have a blues trio gig with no drummer at a bar in SoHo that started at midnight. Kevin came to the gig, sat at the bar, and listened. On our first set break, he handed me a manila envelope containing charts and a cassette tape of Shirley's live show. I had the gig.

What I didn't know until much later was that the gig was in Massachusetts, a five-hour van ride from New York. There were no hotel rooms. So this would be a day trip, 10 hours in the van with a two-set concert in the middle. There was also no rehearsal. I was expected to learn the material from the charts and the tape, and to show up ready to hit it cold.

The gig was anything but cold. It was in the middle of summer, outdoors in the parking lot of a church that was host to a traveling family fun fair. The fun fair was run by a dude named Uncle Bob, whom we came to know and love. We did dozens of shows for Uncle Bob over many years until he passed away.

Let's not put too shiny a coat of paint on it. Even with our tuxedos and slippery dress shoes on, we had basically become carnies.

Kevin knew fully the parameters of this particular gig. When he came to "audition" me, he figured the chances were good with my just being out of music school that I could read the rudimentary chord charts he gave me to study. Basically, if I could play my instrument at all, he was going to hire me for at least this one gig. Whether I was able to sink or swim or warrant a second booking was another deal entirely.

Even though I hadn't yet absorbed all the minutiae of undercurrents to my newfound employment, I had an absolute blast on the gig. Shirley is a legend. I knew many of The Shirelles' hits from my youth and loved the music. I love playing with Shirley and love seeing her to this day, more than 28 years later.

Shirley was my first classic soul, old-time rock & roll, or oldies circuit gig, whatever you want to call it. Getting hired sight unseen like that turned out to be the key to most everything that has followed. One of the reasons for this was the drummer on the gig, the late Crusher Green. I'll discuss more about Crusher in a moment.

I was playing hit songs with the woman who sang on the records and made them famous. Although we were set up next to the crazy slide at the carnival, it felt like, yeah, this was me starting to make it.

Crusher Green liked my playing and the preparation I had done for the gig. I really did my homework thoroughly and knew the show as well as anyone else in the band. I had the charts to read. I hadn't memorized the music. But I was able to play the show without any major mistakes.

Crusher had played with The Shirelles on and off since the 1960s. He had also been the drummer and music director for Wilson Pickett since 1965. This was a seriously funky and soulful cat.

On a dark desert highway (OK, it was really Jersey), we were on the way to a gig in the back of Shirley's van, a well-worn 1978 Dodge Ram passenger van we affectionately called "Brown Betty." She occasionally showed up to the gig on the back of a AAA flatbed truck, old Betty. But she was a trouper.

In the van, Crusher put a pair of headphones on me to have me listen to a recording he had just played on. It was a song called "Imaginary People" by a group called The Uptown Horns Revue. This track was a slamming funk fest played by an aggressive horn band that sounded like it should have been recorded by James Brown. I loved it on first listen.

In a bizarre turn of events, I came to find out later that this track had been written for Mr. Brown by Dan Hartman and Charlie Midnight. It was a song that didn't make the cut for the *Gravity* album, which featured the hit "Living in America." The horn section on that album was none other than The Uptown Horns. In the "small world" department, that was also the album that Mr. Brown was promoting the day I took him around to interviews back when I worked for his record company.

The song was so banging that The Uptown Horns decided to record it on their own album with Bernard Fowler singing lead. Bernard had just then joined a touring outfit out of the U.K. called The Rolling Stones. The Uptown Horns had just finished the Stones's *Steel Wheels* tour as their horn section as well. These cats were no joke.

About a year after my first Shirley gig, The Uptown Horns found themselves in need of a bass player, kind of last minute, for a big show they had booked at the legendary Bottom Line in New York City. Because it was rather short notice, Crusher, knowing that I would diligently do my homework, recommended me for the gig.

I had already met their alto sax player, Crispin Cioe, on a separate $50 blues gig, and they agreed to hire me.

I arranged to meet their trumpeter, Larry Etkin, on the sidewalk on 24th Street in Manhattan to get a normal bias (read: from the 99¢ store) cassette tape of their album to learn the songs for the gig. I had a week to transcribe everything and write my own charts.

We had one rehearsal. Then we played two sold-out shows the very next day, which included the great song "Imaginary People" that I had heard in the back of Shirley's van. The Uptown Horns had a powerful nine-piece R&B revue with multiple singers and special guests joining in, including: Soozie Tyrell and Charlie Giordano (now both touring with a very famous act from New Jersey), Bernard Fowler (Rolling Stones), Vernon Reid (guitarist from Living Colour, another of my former clients at my record company job), and starring Peter Wolf from the J. Geils Band.

This had to be making it, right? It certainly felt that way. The band was on fire. The crowd ate up every minute of it. I dug the shit out of it.

I have been the bass player with The Uptown Horns since 1994 as a result of that one gig. They have hired me to back up so many legendary performers, including: Buster Poindexter, Martha Reeves & The Vandellas, Sam Moore, Ben E. King, Gary U.S. Bonds, Percy Sledge, Rufus & Carla Thomas, Solomon Burke, Gene Chandler, Howard Tate, and many others.

Man, I'm glad I did the homework for that first Shirley gig. I had no idea how much it would eventually pay off.

We played the Bottom Line many times after that. I always liked that venue. It was a great listening room. The backstage catering was consistent to a fault: a basket with two apples, two oranges, half a dozen Hershey's kisses, and a pitcher of water. It didn't matter if you were a folk duo or a 15-piece band. It was always the exact same rations. I think they gave you half price at the bar, too.

Shirley Alston Reeves eventually called me for a gig at Shea Stadium. Now, tell me that's not the big time. The Beatles played there. The Beatles also covered The Shirelles twice on their records, incidentally. Shea is quite literally the big leagues.

Well, it wasn't the big leagues for us that day. It turned out the gig was in the parking lot of Shea, not inside the stadium itself. And it turned out that we were the entertainment at yet another traveling fun fair. We were back to being carnies.

We were alternating sets with a DJ who had these giant deafening subwoofers that forced you to breathe in time to the dance beat. It was that loud. When it was our turn to play, the deafening bass cabinets would be silenced so that we could do our set playing through a stick PA, which consisted of two 12-inch speakers on foldable aluminum stands. Needless to say, the sonic impact of this felt quite paltry by comparison. Never mind that we were live musicians backing a rock & roll legend.

Plus, depending on the direction of the wind, Shea Stadium is right in the flight path for planes landing at LaGuardia Airport. Of course, it was an ill wind for us that day. Every couple of minutes, we were completely drowned out by a low-flying jet engine for several seconds. We would have to play those passages of the songs using only our sense memory since we couldn't hear a note of it.

Yeah, we played Shea Stadium.

There have been many instances over the years that felt like proper successes as a musician. These times were sprinkled in between thousands of other working-man's gigs. Of the nearly 4,000 shows I must have done, maybe less than 10 percent of them felt at all rock starish. That's not bad, right? That's maybe 400 cool gigs in 40 years, almost 10 per year average.

I would estimate that close to half of all the gigs I've played felt decidedly un–rock starish and to some extent like punching the clock. There is absolutely nothing wrong with punching a clock. I'm proud to work for a living and proud to be employed in my chosen profession. But the working-man's gigs don't feel like fame.

After a decade and a half of gigging in New York, I finally got two chances to play at the almighty Carnegie Hall. All that practice, practice, practice finally paid off.

The first time was with a really funny musical comedian named Stephen Lynch. He sold the joint out with his legions of college-kid and YouTube fans. I played acoustic bass along with a six-piece ensemble behind his folksy songs with comedic lyrics, which he played on acoustic guitar.

In terms of technical playing demands, the music was fairly simple and pretty gentle. I was glad about this because it was a very high-pressure gig from just about every other standpoint. I don't care who you are. Carnegie Hall is a big deal. There are a lot of expectations riding on you when you step on that stage and plenty of nerves to go with it. Not having that complicated further by requiring massive amounts of chops to pull off the gig was a bonus. It was a great night.

The next time I played Carnegie was a year or two later with a well-known classical violinist named Alexander Markov. He had been playing Carnegie since he was a teenager with traditional repertoire. But I wasn't hired to play symphonic bass. Markov had written a rock/classical crossover called the *Rock Concerto*. I was hired to be the rock guy.

The piece consisted of an electric violin played very loudly through a Marshall guitar amplifier by Markov, a rock drummer, a lead singer, an electric rock bass player, who also doubled on some simple synth keyboard parts (played by yours truly), a 66-piece symphony orchestra, and a 40-voice choir. It was quite a spectacle. We had been performing this piece for about six years before we played Carnegie. So we were ready when the time finally came.

Markov sold the place out. We members of the core rock band were all featured soloists on the show. The audience gave us a standing ovation. There were flowers, autographs, photos, and a nice review in the *New York Times*, the whole deal. It felt very rock starish indeed for the night. It was another great evening personally and professionally. The fame lasted from the stage door at least all the way to the corner of Seventh Avenue.

Fortunately, the next night I played a Russian wedding at a catering hall in New Jersey so that my ego was brought right back down to size.

Just in case we were prone to any long-term head swelling from our triumphant Carnegie Hall performance, a couple of years later the *Rock Concerto* was part of a much longer program by the World Peace Orchestra at Lincoln Center's Avery Fisher Hall. It didn't go very well for a number of reasons, only a few of which were truly our fault.

The *New York Times* reviewed that show as well, calling it less like world peace and more like a "hostile takeover." The reviewer called the performance "baggy" and commented that Markov was wearing the same jacket he had worn at Carnegie three years earlier (as if that mattered). He said we "sent streams of audience members fleeing up the aisles."

We did. But it wasn't all because of us. The program lasted three hours. We only "blared" at people for the last hour of that. The reviewer concluded, "There's nothing wrong with bringing young people together in music. But next time, leave Mr. Markov and his concerto at home."

Ouch! Just when you think you hit the big time: ego duly checked.

That being said, I have enjoyed many wonderful successes over the years. I'm really thankful to be able to do what I do. I say at the end of every calendar year, "Well, I fooled them again." I feel like I'm getting away with something every year that I continue to be able to pay my rent with a bass in my hand.

But then there are those other times …

Warming up at Carnegie Hall

19 YOU'RE FIRED!

For every resounding success in anyone's career there are even more failures. Most failures are small things like not getting called for a particular Saturday night gig during the summer busy season. That happens. More often, you just don't get called back for a gig you once had. There are no reasons given. There may be no specific reason other than the dude's cousin also plays bass and lives closer to the gig. It's not always something that is someone's fault.

But there are other failures that feel colossal. These are the ones that make me question every choice I've ever made in my life, not just my career decisions. They can feel like a gut punch. Often too these epic flameouts aren't necessarily anyone's fault. Things just happen, very often circumstances beyond anyone's control. That doesn't make it feel any better though.

Sometimes you get a dream gig. You're sitting on top of the world feeling invincible. And still you get fired. I've often said that I've been the guy who's been fired. And I've almost as often been the guy who's been hired to replace the guy who's been fired. It's the nature of the music business in a way.

Things change. Band personnel changes. Artistic trends change. Budgets change (that's a big one). And people get fired. What follows are accounts of some of my more memorable terminations.

One of the early ones was a pub gig when I lived in England. I was playing with a bar band called The Dublin Cowboys, who found my classified ad in the music paper.

They rang me up and said, "The gig pays £27.50 a man, no rehearsal. Be at the Consumptive Friar pub at half 8."

It was a fun band that did classic rock covers by the seat of their pants. The chord changes were fairly simple, often intuitive, and always easily discernible by looking at the guitar player's left index finger. They played a lot of salt-of-the-earth working-man's pubs next to some pretty colorful council estates all over London.

We got hired to play a birthday party one Saturday lunchtime at a pub in south London. We set up and played our first song. The party host came over to us and said, "It's a bit loud. Turn it down, please." We turned our amps down.

We played a second song. The host came over again and said, "Still really too loud. Please make it lower." We turned our amps down again.

We played a third song. The host came over and said, "Here's your money. You're done. Go home."

We were fired and paid not to play.

Much later in my career, I was called by a producer friend of mine to some play arco (bowed) upright bass on a music track by comedian Steven Wright. He was doing a songwriter album, not comedy, apparently.

I told the producer quite honestly that arco was the least spectacular of my many parlor tricks. He assured me that it would be fine. All he needed was some footballs. He meant long tones because written whole notes look kind of like footballs on the musical staff.

I turned up to the session with my upright and my bow. He started playing me the track. I began trying to drone along with it. About 20 minutes into it, the producer said, "This really isn't flowing. Let's just call it a day. I'll pay you for your time."

I felt really embarrassed and inadequate even though I had told him that I'm not great with the bow. I also refused his money. I wasn't going to make him pay me for that abomination, although it did take me most of the afternoon to transport my upright to the studio on the train. It wasn't his fault I sucked.

A couple of years after, that I began to woodshed my arco playing heavily in order to be able to sub in the pit of a short-lived Broadway show called *Amazing Grace*. That score was 95 percent arco. It required me, a rock and soul electric bass player with no classical training, to practice three hours a day just to be adequate with the bow. I ended up playing that show six times before it closed. I barely got away with it, I think.

I also learned an important lesson at that recording session. The so-called easy footballs that the producer had called on me to play are some of the most difficult things to execute cleanly on a recording. Faster moving passages with lots of notes are easier to play than long tones.

There was another high-level theatre experience I had, which shall remain nameless. I will neither confirm nor deny whether it was actually on or off of the Broad Way.

When I started subbing on this particular show, the music director told me that my approach was a little more aggressive than the guy I was subbing for, but that he liked it.

Cool, I thought. I'll keep playing the show that way. The boss likes it.

Skip ahead a year. I had played the show about once a month and had successfully done about 14 performances. But then I had one particular show that wasn't so great.

The guy I was subbing for called me about two hours before curtain time saying he was sick and asking if I would do him a solid and fill in last minute. Ordinarily I would have liked to review the score at least once at home before I went in just to make sure that it was fluidly under my hands. I also preferred to read the show off of my own copy of the book in my own binder. This allowed me to practice my page turns throughout the show.

Neither of these conditions were met that day. I went in to play without being able to review the show. I hadn't played the book in a few weeks. When the guy called me, I also was out and about, and there wasn't enough time to go home to pick up my binder before going to the theatre to make the curtain time. I would be forced to read off of his score that night with all of its different page turns, which I had not practiced.

My stress level was high. But I knew I would be all right if I just stayed focused, leaned forward a little, and dug into the book. I made it through the show without any major mistakes and felt proud of myself for rising to the challenge.

But then I was fired.

Actually, I wasn't fired. The music director told the guy I was subbing for that he could use me, but that it had to be a lot less often. It took a couple of years for me to realize that "a lot less often" had effectively turned into "never again."

I had a couple of emails with the music director and with the player I was subbing for. What I think happened is this: Over the course of a year, the music director went very gradually from liking my more aggressive playing to not liking it. Yet he never told me this until he decided that he was fed up with me.

Meanwhile I had been consciously digging in when I subbed over there because he had told me initially that he liked it. It was basically a miscommunication that never got resolved in time to keep me on the sub roster at that show, unfortunately.

Also unfortunate was the fact that this unofficial firing shook my confidence quite a lot. Other gigs that I knew like the back of my hand suddenly felt shaky and alien to me. I began seriously to question my abilities to play bass in public at all. It was a tough time for me for a few months. I gradually talked myself down off the bridge and recaptured the confidence I felt I had earned after decades of professional playing. But it took a minute.

20 CATAPULCO

Gloria Gaynor and her band got hired to play in Acapulco, Mexico, at a private party being thrown at some billionaire's crib. You know, as one does.

The crib was way up on top of a mountain on a sharp ridge overlooking the beautiful bay and the Pacific Ocean. Billionaires like to build up high. It assists them in looking down on people.

When the band arrived at the venue for sound check, we were greeted with a disturbing sight. The stage had been built above the large outdoor patio at the home. But because this was the very top of the mountain, the patio was a long thin strip of concrete along the ridgetop. The stage was twice as wide as the narrow patio. Half of it was literally suspended in midair atop metal trusses that ran at a 45-degree angle back toward the hillside.

Half the stage was about 6 ft. above the patio. The other half was about 40 ft. above the street below. The street then proceeded to wind down the roughly 1,000-ft.-high mountain to the sea. It looked scary as hell.

We had to put an 11-piece band with all of our gear up on this temporary structure and would have to jump up and down on it while performing an animated disco show. You know, as one does. It seemed sturdy, but at the same time a little bouncy.

Also, construction and building codes in Mexico are not exactly what we're used to in the United States. The infrastructure of the entire country feels a little suspect, as do the roads and sidewalks, which are permanent thoroughfares on level ground. A temporary structure suspended in space off of the top of a mountain inspired no confidence in us whatsoever.

One by one we went up on deck. We all test-bounced in place to feel just how much give the platform seemed to have. Eventually we got loaded in and finished our sound check.

Normally, I'm fairly active onstage. It is very difficult for me to stand completely still, especially while playing dance music. I like to bop around and feel the rhythm with my whole body. It's more fun that way.

On this platform, I was as still as a mannequin. We all were. We were taking no chances. None of us wanted to be the straw that broke the camel's back. We also each independently mapped out personal escape routes for ourselves should we feel the structure beginning to topple. Assisting one's fellow compatriots be damned. This would be every woman for herself.

With the drums at the center of the state, the half of the band who were standing to the left side of the stage were over a concrete patio. In a disaster, they might fall only 6 ft. Besides spraining an ankle or two, the horn players and the keyboard player would live to play again.

The other half of the band who were standing on the right side of the stage, including me, were suspended 40 ft. above the nearest landing spot. The guitarist, the background singers, and I had a rough fall ahead of us should anything go awry. The drummer, sitting right in the middle, could potentially fall either way.

I decided that my best escape route would be to run at full speed all the way across the stage at the first sign of trouble. My plan was to jump off the keyboard player's side and hopefully only fall a few feet. But that's when uninformed thoughts of engineering and geometry started to bubble in my head. My plan wouldn't work.

The way the structure was built, if it started to fall, the drummer would be sitting right in the middle of what would then become a giant seesaw. We, the half of the band on the low end of the seesaw, would surely fall 40 ft. to certain maiming and our likely deaths.

The keyboard player and horn players, who would now be on the high end of the seesaw, would be launched as if from a catapult. I imagined that it would send them flying through the air and possibly hurtling down 1,000 ft., all the way to Acapulco Bay.

A catapult in Acapulco? We were performing on Catapulco.

I'm not sure which half of the band was better off. But I knew for sure which half of the band that I hoped the YouTube clips would capture in the unfortunate eventuality of a disaster.

Billionaires like to hire big music stars to play at their swanky parties to demonstrate to their guests how cool they are even if the guests just end up standing there the entire night staring at the stars with their arms folded.

That's what happened in this case. A patio full of rich people seemed genuinely inconvenienced to have been made to sit through an interruption to their enjoyment of a DJ playing loud 2010s techno dance music.

They were forced instead to endure an entire concert of some lady whom they didn't seem to know, except for the last song in her show, singing 1970s disco dance music. As soon as we finished, they went happily back to their "unka-unka" dancing, relieved that we were finally done.

With shaking knees, we descended the stairs down from the catapult stage and beat a hasty retreat back to our sea-level hotel. And though it felt like we possibly risked our lives for naught, we lived to play disco music another day.

The catapult stage

21 SERIOUSLY, MAN, YOU'RE FIRED!

I had another incident that involved a large touring ensemble, one that I had been working with for a number of years at the time of my unforeseen termination. There was a new concert promoter who got involved with us a few years into the project. This guy was a mover and a shaker in the industry, ran a successful company, and had a great deal of credibility. The guy was also a word-slurring drunk.

We didn't know this at first, of course. He threw a couple of parties to introduce the act to industry people and also to announce a big upcoming show we had. At each of these events, the guy got so polluted drunk that it was impossible to understand him by the end of the evening.

I am not judging recreational chemical usage. The problem was that we were in a roomful of professional colleagues. This visibly intoxicated idiot was supposed to be our representative. It was very uncomfortable.

Compounding the bad public behavior was the fact that this guy, like so many others who were guitar players back in their high school days and were frustrated that they never got famous, wasn't content with just selling tickets to shows, which was what he was eminently qualified to do. He also fancied himself a musical collaborator and tried to insert himself into artistic decisions. Whether he had any valid artistic ideas or not is kind of immaterial. The trust in someone's judgment must be earned. He had absolutely no track record doing anything artistic at all. There was no reason to have any confidence in his ideas, especially being delivered when he was hammered and could barely speak.

Complicating the situation even further was the fact that not only did he fancy himself a non-performing member of the band, but he also appointed his sister as our band's stylist and insisted that we hire his brother-in-law as our "world" percussionist.

The sister had been a stylist on a few rap videos that in no way resembled anything we were trying to look or sound like. Oh, and she was also a raging drunk. I guess it ran in the family.

The brother-in-law was a rock drummer who held a world record for the fastest single-stroke drum roll or something goofy like that. Yeah, good luck with that skill set, kid. That doesn't make you qualified in any way to play hand drums and world percussion.

The leader of the band was willing to roll with all of these punches just to be able to have access to the promoter's ticket-selling ability. Fine. Understood.

When we did our first gig under this new arrangement, I was fed up with the new hangers-on before we even arrived. I decided to keep to myself, stay out of their way as much as possible, do my job, get paid, and go home. It was a far less cheerful situation than any of the previous gigs we had done without this guy and his nepotism. But I was resigned to the reality of the situation.

It kind of went fine too until the very end of the evening when I had to get paid by Mr. Drunkie McDrunkington. He wrote me a barely legible check for only two-thirds of my previously agreed upon salary. When I brought the discrepancy to his attention on the spot, politely, he went into a tirade about how I didn't want to make an enemy of him. He said that I needed to treat him like a band member. He knew I didn't like him.

My hatred must have been going through him like daggers as he scrawled me an even less legible check for the correct amount during the chastisement. It was a charity gig, but we were still being paid for it. He was berating me for taking money from the charity. If someone wants me to do a gig for free or for a reduced salary because it's a charity, those arrangements are made at the time of the booking, not after the fact when I'm trying to get my damn money.

As far as I was concerned, he was wildly disrespectful to me. I had done my job and done it well. Then when he drunkenly tried to get funny with the money, I saw red.

I complained bitterly about it to the bandleader. I told him that I couldn't remember feeling so professionally denigrated in my entire career as I had been while being admonished for bullshit by a lush who couldn't even stand upright.

The next day, the bandleader emailed me and told me to take all future bookings with this group officially off my calendar. That was his way of firing me.

Apparently when it came down to "it's him or me," even though I made no such stipulation, the bandleader chose the promoter over the bass player. From an economic standpoint, he may have been right. From a human standpoint, there should have been a much longer walk from being a trusted collaborator to being fired.

After digesting this news for a few minutes, I wrote back to the bandleader and said some words that I will forever regret to the end of my career. I said I was sorry. I managed to backpedal sufficiently enough to get rehired within about eight hours.

I wasn't sorry in any way, of course. But my economic reality got the better of me. I figured it would be better to kowtow to the whims of a drunken idiot than to be righteously unemployed.

We ended up doing only a couple of other gigs after that before the whole band finally imploded. One of them was a high-profile gig that I was super glad I was able to do. It paid really well, too. The other was a disaster that I wished nobody ever saw me on.

Was I right to apologize and get my gig back? I'm still not entirely sure.

I did know that from then on, that bandleader wasn't my friend or a collaborator as previously advertised. He was ultimately out for his own interests as we all are to some degree. It was just an unpleasant denouement.

22 EXACTLY WHERE I WANT TO BE

Back in my early days in New York, I had a firing that felt like my career was over before it even began, that my dreams were crushed. Let's call the guy I was working for: Former Lead Singer of Platinum Rock Band, or FLS of PRB for short.

I had worked for PRB in my record company days. So I knew the cats in that band well and had been helpful to their success from the business side of things before I quit my job and went to music school in Boston.

Once back in New York after graduation, I found myself in FLS's new band created after the demise of PRB. It was a golden ground-floor opportunity. Even though PRB had broken up, FLS was still under contract to the record label and was expected to deliver new material for a debut solo album.

We had big plans. We rented a rehearsal space, started to assemble a set of music, and began collectively writing new songs. A few months into this process we were ready for the debut solo gig of FLS. It was an opening spot for an established band at a major rock nightclub in Manhattan.

I remember sitting on that stage that day during sound check and saying to FLS's face, out loud, in English, "This is exactly where I want to be and what I want to be doing." As far as I was concerned, I was on my way with him to rock stardom on my own terms with the corporate world now history. Though I was still a temp secretary during the day to pay my rent, I saw this band as a clear path to my eventual success.

The place was sold out. The air was electric. We took the stage. It went well, not astoundingly, just well. The last time FLS had been onstage was with PRB, which was a much bigger deal than an opening slot at a nightclub. From his perspective, the show didn't go well at all in comparison to his recent former glory. He had a point.

We were writing songs by committee in the new band, which isn't necessarily the most effective way to do that. The band members were also mostly FLS's friends rather than the absolute baddest cats in town. So the performance wasn't as strong a solo debut as he had hoped for.

In his mind the solution was simple: Fire the bass player.

I got the call the next morning. I was devastated. I felt the air squeezing out of my lungs like it might never return again. I just didn't understand it. Of all the cats in the band, I was the only one who had any formal training. I hit all of my marks, sang all of my parts, and played my heart out that night, only to have it ripped out of my chest and held before my face still beating before being thrown on the ground.

That was a tough day.

Over the next year, several interesting things happened. For one thing, I was reminded about an incident in the career trajectory of PRB. When things weren't going well for them in mid-career, they also fired their bass player. That was supposed to solve their problems. It didn't.

I guessed, correctly it turned out, that FLS's firing me was a repeat of that pattern. It was supposed to solve his new problems. It didn't.

I was just the first one fired from that new band. One by one, each of the other cats got fired every time FLS ran into some new problems with his still yet-to-be-launched solo career. Each time, the inherent problems with his new act were still not solved.

The record label ended up dropping him too, though he eventually signed to a new label with, by then, a completely new backing band.

Two of the songs I had cowritten by committee were nonetheless included on the album that was ultimately scheduled for release. I owned a 25 percent writer's share of one song and 20 percent of another. I kept getting calls and faxes marked "urgent" from FLS's lawyer telling me that I needed to sign my publishing rights over to his company immediately.

The lawyer also said some BS about it being necessary for me to accept only half of the normal royalty rate for my share of these songs. This was standard business practice, he claimed. FLS would then allegedly collect the publishing monies for these songs and pay me my share of the royalties. He seemed to have forgotten that I had been fired and had no interest in cooperating.

Thanks to some competent legal advice I got from an old classmate, I knew how to proceed.

I did nothing.

The album finally came out. My writing credits were listed on it. I had still signed nothing even though the frequency and intensity of the threats in the faxes from his lawyer and management company increased. But there was nothing either of them could do about it. I was a lone wolf.

Instead I got a recommendation on how to create my own publishing company through ASCAP and secure my own publishing administration deal through Bug Music. That company would take a 10 percent administration fee on any money it collected on my behalf. Ten percent I could handle, versus giving away half of my money. Also, the half that FLS's company would owe me I might never even see. Those people had no allegiance to me either.

Though I don't know it for a fact, I suspect the following events probably happened. The rest of the guys who were still in that band probably signed the initial publishing deal with FLS before they were fired. When the album finally did come out, it did very little business.

It turned out that the dream gig with FLS wouldn't have been my path to stardom at all. I suspect the other guys in the band received absolutely nothing in royalties. Over the course of a few years and thanks to monies collected by Bug Music from the record being played in elevators in Finland and things like that, I have made tens and tens of dollars on that deal.

Who's laughing now?

23 OMG, You're Fired!

I am an officially licensed Soul Music bass player. I have literally traveled all over the world backing a whole bunch of rhythm & blues stars who became famous during the heyday of the 1960s soul music craze. I adore it. It is fantastic music and pure joy to play.

One of these soul legends, and I've worked for a lot of them, has fired me not once, not twice, but several times. There are probably three or four firings I know about for sure and likely a couple of others I just never heard about because I was rehired before I even knew I was fired.

A memorable occasion involved this legend recording a new album with a new producer and a new record label. The next logical step was to replace me and get a new live band. I would have understood. It wouldn't have shocked me. The music business often moves that way.

A more famous bandleader than myself was hired out on the West Coast. Everything was given the green light and ready to go until said bandleader named his retainer price for putting together a completely new live act from scratch: $30,000.

"Yowza! Hey, why don't we call Ivan?"

Mind you, I had already been the music director for this legend for a number of years, working much more cheaply, I can assure you. Now I had to get flown out to the West Coast to meet the new producer to basically audition for my own gig. It was just a meet-and-greet. But I got the job back that I hadn't yet realized I had lost.

Even though I was the new man for the old job, the artist's management did want the band retooled somewhat. Remember Kevin, the bandleader from the earlier story about Shirley Alston Reeves, Original Lead Singer of The World-Famous Shirelles, who gave me my first big gig in New York based on nothing more than a secondhand recommendation? He and I had become very close friends and had worked together in countless situations for about a dozen years by this point. We were tight personally and professionally. When I got the gig music directing for the soul legend, I hired Kevin on guitar in the band.

Now I was told in no uncertain terms by management that Kevin was not to be a part of the retooled band. It put me in a bad spot, to be sure. But I had also been around the business enough by this time to know that it wasn't anything personal. It was just business, for whatever management perceived the need to be, misguided or otherwise. I didn't agree with the decision and fought them on it, but to no avail. Kevin was out. And I was to be the one to break the news to him.

I fired him as a guitar player. In return, he fired me as a human being. After hours and hours of heated discussion about the situation, it basically came down to the fact that Kevin felt I should have resigned in protest over his firing. I told him in no uncertain terms that if the situation were reversed, I would never allow him to quit on my behalf. People get fired in this business all the time. That's just what happens. He hasn't spoken to me since. It's been 14 years.

Another time I got fired from the same soul legend's gig was when we played a late-night major-network TV appearance promoting the aforementioned new album. This was in the very early days of YouTube. People didn't have it all figured out back then. The networks didn't have their own on-demand rebroadcast links yet. A certain faction of the old-school music business saw YouTube and outlets like it as "bootlegging" because it wasn't monetized in any way at that time. I get that.

My perspective on it was that it was my first time appearing on national network television. I wanted a way to be able to show the clip to my family and friends and anyone else who wanted to see it, yet who hadn't been awake or tuned in to that particular network at 1:30 a.m. on a school night. I uploaded our three-minute music performance portion of the show to YouTube.

Band management found out about it. I was so fired. This time it was with screaming and threatening phone calls. Oh, it was ugly. I took the clip down and retreated to my house to lick my wounds.

Within weeks I got a call from management about the next gig. It was as if nothing had happened. Apparently, I was unfired and didn't even know about it.

A few years later after YouTube gained some credibility, another former band member uploaded the very same video clip. It's up there to this day if you can find it. It's not easily searchable. I guess making it a little harder to find was the main lesson I learned there.

Like I said, I don't really know how many times I've been fired from that gig. I know about three or four of them for sure. I expect there may be others that I never found out about.

Most of the time a firing merely involves the fact that you just don't get called for the next gig that an artist does. This can be due to any number of circumstances that may have nothing to do with you as a player or as a person. The business moves in mysterious ways.

I've been not called back for gigs. I've been fired via very cordial telephone calls that were aimed at keeping me friendly should the band ever require my services again in the future. I've been fired by equally cordial phone calls that left no mystery around the fact that a certain act and I shan't work together again. And I've been cursed out with venom, vitriol, and invectives, then angrily hung up upon.

I'll be honest. I'm not sure which method I prefer.

24 WHAT'S IN A NAME?

S ome dude from England once said, "A rose by any other word would smell as sweet." I forget what band he was in.
He was absolutely correct when it comes to horticulture. But when it comes to the music business and marquee value, everyone knows, "A band by any other name don't make as much damn money."

Names in the music industry are valuable and legally protected trademarks. If a band works hard to attain success and notoriety, their trademark is the main thing that makes people want to buy the next album or concert ticket. There are managers and lawyers who recognize this very well and who tirelessly toil to procure and protect these naming rights. This can be done with varying degrees of integrity since it's all about the bottom line. Marquee value equals money.

Let's say, for instance, that four young women attending high school in Passaic, New Jersey, enter their high school talent show as a doo-wop singing quartet called The Poquellos. Let's say they win that talent show with a song they wrote just for that show. Let's say that one of their classmates' moms is a Jersey housewife with aspirations to be in the music business.

Let's further imagine that this housewife signs the high school girls to her record label that she runs out of her house. The housewife changes the name of the group from their talent show billing to a name that uses the first name of the lead singer.

Continue imagining this fairy tale, if you will, to its logical conclusion. The group go on to have the very first *Billboard* No. 1 hit by any girl group and seven top 20 charting hits. They sell millions of records worldwide. Millions.

It was no fantasy. That group formed in 1958 with the name The Shirelles. Their lead singer, for whom they were named, was Shirley Alston Reeves. It was all peaches and cream … until it wasn't.

Shirley left the group in 1975 to pursue a solo career, according to the Wikipedia page. I don't know exactly what happened. I wasn't there. She may have departed the group for maternity leave. But whatever happened created enough of an environment whereby the remaining members of the group were able to legally take over the trademark "Shirelles." Shirley can't use that band name to this day.

That is why her full legal billing is "Shirley Alston Reeves, Original Lead Singer of The World-Famous Shirelles." The typeface for the word "Shirelles" has to be 10 points smaller than her name, or she runs the risk of being sued. Many times, she has been served cease-and-desist papers on the road when an ambitious and possibly underinformed concert promoter has incorrectly advertised a show.

I wasn't present for any of the group history. When I was on the road with her, we had instances when we showed up in the van to gigs where it said "Shirelles" on the marquee or on a backdrop behind the stage. Understandably, this was very upsetting to Shirley. Her contract was explicit about her billing.

She would have to refuse to perform unless the sign was changed or taken down, or run the risk of yet another court appearance. If it had been an incorrectly worded newspaper ad that was too late to retract, she would go ahead with the show unless legal papers turned up, which I understand they sometimes did. Even if they didn't, she would be worried the whole time.

It's a stressful and unsavory situation for her. It's based on lawyers trying to make money on some bad blood that goes back almost 60 years to four girls in high school. I can understand both sides of the argument. But it still makes me shake my head and feel sad thinking about it.

As I've said, I have toured with Shirley on and off for more than 28 years. I love her dearly. She is exactly the same age as my late mother would have been. I think of her almost as a surrogate parent. It's upsetting to see that she is legally prevented from doing business under the group banner that is derived from her name, singing the songs she made world famous. She doesn't like to talk about it. But that's the situation.

If you look at the credits on my résumé, you will see "The Shirelles" listed. This is not out of any sense of righteous indignation on Shirley's behalf, though I certainly possess that. It is merely a reflection of the fact that on just one occasion in the late 1990s, I backed up Ms. Doris Jackson on a show playing all of The Shirelles' hits. On the original records, Ms. Doris sang lead on only one of their many hits, "Dedicated to the One I Love."

Ms. Doris, who is now deceased, was one of the two surviving original members of The Shirelles who had rights to use the name. So technically I played with "The Shirelles" once even though I have done hundreds of shows playing all of their hits with their original lead singer.

In the 1990s I was starting to gain a tiny amount of traction in the classic rhythm & blues and oldies rock & roll music markets as a sideman for hire. I began working with many groups, including, but not limited to, The Coasters, The Drifters, The Platters, The Marvelettes, and The Shangri-Las.

I mention these groups specifically because all of them were doing business as trademarks owned by a couple of music promoters who had no connection to any original members in any of them. I don't know all of the legal machinations that made this possible, though I suspect that if someone owns a trademark like Kodak™ or Jell-O™ that this person is also technically at liberty to sell the trademark to the highest bidder even if the inventor of the camera or of sweet rubbery desserts has retired from the industry.

This is what apparently happened with all the music trademarks I have just mentioned. They were sold or licensed to other people to administer.

Gene Simmons of KISS envisions a day when he and Paul Stanley will retire from their band. They're already in their 60s and 70s, respectively. Gene assumes that the trademark, the songs, the makeup, and the costumes will have a life far into the future. That's fine if that's your corporate credo. But I'm not sure that singers and musicians who got famous in their high school band were thinking that far ahead.

One of the management companies that owned several trademarks would try to book package shows of its artists whenever possible. I played many double and triple bills of varying combinations of Drifters, Platters, Coasters, and Marvelettes. The pay rate for a sideman would be $125 for backing the first act, no matter where the gig was, New York City or an eight-hour drive to Pittsburgh. You got an extra $25 for each additional act. A triple bill meant $175 for a three-hour concert. Good times.

Furthermore, if the owners of The Coasters trademark, for instance, had multiple bookings for the same night, they could put out any four cats in matching suits and call them The Coasters. I know this because I backed up a lot of B-team and C-team Coasters (and Drifters and Platters and …). By the time they called me to play bass as a sub, it meant they might have already been on the second or third version of the group for the night.

I have all these groups listed on my résumé for a couple of reasons. Though I haven't necessarily played with any of their original members, I have played their music faithfully under a legal marquee bearing the name. Even if they were really just tribute bands, they still had fair use of the trademarks. As a sideman for hire, I take these credits.

In the case of The Drifters specifically, in addition to having done many trademark Drifters shows, I have also played many times with original members Ben E. King and Charlie Thomas. Although Ben E. and Charlie shows weren't billed as Drifters shows, we played many of the same songs. It just makes me feel I have more of a philosophical and moral right to claim that I have indeed played with The Drifters.

The company that owned The Drifters trademark during the time I speak of at one point inserted a former Drifter, Rick Sheppard, into their bookings to legitimize challenges to their trademark. Rick was a late-season replacement in The Drifters in 1966. He sang on none of the group's top 40 charting hits, and sang lead on nothing. I didn't really get to know him that well. I did only a couple of shows with him. He seemed to enjoy his own company a lot, though.

Our old friend, Bowzer, spearheaded legislative battles to get laws enacted to prevent groups from using trademarks if they have zero original members present. It is called the "Truth in Music" bill and has passed in a bunch of states. Subsequently, these trademark gigs have dried up for me. But I'm OK with that.

Charlie Thomas of The Drifters – Rock & Roll Hall of Famer

25 DUDE, YOU ARE SO FIRED!

I am a board-certified Disco bass player. I have literally traveled the world backing a whole bunch of different stars who became famous during the 1970s disco boom. I love it. It's great music and a ton of fun to play.

One of the famous disco divas, and I've worked for a lot of them, has fired me not once but twice.

The first time I was only a couple of years out of music school. I got recommended to the diva and was asked to be her music director and put together a young new backing band for touring. I assembled a crew of players whom I knew from around town. We were pretty green. But we played well and were hungry enough to agree to travel to foreign lands for probably much less money than more experienced players would have done.

We did half a dozen shows over a 10-day tour of Brazil that took us from the beaches of Ipanema all the way north to the Amazon basin. The venues ranged from very urban cosmopolitan theatres to some fairly primitive semi–open air venues up north. It was interesting, and the gigs were great.

The next booking was a one-nighter in Singapore. This consisted of 24 hours in the air, less than 48 hours on the ground, and another 24 hours right back to New York. But at least it paid only $450 per person for four days of hard travel. The band was a little warm about it and made it known to me in no uncertain terms.

I decided to have a face-to-face with the diva's manager/husband in Singapore because I felt that asking for a raise was a delicate conversation best had in person. Plus, the way they ran their operation, access to the diva and even to the manager was quite limited. It was impossible to get him on the phone. I always had to speak to his lackey nephew, who would then relay the message to the manager, then call me back with a response. This situation was less than ideal. Knowing that I could get face time with the manager in Singapore seemed to be the easiest path to having an actual conversation with him.

Fast-forward halfway around the globe, 13 hours' time difference from New York City. We had to adjust to day flip-flopping to night, not to mention the sheer bewilderment of just emerging from a 24-hour flight. We were doing the sound check in a hotel ballroom where we would be playing the wrap party for a golf tournament. Yes, it was every bit as confusing as it sounds.

As we were playing a song, I heard behind me from the drum riser a long "brrrrrriiiiiiing." The drummer had decided to use the wind chimes in the middle of a song in a weird spot. It was odd, but not concerning. Maybe he was checking his gear as we all were. Then the wind chimes went off again. And again. And again. I finally turned around to give the guy a look and tell him to knock it the hell off so we could concentrate on getting the sound levels set.

But when I turned around, I saw that the manager had climbed up onto the drum riser and was gleefully playing the wind chimes over and over again. I gave him a smile and laughed as if to say, "Oh, yes, that's very funny. It's great to have you jokingly playing in the band."

Any muttered obscenities were done quietly to myself. You don't want to argue with the boss unless it's absolutely necessary. This wasn't the hill to die on. It did tell me, however, that he was in the building and therefore would be available for a meeting to discuss the money situation. Fine.

After we finished sound check, I looked around for him. He was nowhere to be found. I couldn't believe it. I really needed to talk to him. The mood in the band was deteriorating rapidly. I never saw him again, even after the show that night.

It wasn't until the next day that I finally found out where he went. Hotel ballrooms very typically have portable 2-ft.-high stages that they can move in and out quickly for various function floor plans. We were set up on some of these platforms.

Though we didn't realize it at the time, it turned out that the manager was completely drunk, which was probably why he was playing the wind chimes so vehemently. We didn't see this happen but were told that he fell off the stage platform, breaking his foot in the process, and somehow managing to fall face-first onto a board with a protruding nail that punctured his cheek.

He wasn't available for my salary meeting because he was in the hospital. The diva and her husband weren't with us on the plane the next day back to New York because he had to stay in Singapore a couple of days to get stable enough to travel.

The face-to-punctured-face meeting was now out of the question. I was forced to call the nephew on the phone to ask for more money before the next overseas trip, which was scheduled for a few weeks later. I asked for $50 more per person. The nephew took my message, relayed it to the manager, and called me back the next day to let me know that we were all fired. Our tenure with the diva had lasted only about three months.

This firing took place on the Wednesday before we were scheduled to leave on Saturday for Germany. Plane tickets had been purchased and everything else arranged. They ended up getting a band out of London instead, whom they had worked with before. But they wanted to hire my horn section for that gig anyway.

The tenor sax player called me to ask for my blessing to take the gig even though he knew we had all been fired. He said that the weekend booking was ruined and that we were all unexpectedly out of work with too little time to find other bookings. He asked me if I wouldn't mind if he went to Germany anyway to take their money. I respected what he said and didn't want to take food out of his mouth. I told him to take the gig.

The next gig after that, the manager called up the rest of the band and offered them the same low money they had all been complaining about. And they all took it. They got another bass player and went out without me after I had stood up for them and asked for a raise.

I never spoke to or worked with any of them again. The only one I stayed friends with was the tenor sax player who had the decency to call me and ask if I would be upset if he took the gig. I've always respected him for that move. The rest of them can eat my left ball.

A mere 15 years after this brief but meteoric episode with the diva, I got a call from a keyboard player and music director who wanted to hire me to play bass as a sideman in a new band he was putting together for the very same disco diva.

I asked him one pertinent question, "Is the husband still the manager?"

"No, they're divorced," he said.

"Then I'm in."

I didn't tell him about my previous tenure.

We were on the way to Virginia Beach, the first gig with this newest new band, when I decided to tell the music director that he probably shouldn't mention my name to the diva because I wasn't sure what her reaction would be. A lot of water had gone under the bridge since my initial employment. She had worked with hundreds of people since then, as had I.

I envisioned one of four scenarios playing out when she re-encountered me: either she would remember me or not, and this would be either a good thing or not. Three out of the four scenarios would allow me to still have the job. So I thought I would play the odds.

As we were getting ready to go onstage, we were finally introduced to our star, meaning it was too late for her to fire me at least for that gig. She genuinely seemed to not remember me.

I said to her, "I played with you once a long time ago."

She asked, "Where are you from?"

"New York," I said.

She smiled. We shook hands. Nope, no memory of me at all. Fantastic. I stayed in the band for two years that time.

With regard to our new employment situation, I told the guys in the new band, "Understand this: we will all eventually be fired."

"Nah," they said, "you're crazy."

"Trust me," I said. "This is my second time around."

They started to believe me very quickly because right away heads began to roll. The guitar chair in that band was like the exploding drummer chair in *This Is Spinal Tap*. For about a year, there was a new cat standing in that spot on every single gig. Something was wrong with each one of them.

The band played an AARP convention in Florida, complete with a scooter and wheelchair parking section. The guitar player du jour showed up with a 1980s pointy heavy-metal Jackson guitar. We knew he was fired before he even played his first note. Horn players or backup singers would also get canned one by one.

Eventually, I got refired. There was no particular reason given at the time, though much later I found out that they wanted an African American face in the bass chair. I understood this inclination. Basically, it got to be my turn to go (again). Of that 11-

piece band, exactly two members made it past the two-year mark. That's got to be a longevity record with the diva.

My postmortem analysis from my original tenure in the band was that the husband/manager was insistent about exercising total control over all aspects of the diva's career and, more specifically, the finances. One of his methods for keeping command of the situation was to never let anyone get near the diva to give her career advice, suggest any kind of changes to the status quo, or even befriend her in any way. As soon as anyone seemed to be entering the inner circle, he or she was fired.

This got to be such a way of life for them that it became the solution to any problem, actual or perceived. If a show in Tucson didn't go well: fire the drummer. If a tour was difficult due to weather delays: fire the road manager. If the diva's shoes hurt because they were too tight: fire the backup singer. This was such a prevalent pattern for so many decades that even when the husband was out of the picture, the old habits continued. At least, that's my armchair psychiatrist analysis of the situation. I'm just guessing.

The punch line for me is that they've called me back twice to come sub in the band last minute. Neither time was I available. I only hope that they keep trying me so that I can get fired a third time. That would really be an achievement.

Disco essentials

26 GROUPIES

L et's talk about sex.

Yes, I'm talking to you, casual reader in the aisles of the bookstore (or surfer of YouTube). I know what you did. You saw my handsome face on the cover of this book and picked it up. Intrigued by the blurb on the back, you decided to have a peek inside to see what dirt gets dished on which rock stars. Then you looked at the table of contents and realized this would certainly be the dirtiest chapter. So you flipped directly to this page. Don't worry. I would have done the same thing.

Now get ready for the shortest chapter in the book.

As a journeyman musician in this business we call "show," I have gone from "nice to meet you" to naked within the same night exactly two times in 40 years. It happened once on a gig at a bar in Manhattan. And it happened once again on a gig overseas. That's it. The glamorous life may not be all that you imagined, eh?

I think if I had more self-confidence as a younger touring musician, I might have been able to close the deal a couple of other times. But even then, it would have only been a handful at most.

It might have been different if I were a huge star. There are certainly legion examples of this. But even if I had been in a huge rock band, the groupies mostly aim for the lead singer or lead guitar player.

Do you even know who plays bass for Alice Cooper? I don't mean Dennis Dunaway, who played with him from 1969-1974, if you've heard of Dennis. He's a nice guy. I mean anyone who has played with Alice in the past 40 years. No? Exactly.

In moments of utter desperation and complete loneliness, I have gone so far as to tally the number of sexual partners I have had in my life. I'm not proud of these moments. But they exist.

I'm at about 70 career partners. This might sound like a medium high number for the average L7 (square) person. But let's look at some famous showbiz examples.

Gene Simmons of KISS claims nearly 5,000 partners. NBA star Wilt Chamberlain claims upwards of 20,000. That seems a little ambitious. But I wasn't there to keep score.

My meager 70 doesn't sound so promiscuous in comparison. But let's do some further math, shall we?

I lost my virginity at age 15, though I didn't have my second encounter until I was 18. I went to an all-boys high school, remember. If I had liked boys, I would have been all set. But, alas, my preferences lie elsewhere. So let's subtract two years for ages 16 and 17 when nothing happened.

Let's also figure in that I have had four "long-term" relationships that lasted an average of four years each. Let's subtract 16 more years and four partners from the grand total.

That leaves 66 partners in 24 sexually active years. That comes out to less than three one-night stands in any of those calendar years.

Making the hot monkey love just three times a year isn't exactly the stuff that rock legends are made of.

27 GIGS I *DIDN'T* GET AND WHY

I have a section on my website and résumé with this title. I only have about half a sentence by each of the names on that list. I figure those stories are at least as interesting as the stuff I have done, maybe more so. People always write about their myriad successes. But few people seem to admit that there might have been a few thousand bumps in the road along the way.

I'm here to tell you that the gigs I haven't gotten are too numerous to mention. But here are a few of the better-known artists with whom I had a near or not-so-near miss. Some of these instances were funny. Some of them had nothing to do with me, nor was there anything I could have done differently. And some of them were downright heartbreaking.

Santana – I got called by songwriter Eric Bazilian of The Hooters to come down to Philadelphia to play on three songs he had written for a new Santana album. We had a great session. Carlos wasn't there in person. But his guitar was on tape. So I was "playing" with him in my headphones. That was a thrill. I was in.

Eric took the tapes from that session out to the Bay Area and ended up completely rerecording the same songs but with Santana's live band instead of the Philadelphia studio band. Just like that I was back out.

Eventually two of the three songs got scrapped by the record company. But the third one was a keeper. Not only was it all set for the album, it was also to be the lead single from the release. Furthermore, former Santana lead singer, Gregg Rolie, had been brought in for this song. He was the guy who had sung on "Black Magic Woman" and "Oye Como Va." I was still out. But at least my pal Eric was in.

Still not quite satisfied with the track, Eric brought the session tapes back to Philadelphia and called me to come record the track yet again. We recut it with the East Coast band playing along with Santana's guitar and Rolie's voice on the tape.

The record label even went so far as to send out a teaser press release saying that the new Santana single was coming out shortly with Rolie once again on lead vocals. I was back in.

Then at the last possible minute, the record label completely dropped the track. I was back out.

That album was called *Supernatural*. It was Santana's first album in seven years. It went on to sell 30 million copies and win eight Grammys.

Doh!

Somewhere there's a rough mix of me playing with Santana. But I don't have it. And I can't prove it. You just have to take my word for it. Or you could call Eric if you don't believe me.

Joan Jett & The Blackhearts – The Blackhearts were signed to Blackheart/CBS Associated records when I worked at that label during my record company days. At some point during that time, they needed to replace their bass player. I sent word through proper channels that I would be very interested in auditioning since answering phones and making Xeroxes wasn't my ultimate career goal.

Word came back to me through those very same channels that I was never going to be allowed to audition for that band for any reason since I was 6 ft. 5 in. tall. Joan was only 5 ft. 2 in. I towered over her. It would have looked too weird onstage. So it would not be allowed. It was a fair point.

In an unrelated coincidence, decades later my buddy Hal Selzer plays bass for The Blackhearts now. Besides being a great musician, he's also a much more reasonably sized human being.

Wilson Pickett – My old pal, the late Crusher Green, was Wilson's drummer and music director. He had been throwing down with the Wicked Pickett since 1965 when "Mustang Sally" was on the pop charts.

In 1999 Pickett released a new album and was touring heavily behind it, not that he had ever really stopped touring since the '60s other than the year he spent upstate in the early '90s on a drunk driving charge. But that's another story.

Wilson's bass player was having some health problems and was finding the air travel to be difficult. Crusher called me and told me to memorize all the songs on Wilson's set list and to wait by the phone.

I did my homework. I was on deck, in the wings waiting to go on. My passport was current. I was just waiting for the phone to ring at any time.

It never did.

I'm pleased to say that Wilson's bass player's health improved to the point that my services weren't needed.

Crusher's health took a turn for the worse, however. He passed away in the winter of 2002, less than three weeks after my mom died.

That was a tough year for me. My fiancée dumped me that summer. Then 9/11 happened. Then my mom died. Then Crusher.

I'm sorry that I never got to play with Pickett, who passed in 2006. But other events in my life clearly eclipsed whatever disappointment I might have been feeling at the time.

Keith Richards – I had a series of conversations with his drummer/producer in the late '90s. He was saying things like, "We'll have to have you up to the studio to play."

This was an exciting prospect. But our schedules just never aligned. That drummer ended up getting a major road gig with a huge artist and hasn't really been seen since other than onstage with that artist. So my connection with Keef left town, as did my hopes of ever meeting him.

Hubert Sumlin – This same drummer/producer was doing some tracks for blues legend Hubert Sumlin. There was one track that Keef had also played on that they were having some trouble with. The producer booked me to come in and rerecord the bass part on that one song.

The night before the session, he called to say they had decided to go another way with the part or maybe scrap the track altogether. I never got to meet Mr. Sumlin. And strike two with Keef.

Ronnie Spector – Her husband/manager called me to do a one-off Christmas gig with the former Ronette on the very kind recommendation from my friends in The Uptown Horns. Unfortunately, I was already booked and couldn't make the date. The conversation I had with her manager was kind of funny though.

As he was inquiring about my experience, I said, "Yeah, I'm familiar with The Ronettes. I do a lot of oldies gigs."

"Let me stop you right there, Ivan," he interjected quickly. "We consider Ronnie to be an artist of today."

Oh, boy, I touched a little nerve there. He was right. My wording was unfortunate.

I never did get to play with Ronnie. But I was on the same bill with her one time. We both played Joey Ramone's birthday party at Coney Island High on St. Mark's Place in Manhattan.

I was there with former '80s Playboy Playmate and accordion wunderkind, Phoebe Legere. That's a whole story in itself. There was a little person involved. Don't ask.

Jonathan Richman and then Ronnie Spector played right after us. Joey and his mom were holding court all night. It was quite a scene.

Rod Stewart – I ran into a pal of mine who told me that he wanted to recommend me for Rod's band. But he claimed that he couldn't find my number in time. The dude whose number he did find in time has been playing bass with Rod since 2002. He's a great bass player, a cool dude, and a good pal of mine. I ain't mad at him for nothing.

But dude couldn't find my number? I'm not sure if I believe that 100 percent or not. I'm in the phone book. Dial 411. Google me. I can be found. And if all that was indeed true, there was probably no reason to tell me about it. Even if he meant it as a compliment, it was a backhanded one at best.

Al Di Meola – In my early days in New York, I auditioned for fusion guitarist Al Di's band. He wasn't there at the audition. They were being run by his guitar player/music director who played exactly like Al Di.

It struck me as odd that a guitar player would have another almost identical guitar player in his band. You've got that chair covered. Get someone who does anything else. But whatever, that was the situation.

At the audition we were presented with lengthy and complicated sheet music of Al's original compositions to sight-read. My sight-reading is only OK these days. Back in those days, it was somewhere between barely OK and not at all OK. Upon seeing the charts, I started to sweat profusely, indicative of the stress I was feeling, which effectively diminished whatever paltry level of reading ability I had up until that moment.

Using some combination of reading the charts, my ears, trusting my instincts, and following the guitar player, I barely survived the songs. I wasn't great. But there were no train wrecks either. Luckily for me they had a second drummer coming in that day without another bass player. So they asked me to stay and go through the songs again with the new drummer.

This was my big chance, I thought. I had a better idea of how the songs went after the first cold read-through. This would give me the opportunity to play the music again being more relaxed this time. I thought that would allow them to better hear what I could offer as a musician.

Al Di is famous for playing a lot of notes very fast. That's what he does. His clone music director also played a lot of notes very fast in the audition to demonstrate what the boss would do if I indeed got the gig.

Somewhere in the second run-through of one of the tunes, I knew for a moment where I was in the music. With complete confidence, I took it upon myself to play a gentle pentatonic scale fill at the end of a phrase setting up the next section. I was proud of myself for adding something to the music, even though it was a skill covered in Folksong Bass Accompaniment 101 class.

At the end of that song, the music director, the one who had been playing a million notes very fast, looked at me and said in all seriousness, "Hey, man, it's not a bass solo."

Wow. I had played four notes that weren't actually written on the chart against his barrage of sound and had gotten chastised for it.

Soon afterward I was telling this story to Stanley Clarke. Stanley and Al got famous together in the 1970s playing a lot of notes really fast. I told Stanley about the audition and the charts and how I was kind of faking my way through them. He had just finished a tour with Al that year and had been reading off of the same charts.

He told me it was a good thing I was using my ears because the charts were wrong.

I did not get the Al Di Meola gig. I guess I played too many notes.

Stanley Clarke – There were a few years when Stanley was using a "rhythm" bass player in his live band so that he could concentrate on being a soloist. I knew already that I was no Stanley Clarke. But the rhythm bass chair was one I thought I could handle.

Here's how much of a pal Stanley is. He gave me an audition. That's a friend right there. He didn't have to do that.

I flew out to L.A. and went to his house up in Topanga Canyon. He and his wife kindly let me crash in the room of one of the kids who was away. He had his touring keyboardist and drummer come over to the house for the audition and a little play around.

As we were playing, the way we were physically set up in the room, I could make eye contact with Stanley and the drummer. But the keyboard player was forced to play with his back to us. I had a great vibe with the drummer. We were smiling and communicating with each other. But I couldn't make any contact with the keyboard dude. I couldn't get any chemistry going with him at all.

The next week Stanley called me and asked how I thought my audition went. He said one of the guys in his band really liked me, the other not so much. I told him that I knew exactly who was who because I knew the vibe I was catching in the room: drums = yes, keys = no. He said I was very intuitive.

That was it. I wasn't going to be in that band. He gave me a shot. I didn't quite make it over the wall. I thanked him for the opportunity. We have stayed good pals.

Ernie K-Doe – This was an interesting one. I never played with New Orleans soul legend Ernie "Mother-in-Law" K-Doe, né Ernest Kador. I wish I had.

Back in my college radio days, I was an extremely minor local celebrity. Among the thousands of people who listened to the mostly alternative rock 1,500-watt radio station where I was the music director and a DJ, literally dozens of them knew who I was. I'm talking minor celebrity.

One of the many duties one had whilst being a celebrity such as myself was to make the talk show circuit to promote whatever one was selling at the time. I don't even remember if I was selling anything other than perhaps the college radio station itself.

I got invited to be on a panel for the Bunny Matthews show on New Orleans public-access cable TV. Bunny was a local music journalist and cartoonist whose TV show had zero budget and was seen by literally tens of people.

Also guesting on my same episode was the great soul singer King Floyd, who lip-synched to his hit "Groove Me." The playback for his performance was coming from a cassette tape in a boom box on the ground. I never saw the finished show. But I know the sound quality on that must have been amazing. No one could have possibly questioned the fact that he wasn't singing a 12-year-old song live with the exact inflection of the original recording.

During my interview segment, Bunny asked me if I wasn't indeed also a bass player in addition to being a college radio DJ. Ernie K-Doe, who was also sitting on the panel just having been interviewed himself, jumped into the conversation saying, "Yes, he is. He played with me."

Confused, I said, "No, I don't think I did." I wasn't confused about having played with him. I never had. I was confused about why in the world he would say that.

K-Doe, known for his gift of gab, was insistent and emphatically went on, "Yes, yes, you did. I'll tell you what will make you remember: It was in the east."

I thought to myself, Ah, yes, the east. Of course. How could I have been so stupid not to have remembered? Wait, the east of what?

I just kind of mumbled an agreement and got on with the interview.

For years I had Ernie K-Doe listed on my résumé. I figured that if he claimed it was true on television, who was I to refute him?

There are so many other gigs I didn't get. Here are brief synopses of some more:

CHIC – They only let me conduct the band for their special guest, Sam Moore, for whom I was music director. I did not play

Am I Famous Yet?

bass with them. It was still a thrill waving my arms in front of them like an idiot.

Larry Coryell – I was told that he allegedly said he would call me. For whatever reason he never did.

Little Anthony & The Imperials – They called me for a gig. But I was already booked. Ten years later, they called again. I finally got the gig.

Little Eva & Little Peggy March – I was booked to back both of them on a one-night gig. But another weeklong gig came in that preempted it.

Darlene Love – I was called to do a last-minute recording session. But I was out of town. Two years later, I finally got to play with her.

New York Dolls – They wouldn't audition me because of potential schedule conflicts I might have had with their tour schedule.

Tower of Power – They were given my number when Rocco was sick, but never called. I don't know how serious a recommendation I was given. But I do know that my information was sent.

Pat Travers – I got called to do a gig with him. But I was already booked. I ended up jamming with him at a fund-raiser years later.

Johnny Winter – His manager kept threatening to call me to fill in with the band. The opportunity never arose before Johnny, unfortunately, passed away.

Below the "gigs I didn't get" heading on my résumé, I also have a section called "early jobs." I wanted to illustrate that my "career" in showbiz didn't automatically start onstage. Here's what I have listed in this section:

158

Early Jobs

- Dishwasher at a Dude Ranch, which I maintain to this day is my only truly marketable skill.
- Envelope Stuffer as an hourly temp. That was a good paper cut gig.
- Oldies Nightclub DJ, spinning your favorite classics at a '50s-themed meat market in a New Orleans suburb.
- College Radio DJ/Music Director, WTUL, New Orleans, my initial claim to "fame."
- Record Label Promotions College Rep/Intern, making phone calls to other college DJs for $50 per week and, more importantly, reimbursement of my long-distance phone bill.
- Record Label Publicist, Manager of West Coast Publicity for Epic Records/Sony Music. I was a real-life junior executive with a corporate Amex card and everything.
- Record Label Publicity Assistant, the per diem phone-answering and Xeroxing job that led up to the corporate Amex gig.
- Record Store Clerk for which I had to take a polygraph test to prove I wasn't stealing from the cash register.
- Security Guard at the World's Fair in New Orleans, graveyard shift, midnight to 8 a.m.
- Temp Secretary typing résumés for the people the phone company was laying off. I "temped" at this same gig for three years while I was trying to get my freelance music income together.

Little Anthony & The Imperials – Rock & Roll Hall of Famers

28 WEDDINGS, FUNERALS, AND BAR MITZVAHS

I have a long-standing joke that I tell when asked what gigs I'm playing lately. I say, "Weddings, funerals, and bar mitzvahs." It makes people smirk or occasionally giggle.

Then there is a certain kind of literalist who asks, "Funerals?"

Yeah, funerals.

There is an old tradition of New Orleans brass bands playing funerals. The jazz funeral is often the highest honor that a musician can receive while being accompanied to his final (aboveground) burial.

In fact, the "second line," which is an entire genre of music and its own unique rhythmic style, comes from the New Orleans brass band funeral tradition. The march to the cemetery consisted of somber dirges. But the walk back from the cemetery, or the part of the procession after passing the slave owner's house, depending upon which version of the traditional story you've heard, broke out into joyous parade music with dancing and shouting.

To this day, the New Orleans funeral tradition involves jubilation. When my mother passed in 2001, I remember my New York friends sending their condolences. But I also remember my New Orleans friends, specifically singer Frankie Ford and his manager, saying to me, "Celebrate."

Death is a part of life. It's part of the deal we make by being here on this planet. I find the New Orleanian method of processing grief to be the healthiest I have thus far encountered.

While I certainly have played many wakes and memorial jam sessions for our fallen comrades in music, that's not the specific intent of the weddings, funerals, and bar mitzvahs joke.

In fact I'm referring to the reality that I'm playing with private party bands that do mostly weddings but also other functions where someone might want to hire musicians. Many of us do these gigs in between our rock star sightings and world tours because they pay well. They also keep an instrument in our hands and keep our fingers nimble.

In and around New York City, these gigs are called club dates. I'm not exactly sure why. They usually occur in catering halls, not nightclubs. They often occur in golf and country clubs, but not exclusively enough to require that every private party gig be called a club date. This is a regional quirk, it turns out.

In the Boston area, these same gigs are called general business or "GB" bands. In Nashville they're called "formal" gigs. In LA the same gigs are called "casuals." In London they're called "function" bands.

It's confusing. But all these words signify the exact same type of gigs. I know one drummer in New York who refers to any private party as a "corporate" gig, regardless of whether a company or an individual has hired the band. And though that nomenclature doesn't quite fit, everyone knows exactly what he means by it.

There is an actual corporate type of gig we typically call "industrials." These can be some of the highest paying gigs ever. I got about a thousand dollars once to play for eight minutes at 8 a.m. for the opening of a rah-rah sales meeting for a big telecom company.

The Uptown Horns band had to synchronize an intricate medley to a video presentation in the days before ubiquitous click tracks. This was concurrent with a lot of pyrotechnics, fire shooting from everywhere, and acrobats on stilts. It would have been a giant payday if not for the 12 hours of rehearsal that was booked for it. The tech call that morning was for something like 5 a.m. So I guess if you break that down hourly, it wasn't such a huge payday after all.

I played a corporate gig with Martha Reeves & The Vandellas in Baltimore on the occasion of the Corrections Corporation of America national convention. That's right. We entertained a hotel ballroom full of for-profit prison owners. Despite the name over the door, the folks inside were not unlike any other convention audience. There were 750 people in a ballroom eating rubber chicken and waiting for the speeches to end so they could dance in the streets, as it were. It was fairly unremarkable except for a souvenir handbill for the evening that I took home with me.

Beautiful downtown Baltimore is a rough town. You may have heard other people mention this fact. The morning after that gig we were waiting in front of the hotel for an airport pickup. Our luggage was stacked against the wall of the building, which included all of Martha's sheet music, the gowns, the makeup, everything. Oh, and my bass.

There was a dude just kind of leaning against the wall of the building a few yards from us. There was nothing notable about that. A few minutes went by. I noticed that he was a couple of feet closer to the luggage and, you know, my bass, than he was moments before. Now my New York City street sense kicked in. So I was keeping a nonchalant eye on him. Another minute later, he was a couple of feet closer. You know, just hanging out, watching traffic go by. By this time, he and I were about equidistant to the luggage.

No longer satisfied with our sense of security, I pretended to walk over and pull something out of my bass bag. In my fake efforts to dislodge whatever I was pretending to retrieve, I was forced to pick up and move the bass back within range so that I had my hand on it. I was also now positioned closer to the luggage so that he no longer had the jump on me should he decide to grab something and make a run for it.

Within a couple of minutes, the dude magically decided he wasn't interested in hanging out in front of the hotel anymore and casually walked off. Ms. Lois Reeves, a Vandella, witnessed this entire interaction, nodded at me, and said, "Smart." Ms. Lois is from Detroit. She knows about street sense.

I just thought that it would have been really ironic to have had our luggage or my bass stolen in front of a hotel filled with corrections officers.

Several years before that, I had also been in Baltimore for a corporate gig with The Shirelles at the Convention Center. It was another huge decorated ballroom that could accommodate 1,000 or more people for the dinner at the end of a national convention. There were vendor booths on the convention floor, seminars in meeting rooms, the whole shebang.

The ballroom was outfitted with a big stage, lighting, and huge video screens to project the four-camera TV rig for people in the back of the room to see the close-ups, like at a Bon Jovi concert. Only instead of Bon Jovi it was The Shirelles and The Drifters. It's a different demographic. But the show business production trappings are the same.

This was the NFDA annual convention and dinner. We were there for several hours loading in and sound checking before we realized what NFDA stood for: The National Funeral Directors Association. We were playing for 1,000 morticians. Suddenly all of the gentlemen walking around with red satin shirts and ties and the sales booths for embalming supplies started to make sense.

I'll say this about funeral directors: Those cats need to let off some steam. When they're away from their customers, them dudes know how to party. I can't remember a wilder or more raucous crowd at any gig. They were hooting, hollering, screaming, dancing, practically bouncing off the walls and swinging from the chandeliers. Those folks cut loose. It was a blast.

Afterward we walked out with a souvenir videotape of the four-camera shoot of the gig. It's some of the best footage I've ever been in of a genuinely fun but strange gig.

There was a megachurch gig with Martha Reeves & The Vandellas in Wichita, Kansas, once that had a similar multi-camera setup. The church's media rig was designed to broadcast weekly church services to the masses. So it was a pretty sophisticated rig. Likewise, we walked out of that gig with a freshly burned DVD of the evening's performance.

The Funeral Directors' convention wasn't the only time we played for morticians with The Shirelles, either. We played a catering hall in New Jersey with lots of mirrors, marble, and chandeliers. This time it was a birthday party for a successful local businesswoman who owned a funeral parlor. It was a dinner for 250 of her closest friends featuring a classic soul music performance at the end of the evening.

It is standard practice for a master of ceremonies to introduce the guest of honor at events like this as he or she makes an official entrance into the room. This is true of weddings, bar mitzvahs, and even occasional birthday parties. This is accomplished through a PA system at crushing volume, usually accompanied by lots of flashing lights and very loud disco music.

"Ladies and gentlemen, please welcome our hostess and tonight's guest of honor. Give it up for Miss Madonnaaaa!" (That was the mortician's name, not the singer of a similar moniker.)

Now, my memory of this evening is cloudy. I don't think there was an actual casket in the room. And I don't think she was wheeled into the room in the casket only to emerge from it upon her introduction for dramatic effect. I don't think that happened. But it might have.

I know that we bandfolk certainly laughed about that entrance. So we might have invented or embellished it. But we definitely played a gig for Madonna, her funeral home employees, family, and friends.

Perhaps we conflated Madonna's entrance with Screamin' Jay Hawkins's standard stage entrance. I never played with Screamin' Jay. But several friends of mine have. I got to see him perform once, which was amazing.

This particular story came to me from drummer Crusher Green. Though I regret not personally witnessing this, Crusher said that when the curtain went up the band was onstage playing Screamin' Jay's overture. Also noticeably center stage was a black coffin.

The gag was that Jay was preloaded into the coffin with the microphone. As the curtain went up, the front-of-house soundman turned on the mic. Screamin' Jay started doing his thing inside the coffin and popped out, making his entrance during the opening number. It's just good old macabre show business comedy.

The particular night Crusher was describing was a two-show night. I don't care who you are. That second show is always harder than the first. Screamin' Jay was in his later years at the time of this incident. But I have had similar things happen to me at a much younger age.

The announcer crowed, "Ladies and gentlemen, Screamin' Jay Hawkiiiiiiins!" The band started the overture. The lights came up. The curtain went up. The soundman turned on the mic. The entire audience was assaulted by 10,000 watts of an amplified Screamin' Jay snoring. He was out cold. The piano player had to go bang on the coffin lid to wake him up to do the show.

Don't let anybody ever tell you show business is easy.

A wedding band I was working with played a Greek American wedding once at a swanky hotel on the coast up in Connecticut. We were requested to play some Greek traditional tunes at the reception. The bandleader had found some sheet music online for generic Greek folk tunes. The melodies were written in traditional notation. No problem. But the chord symbols were written in the Greek alphabet. Problem.

I ended up combining my two college experiences into one uniquely useful skill. I knew from Tulane about the Greek fraternities and knew what all the letters over the doors of the frat houses were.

Additionally, I knew from a combination of my studies at Berklee about solfège ("do, re, mi" syllables). From my world travels, I also knew that a lot of European music uses a "fixed do" system. As I've previously explained, this means that the syllable "do" always corresponds to the note C on the piano, whereas in America we use a "movable do" system. Do can be the tonic of any key here.

From this I deduced that a chord symbol using the Greek letters "sigma, omega, and lambda" spelled out the word "sol," which is the fifth note of the scale: do, re, mi, fa, sol. If do is C, sol is G.

Yeah, yeah, I know. The band looked at me with that same facial expression that you have right now. Suffice to say I was able to scribble in chord symbols in English/Latin alphabet characters that were familiar to the band. As a result, we were able to start playing our sad approximation of Greek folk music.

As the Greeks do in traditional celebrations, someone smashed a plate on the dance floor and hollered, *"Opa!"* I took this as a sign that we were doing a good job.

The hotel detective, let's call him the house dick, was not amused, however. In general, rich white people in Connecticut do not take kindly to uncivilized destruction of private property. Knowing this, the house dick immediately turned up the lowered party lights to their full brilliance, stopped the band, brought everything to a screeching halt, and called the cops.

The wedding was ruined. The bride was inconsolable, crying buckets of tears. It was not going well. It took several phone calls to find a hotel manager since it was late on a Saturday night. They had all gone home for the weekend leaving only the dick in charge of the property.

After about a half hour of just standing around in silence with the bright lights on while conferences were being had in the hallway with the family, the cops, the hotel dick, and the eventually located manager, the party was allowed to continue for the final 15 minutes of our booking.

Somehow lost in translation from Greece to suburban Connecticut was the fact that the celebrants had every intention of paying for all of the smashed stoneware. This is a standard cost for a Greek wedding, like the floral centerpieces for each table are at every other wedding. The dick had apparently missed that day at cultural awareness school. As such this family ended up saving a bundle of cash because they only got to smash one plate.

As the party resumed, they rushed into the cake cutting ceremony because they were now way behind schedule. The groom tried to make light of the ridiculous situation by doing the smash the wedding cake in the bride's face comedy shtick. I've seen this work many times at other weddings when it was a mutual joke. This particular day it wasn't since the bride had already seen her magical night ruined. It only generated more creamy frosted tears.

We played three more songs, got paid, and went home.

And then there was the Hannibal Lecter wedding.

Well, that's what the band came to call it. It was an odd affair to be sure. We got called to provide an acoustic trio for a wedding gig, which was unusual to start with. It's not common to have a raucous dance party with only an acoustic guitar, an acoustic bass, and drums played with brushes. I suppose it's possible, but unlikely.

The venue was familiar to us. It was a 150-year-old gothic-style converted synagogue on the Lower East Side of Manhattan. It's a beautifully decrepit building, very ornate, spooky, and creaky. Depending on the lighting and the spirit of the gathering, it can range easily from joyous to downright creepy. This gig was more in the creepy category, though it wasn't initially apparent why.

When we arrived, the venue was beautifully lit with colored feature lights scattered throughout the building, making the ornamental columns more dramatic and elegant. In the center of the floor was a specially constructed platform surrounded by a water tank forming a moat around it. In the center of the platform was a beautiful bride's table set for two.

There were real trees brought in to hang over the table in one of the more elaborate florists' constructions I've ever seen. The place was decked out to the nines. It was gorgeous and clearly very expensive, well into six figures for the evening for sure.

This synagogue could hold probably 300-400 people seated and maybe 750-1,000 if it was set up for standing room and the balconies were used.

But not this night. This night the list of attendees included exactly two people: the bride and the groom. That's it. No guests. It was the most bizarre thing I've ever seen.

There were plenty of staff on-site. There were caterers in the basement whipping up a five-course gourmet meal. There was a wedding officiant, a photographer, a videographer, waitstaff, all the trappings of a normal wedding ceremony and reception. There were just no guests.

It's the only time I can remember at any wedding gig that the size of the band outnumbered the audience. And we were just a trio.

To say the energy in the room was awkward is an understatement. We played quietly in the corner all night, including the first dance and all of that. People would come in and out of the room as necessary to perform the wedding ceremony, help with the cake cutting, or serve the meal. The only thing that wasn't done was the bouquet toss. There was no one there to catch it. So there was no point, really.

At one point the groom left the room to use the bathroom. We were playing "Fly Me to the Moon" at the time. Out of nowhere, the bride spoke directly to us, saying, "That's a song from our favorite anime cartoon."

Oh, shit, what were we supposed to do? She spoke directly to us. Do we answer her? Do we make eye contact? Anime? Do we just let that comment go by unremarked? That wasn't even nearly the oddest thing about the whole setup.

"Oh, yeah, great," was all we said.

That was the end of our interaction with the couple for the evening except for a thanks at the end. Her speaking to us as if we were normal human beings in a normal situation only served to amplify the creepiness of the whole thing.

I'm not sure why we decided to call it the Hannibal Lecter wedding, other than the fact that none of us would have been surprised in the least to read in the paper the next morning that the bride's liver had been eaten by her new husband. Nothing of the sort happened, of course. You know, that we're aware of.

Table for two at the Hannibal Lecter wedding

29 THE GIRL IN THE HAMSTER BALL

Russian weddings are difficult to describe adequately. I have played in many Russian wedding bands for years. I get a lot of questions about the gigs from people who haven't yet experienced them. People ask, "Where are the gigs, in Brighton Beach? Do they play all Russian music?"

Well, no, they aren't. And no, they don't.

Let me back up a second. Russia is the largest landmass country in the world. It covers 13 time zones. The country is so ethnically diverse that there are even Mongols. But based on only a very few Russian expats I've encountered playing weddings in Brooklyn, I fear the entire country. My paranoid unfair generalizations spring from over a decade of experience with a very specific microcosm of Russians: those living in the U.S. who have a spare $50,000-$100,000 to spend on a wedding.

Please understand that this is a very limited and specific set of Russians about whom I generalize. I've never been to Moscow. I've never met very many working-class Russian families who are proud of their art and culture.

Most of those I've been exposed to are a group of people who are wealthy or who want to appear wealthy and have a bizarre sense of entitlement. They are desperately trying to demonstrate to their friends and family how rich and esteemed they are. The wealth seldom trickles all the way down to the band, I can assure you.

Let me be clear. American weddings and the people who spend lots of money on them aren't any better. They're just slightly different. Wedding culture in the U.S. is an industry unto itself. Catering halls the world over, and especially in the northeastern U.S., are remarkably similar in appearance, services offered, style of decor, and especially how they tend to mistreat the lowest form of human existence: the working musician.

Weddings in general have the same cake, the same bouquet, the same speeches, the same shrimp for the cocktail hour and rubber chicken for dinner, the same rented tuxedos, the same white dresses, the same god-awful bizarrely colored satin bridesmaid dresses, and the same time line. They're woefully monotonous and unimaginative. The gigs are all exactly six hours long. We as Americans are just used to them.

There is a large Russian immigrant population in the U.S., especially since the breakup of the Soviet Union. As such, a great deal of oligarch's money has made its way over here with these immigrants.

I noticed early on at these gigs that the vodka on every table, as there must be a bottle on every table to demonstrate opulence, is usually Grey Goose vodka. Made in France. The Russians, who arguably know a thing or two about vodka, are somehow self-loathing Russians and would never serve Russian vodka.

The Russians are an interesting breed of people, particularly the musicians. Though I know this isn't true, it feels like the Russian cats in the band have all been in conservatory since age three. Most of them can sight-read fly shit. But most of them, like most classically trained musicians, become very uncomfortable when the music begins to get improvised.

Wedding gigs in general are notorious for getting "off book," due to the sheer volume of material and range of styles that need to be covered in a six-hour gig. So on these gigs by definition, we have to spend a lot of time improvising and flying by the seat of our pants.

Most of the bands I play in are mixed Russian and American musicians, about half and half. Depending on the makeup of the couple: two Russians, two Americans, one of each, the resulting playlist will reflect this.

If it is a full-on all-Russian affair, the 15-piece orchestra might spend 60-75 percent of the night pantomiming to prerecorded MP3s with only the vocals being live. The music is a lot of Euro-disco pop, mostly in English, but some in Russian, Italian, Spanish, or Hebrew. The instruction from the bosses is for us to "make fun" while "performing" these songs.

Contrary to the meaning of this expression in English, which is to ridicule, what they mean is to smile, dance, and pretend to be playing and having the time of our lives. Many of the musicians will noodle along with the MP3s. The drummer is asked to keep playing regardless. The bass player is generally asked not to play because it just muddies up the sound. So I can potentially get paid to stand there three-quarters of the night and pretend that I'm doing something.

The client pays the band by the number of musicians onstage. If they can afford 15 pieces in the band, they get 15. Five or seven of them may be singers performing only three to four songs a night. But there must be 15 people onstage. If they can afford only nine pieces, they get nine. To my ear and mind anything over about five pieces at these gigs sounds the same. But see earlier where I mentioned the tendency toward ostentation.

There is also a trend at these functions of shooting production videos ahead of time to show to the guests. These seem bizarre on first encounter. They usually involve a "comedic" script about how the couple first met and fell in love. This is slapstick comedy without irony since irony seems to be a concept that is completely lost on this particular demographic. It also requires nontheatrical family members to recite lines, perform on-screen action, and use comedic props.

These videos are god-awful to anyone not intimately acquainted with the family. They're just the worst. But because they star Uncle Boris and the wedding couple, everybody is delighted with their antics. The videos get genuine peals of laughter and applause. More importantly, they give the band a 10-15 minute break.

There are a lot of bilingual speeches and toasts at these affairs. More than once, a mother of the bride has delivered her heartfelt good wishes to her daughter in the form of a song. Once in a while it involves the mom singing along to a karaoke track. This feels uncomfortable to watch.

Several times we have seen a mother completely lip-synch some bombastic song from *Phantom of the Opera* or a similar source, not singing a note. The whole thing is an obvious sham yet completely accepted by the entire room.

When I've spoken to some of the Russian members of the band asking how this is in any way acceptable, they have tried to explain to me how important the appearance of propriety is in their culture. The sense I get is that as long as it looks right, it is right, even if it's completely wrong.

There are analogous incongruities in American culture, of course. Any politician who maintains a sham marriage just to remain electable is participating in the exact same subterfuge. But since we Americans are used to that falsity, it doesn't really register with us any longer. It is only when we get to observe the complacent mendacities of other cultures that it strikes us as odd.

Russians also seem to share a deep cultural love of a good floor show. Almost every wedding includes some type of halftime performance in the middle of the ballroom that has nothing to do with the typical wedding band.

One of the bands I play with most frequently has a feature they call the "violins pop show." This involves a string quartet playing wireless electric fiddles out on the dance floor wearing clothing that is more "rock & roll" than the tux-clad band onstage. The string quartet also has prerecorded backing tracks they perform with. They're usually (but not always) playing live, with embellishment.

They get the couple and the family up on the dance floor and make them part of the show. It's an odd performance from the American point of view though usually well-received by the patrons. But this affords the rest of the band a 15-20 minute break. So we love the violins pop show.

Other floor shows have featured dance troupes with routines that range from tango to hip-hop, often during the same performance, complete with elaborate costume quick changes. One set of dancers had candle chandeliers mounted into their headdresses. I'm not sure what that was about.

There was one performance group in which dancers were dressed as Hasidic rabbis doing ethnic folk dances in unison. One routine had them dancing with wine bottles balanced on their heads. It was amazing to marvel at the skill that must have taken.

Well, it was amazing until the end. The big reveal was when they carefully lifted their hats, letting us see that there were holes in the crowns and that the bottles were strapped securely to their heads. Very funny, rabbis.

They even had a rabbi who did a routine with four life-size puppets all mounted on poles resting on his shoulders. You may have seen the same routine done with Village People puppets or something at halftime at an L.A. Lakers game. All of the puppets follow the moves of the puppeteer exactly. It's a good gag. But I had never seen it done with rabbis.

Another wedding had some sort of circus theme to it. Jugglers and a high unicyclist were introduced into the performance space at the end of the evening. Somewhere during the dinner hour, a group of about a dozen kids all dressed up as clowns came out and jumped around with no particular purpose other than the fact that they were clowns. Yeah, it was a little creepy.

By far the most impressive act that I have seen to date was a contortionist/dancer who did an entire routine on the dance floor while sealed in what can only be described as a giant hamster ball. This was a large rigid clear plastic sphere with a person inside of it rolling around the room and occasionally getting an ankle behind her head.

I don't know how she got into or out of the ball. And I don't know how she got the ball into or out of the ballroom. It might have been an inflatable situation. As ever, these floor shows afford the band probably the only 15-20 minute break that we are going to get in the entire four-hour reception portion of the six-hour event. As with most of them, I didn't stay to watch the whole thing. I probably had to pee.

I'm going to share with you an email that the band received from one of our bandleaders about an upcoming gig. But I want to preface this carefully.

Understand something: I am very grateful to these bands for many years of lucrative employment. I have nothing but the utmost respect for the people who run these bands. As immigrants to this country sometimes facing tremendous language barriers, they have built successful independent businesses up from nothing. They truly are shining examples of people living the American dream.

I also have no quarrel with anyone who is heroically conducting business in a second language. That has to be extremely difficult. I can barely speak English myself. If I had to communicate in another language, I wouldn't be able to get past "yes" or "no." And those would most likely be in sign language, not words.

This email I will share with you verbatim. There were several issues that needed to be discussed involving onstage band decorum that were all based on our previous poor behavior. Everything he was saying was completely reasonable.

The reason I share it is not to ridicule the author, though some of the mistakes are a lot of fun to read. Quite the contrary, I wish to illustrate both the challenges the bandleader faced trying to communicate in a foreign language as well as the additional challenges we faced as non-Russian-speaking musicians trying to decode exactly what our charge was for the evening.

>> VERY IMPORTANT (Orchestra rools):

1). ***Nobody from the all the band members can't use and check your cell phone or Ipad on the stage during the dance sets,just during the breaks (e-mails,Facebook, SMS & voice mail messages)***

2). ***Nobody from the band members can't do the pictures from your phone on the stage during the dance set your (show) working time. ***

3). ***Nobody (singers or musicians) can't leave the stage during the show working time period,only during the breacks.***

   NOBODY from the singers CAN'T use any time the wireless system for your own IPad (only wire). We had a very bad experience and will never use this system any more times.

   Please check the introductions of song "Gozar La Via"/Julio Iglessias,because we had all time a problem to play this song properly from the beginning.

Hope that everyone understand my point and we don't need to return back to talk about these probles. Everyone on the stage must to have a big fun with your work and show to our a new potential clients your energe. Also a good time,including the dancing & smile.
This point will show to the gusts our professional skils and will bring more a new potential clients.

The songs program I'll send you shortly. <<

Did you get all of that? Good. I'll see you at the next wedding gig.

30 TAKING THE TEMPERATURE OF THE ROOM

A great deal of what I do as an itinerant musician involves repeatedly walking into new environments. Though I might play 228 gigs in an average calendar year, unlike going to the same office five days a week, I'm constantly playing venues for the very first time. There are certainly numerous repeat engagements. But even after nearly 30 years of doing this, I play new joints all the time.

When entering a new performance space for a gig, I like to get a feel for what my surroundings are. I take the temperature of the room, so to speak. I look for subtle and not so subtle cues that let me know exactly where I am, how I fit into this scenario, and what type of energy I can anticipate receiving from those around me for the duration of the engagement. That lets me know how welcome I am in this place, how hard I'm going to have to work to get through the night, or how much shit I can anticipate having to eat before the end of the evening.

Almost always, I have to travel over some time and distance to get to a venue. Travel is tiring, no matter who you are. From subway delays to Holland Tunnel traffic jams to long-haul trans-Pacific flights, very often I've been through a little duress before I even walk in the door. This is not a complaint. It's just a statement of fact.

I've learned from years of doing this that nobody cares what kind of day you've had before you get to the gig. They only know or care about dealing with you for right now, which is exactly as it should be for the most part. This is why it pays to leave whatever grief you're carrying with you outside of the venue if possible. But I digress.

When walking into a new dressing room for the first time, if there is a bottle of water waiting for the weary traveler, that tiny gesture of hospitality goes a long way. I guess one of the reasons I remain impressed by being offered a mere bottle of water after all this time is that it so rarely happens.

Usually there is nothing. You should expect nothing. There will be nothing. You'll get nothing and like it! I have a long-running joke about asking people at the venue if this is indeed the hostility suite. I repeat myself a lot. You'll get used to it.

There are other indications besides the (usually non-) availability of food and drink that may indicate just exactly where one has found oneself at the end of one's travels.

For instance, a hotel I was scheduled to stay at in Miami Beach advertised on its website: Bachelorette Party Packages, "your last fling before the ring." Oh, boy.

I noticed upon entering my room in this very cute newly renovated art-deco hotel the easy-to-clean squeegee-friendly plastic flooring. It told me a great deal about the clientele of the hotel and about my chances for enjoying a quiet night's sleep at this lovely establishment.

If the website advertisement weren't enough of an advance hint, the check-in desk would have been the clincher. There was a live DJ in the hotel lobby set up with a full party-volume PA system. Normal conversational volume with the receptionist was rendered impossible, requiring her to scream at me, "I NEED YOUR ID AND A CREDIT CARD FOR INCIDENTALS" with the same ferocity one might intone toward a mixologist in a thunderous nightclub, "GIVE ME A BAY BREEZE AND A JAGER BOMB."

To prevent the need for hollering the answers to my next question, there was a convenient sign posted on the front desk listing the names and shift times of the DJ "talent" in the lobby. It was clear from this placard that DJ Marvin would be spinning until 2 a.m. Even though my room was on the third floor, DJ Marvin and I seemed to enjoy a special relationship in my bed until that hour.

After three days of that town, where a DJ seemed to come pouring out of every business and establishment on the main drag, I had had quite enough of the "unka-unka" music. I said when I returned home, "If I hear the beat drop one more time ..."

Sometimes the room announces its temperature to you before you get a chance to get out the thermometer. Countless times, we have been accosted by a restaurant owner or country club manager as we are physically walking in through the door. They come running up to us basically saying that we are already too loud.

But wait, we haven't played a note yet. How do you know we're too loud?

Then they go into some diatribe about all of the complaints they've gotten in their entire lives about loud bands. I would love to have the chance just one time to demonstrate how softly I can play before I am reprimanded. I'll stand there with my volume knob completely turned off if the gig pays the same amount of money. I've done it before. And I'll do it again.

In New York City this began to get really bad two mayors ago. Blowhard Rudy Giuliani started and Michael Bloomberg continued to criminalize sound. The cops seem to go through varying levels of enthusiasm when enforcing these mayoral dicta. I guess it depends what the boss had for lunch on a specific day.

At the worst point in the enforcement of sound violation, the cops were forced to show up anytime anyone complained at all. Considering the population density of New York and the statistics of general human happiness, one can conclude that there is at least one crank on every single block who will complain. It doesn't matter if your gig is juggling cotton balls. Some idiot is going to think that it's too loud.

This equation is further complicated by superrich people buying properties in Manhattan because they are the only people who can afford them. They want to be in the city because it is the trendy place to be. Yet they forget that the reason it is trendy is due to all the artists and musicians who live and create there.

Then when they buy a million-dollar apartment in the heart of Greenwich Village, they expect peace and quiet. I'll never understand this logic nor the hubris and the sense of entitlement many rich people have, assuming a special right to complain.

At the height of the noise crackdown, the edict was that if the cops could hear just one decibel of sound outside of your establishment, technically you were in violation. The first visit from the cops got you a warning. The second visit by the cops got you a $700 ticket. The third visit from the cops got you a $1,400 ticket. The fourth visit got you a padlock on your front door. The city officially declared you out of business.

It happened to an old concert venue on Bleecker Street called the Elbow Room. Rich people moved into the trendy and expensive neighborhood. The mayor decided that the needs of rich people far outweighed anything else. Somebody complained. The nightclub got padlocked. It's a chain drugstore now.

My regular long-term nightclub gig in the Village had to deal with this problem increasingly through the years. The club kept getting tickets and kept fighting them because the owner's wife was a lawyer. Whatever hell the club owners were catching from the neighbors and from the city they passed directly along to us in the band.

We were even on alert at one point, so that whenever the manager signaled "five-o" to us from the front door, we were to instantly turn down to a whisper no matter what we had been playing. This meant that a cop was outside.

I think the regulations have relaxed slightly from when the situation was at its worst, around the year 2000. But it's still bad. There's another club on Bleecker Street that has been there for decades only recently having trouble with an upstairs neighbor who has lived above the club for decades. Some people just want to cause problems.

In a way I get it when a bar manager comes running over to me and tells me I'm too loud before I even get the bass out of the case. It still doesn't make it any more fun to hear.

When playing gigs in restaurants and in catering halls especially, it's often a fun little game to try and figure out how musician-friendly the management are in any given establishment. Do they like bands or feel compelled to barely tolerate them? Are we going to have an easy night of working in a professional and cordial manner with a maître d', or is it going to be a long and adversarial engagement?

One simple litmus test I like to perform is going up to the bar and seeing if I can get served. Many catering halls have a strict policy about not serving the musicians alcohol. I can understand why having an open bar for bands probably isn't a good idea in general. But I'm over 21. It's legal for me to responsibly enjoy an adult beverage. In a roomful of other adults also enjoying fermented products, it feels oddly punitive if I am not allowed to play in any of their reindeer games.

This prohibition happens so frequently that my standard wedding-band rig consists of a bass, an amp, any sheet music I will need, protein bars for the disappointingly frequent instances that the catering hall refuses to serve me anything non-carnivorous, and a flask with Jack Daniels in it just in case.

On a band break, I will belly up and say to the bartender, "Give me a club soda, please."

I wait a beat.

Then I add, "And give me a shot of Jack to help wash that down with."

Usually they laugh. About a third to a half of the time, they will give me the shot. The rest of the time, they will say they can't serve me because I'm in the band. But I have presented it to them as a joke. So they don't have to get all nasty about refusing.

And then occasionally something else entirely happens.

At one particular Russian catering hall way out in the wilds of Brooklyn next door to a bowling alley that had razor wire across the windows, any attempts to seem opulent, high class, or even gaudy were laughable. It was in a hellhole neighborhood and was just barely maintaining appearances with duct tape and chicken wire.

I went up to the bar and handed my standard line, "And give me a shot of Jack to help wash that down with."

The Russians aren't known for their sense of humor. I guess it's cold where they come from. And by that, I mean Sheepshead Bay.

The bartender deadpanned without missing a beat, "Vee only have Johnnie Valker Blue."

Johnnie Walker Blue costs almost $200 a bottle. Shots of Blue in Manhattan will run $45-$65 each. A scumhole on Avenue X in Brooklyn does NOT have only Johnnie Walker Blue. I would venture to say that they probably don't have ANY Johnnie Walker Blue. Sure, they have the bottle. But whatever is in it is something else.

I told him that would be fine. He poured me the shot. I enjoyed whatever rotgut it was as much as I would enjoy anything else.

Another notable instance of knowing exactly what kind of establishment I was entering happened to me at a modest hotel in Miami. There was a sign by the front desk that said, "No refund after 15 minutes."

Anytime someone has gone to the trouble to make a sign, this means that said behavior or phenomenon is enough of a recurring theme to be an issue. So let us examine what this sign told us about this hotel right away upon check-in.

The very first line of the hotel policy stated that it was a "drug-free environment." That sounds like a sensible position. But again, if it needs to be committed to a wall posting on the very top line, it means that there have been numerous past occurrences to warrant said signage.

"Shoes & shirt required." This is a little more understandable reminder given the fact that the hotel is in Miami, though miles from any beach or pool.

"No alcohol, littering, or assembly in the common area or lobby." Again, that's fair. But the need to say it explicitly means that it needs to be said.

But what's that back up on the third line? "No refund after 15 minutes." Ah, there's the thing that spoke volumes about where we were. It made me wonder how many incidents there had been in the past to warrant such a declaration, what their frequency was, and what the motivation was of the refund seekers.

This was a humble hotel, privately owned, not a corporate chain, located directly across the street from the University of Miami. Perhaps certain clientele booked the rooms sight unseen online and were disappointed with the humble, yet clean accommodations upon first sight. That's possible.

But let's face it. Most of those incidents probably sprang from guests' performing some sex act, imbibing drugs, or, more likely, some unholy combination of the two within a very short passage of time, then demanding their money back from the desk clerk.

Welcome to Miami.

31 OH, THE INDIGNITY! ENTER THROUGH THE KITCHEN

T his is a real sign behind a catering hall in New Jersey. To musicians, at first glance this sign appears to suggest that we might be emotionally handicapped and unfit to use the front door of the place. Is there some implied hierarchy in the ordering of the people mentioned, I wonder? Are they insulting florists or other vendors by lumping them in with lowly musicians?

Yet further examination of the topography of this particular venue reveals the actual slight. This place is built on the side of a hill. The front door is up two steps from the entrance driveway. The back entrance is around the building and down the hill, one floor below the main level, hence the reason one requires an elevator to transport one's bass amplifier back upstairs.

Rather than a disservice to the vendors, the true disservice here is done to the alternately abled. Instead of building a tiny ramp that would allow a wheelchair to navigate the two steps into the main entrance, the owners felt it would be easier or cheaper to send them down the hill and around the back. Though they are invited guests, the handicapped patrons get to enjoy the garbage chute on their way in to the ritzy party. This place has class.

There is a common practice at catering halls, hotels, and other upmarket establishments to have a service entrance for deliveries that is separate (yet unequal) from the polished brass and marble entryways the paying guests use. That's understandable. No one likes to be checking into a five-star hotel as the staff is dragging out the ripe and dripping remains of last night's sushi station from the Vandersnoot wedding.

While the front entrances of these establishments are quite discerning, the service entrances are notoriously not so. If most people entered restaurants via the service entrance past the greasy Dumpsters into the kitchens, they would be far less likely to want to eat there. There's something about walking past the full bouquet of a fermented garbage pile into the steamy ambience of a working industrial kitchen that sets quite an emotional tone for the evening, especially with regard to one's appetite.

Musicians often need to carry amps and gear into an establishment of this type and are barred from using the front door or what I like to call "the white folks'" entrance. It's very common to see the racial demographics of pricey functions such as these laid out in bold terms. Often the only people of color in these joints are the waitstaff and the band. If they're superrich places, this might not even extend to the waitstaff, just the band.

This discrimination is often accompanied by a goofy dress code. After five years of having to wear a shirt and tie every day to preparatory school, nothing makes my eyes roll faster than a "jackets required for gentlemen" sign in one of these dumps.

Some of them go so far as to require that you be in your full monkey suit to load in your gear. Do you know how uncomfortable and ridiculous it is to hump amplifiers while wearing a wool suit? There is no shame in manual labor. There is also nothing wrong with wearing a formal tuxedo. But combine the two, and it's just not a good look for anybody.

On the very day that I wrote this, I received an email saying, "Please don't forget to wear all nice casual attire for sound check if you are not wearing your performance suit." Tortured syntax aside, this is referring to the load-in at the Rainbow Room, a "classy" dive in Manhattan for a wedding gig the following night.

What exactly is "nice casual"? And who cares what I'm wearing while sweating and lifting amps? It's hard to tell if this neurosis is springing from the bandleader, the booking agent, the couple, or the venue itself. Whoever made up the rule, it's guaranteed that I'm in for a fun evening well before I even arrive.

There are further computations that tend to go into just how snooty a particular establishment is likely to be. More specifically, these factors influence how nasty the employees are likely to be to the musicians. Legitimately upscale hotels, restaurants, and country clubs are discriminatory in their clientele to be sure. One cannot be exclusive unless one excludes someone.

Rules and regulations at this stratum of the hospitality industry are extensive and strictly enforced, though usually with some level of decorum. When attempting to roll a hand truck with a guitar amp on it through the lobby, you will be instructed nicely but firmly that you need to use the service entrance.

An interesting thing happens when one travels a few notches down the food chain to catering halls, which are also aptly called "wedding factories." As the overall socioeconomic level of the establishment starts to decline, even while the veneer of opulence and "classiness" persists, the level of pretense increases mightily.

With the increase in pretense comes an almost linear decrease in civility to musicians and other vendors. It gets pretty nasty fairly quickly. There is a clear hierarchy and pecking order among the staff of such catering halls from the maître d' on down to the dishwashers and porters. Ranking below the dishwashers are? You guessed it: the day-laborer musicians.

Interestingly enough, at a more working-class salt-of-the-earth type restaurant or rented VFW (Veterans of Foreign Wars) hall, the staff and clientele are almost always lovely to the musicians. The trouble only really occurs in the middle-class and higher-class joints, which all aspire to be better than they really are. There's a mini class war going on within the ranks of these places that is constant, pervasive, and amazingly similar across so many venues.

As working musicians, we are arguably skilled at our trade and usually hired for a good deal of money for the evening as special entertainers for the patrons. I'm talking hundreds of dollars, not thousands, just to keep this in perspective. That affords us some level of respect from guests at the wedding who used to play guitar in high school. But that's about as far as it goes. Even though we may be getting paid more than the maître d' for the evening, or perhaps because of this very fact, we are often treated with disdain and intolerance.

A quick word about this. I understand completely why someone would treat musicians with contempt. I know musicians. I work with them every day. Every cliché you've heard about musicians is based on a kernel of truth. I assume the reason that musicians aren't allowed to drink in catering halls has a lot to do with past bad behavior. I've seen it. And I don't care for that behavior myself.

I've seen cocktail-hour musicians position themselves between the kitchen door and the patrons so that they can be the first to grab hors d'oeuvres as the food is on its way out to the party guests. This is bad form and gives us a bad reputation.

I'm especially offended by this behavior because as a bass player it takes two hands to properly play my instrument. As such I am unable to similarly pilfer snacks while I'm playing, unlike a pianist or a horn player between solos. It's a little bit of sour grapes on my part. Even so, I dislike the attitude that so many musicians seem to have, "If it's free, it's for me."

I have had to remind some of my fellow musicians, OK, I usually mean singers, that complaining about the food at a wedding really isn't cool because, believe it or not, that food isn't for us. We're not paying for it. It's not our function.

These places charge a lot of money because they know that a wedding is one of the few times it's possible to extract top dollar from clients. After all, how many times are you going to get married in life? (Don't answer that.) The bands charge a lot of money, too. That's part of life in the wedding business.

The catering halls also charge their clients a lot of money to feed the vendors: musicians, photographers, videographers, etc. The most expensive way to feed the band is to buy them a table in the ballroom to sit with the other guests. Though this seems like the nicest way to treat musicians, I actually dislike this option. When I do have a break from the bandstand, the last thing I want to do is stand around in my uncomfortable suit at a party where I don't know anyone and pretend to engage in the merriment. Even if they are feeding us the prime rib. I'm a vegetarian. Steak doesn't entice me, nor does mixing with the stuffed shirts.

There's an old joke that Buster Poindexter used to tell onstage. He was approached by a high-society dame who inquired as to the cost of his band for a party that she was throwing.

"About 5,000 bucks ought to do it," he replied.

The matron added in a snooty upper-class accent, "I must warn you that there will be absolutely no fraternizing allowed with my guests."

Buster replied, "OK, make it 3,000."

The second tier of cost to the clients is to feed the band the same meal as the party guests, but to have them eat it in the kitchen, in a staff dining room, or even just standing outdoors many times, anywhere as long as it's out of sight of the guests.

The lowest cost to the client is called a "vendor meal." This is where it can get interesting. This range of options can be as nice as a pan of leftover whatever from the main party, which can be delicious though just presented in a serve-yourself fashion. Or it can be something a little less nice like the catering hall on Long Island that typically just slops leftovers onto a serving platter for the band.

There is also a prevalent phenomenon known as "bandwiches." This feels like a begrudging acknowledgment that we are indeed human and in need of sustenance. But clearly all expense possible has been spared to provide us with the bare minimum number of calories necessary for us to finish the job and exit the premises immediately afterward. This option can even be scaled down to boxed or bagged lunches with an apple and an individual serving packet of potato chips, if you're lucky.

Don't get me wrong. There is absolutely nothing wrong with eating a sandwich and potato chips. The sense that something isn't quite right comes from trying to balance a bagged lunch on the fender of a car parked out by a juicy Dumpster, trying not to slip in the grease while wearing dress shoes and a tuxedo as other people not 5 feet away are feasting on lobster and roast beast.

There is an institutionalized inhumanity and disparity featured at these moments that can feel like anything from a cultural educational moment to an absolute "fuck you" from a maître d' who has growled at you and tossed a sandwich at you like a zookeeper tossing raw chickens to the crocodiles. It's often the intent and execution of such feedings of the animals that dictate the tone of the evening's proceedings.

Additionally, there is one lower cost option I failed to mention: not feeding the band at all. This has happened more times than it ever should have. We fight it constantly and complain loudly about it when it happens. It's more than just rude to expect an employee to be on a job site for six hours with no available nourishment or breaks. Yet it certainly happens.

We've been fed dry ham on white bread at famous five-star hotels. We have seen more sweaty lunch meat deli platters than you can imagine. And we have occasionally been offered all we could eat of the very best that the place has to offer. It runs the gamut, though it is definitely skewed toward the lower end of the spectrum, believe me.

I mentioned being a vegetarian. This is a voluntary dietary choice I have made and kept for the past 30 years. I'm not militant or proselytizing about it. You eat whatever you want to eat. Just allow me to eat (or not eat) whatever I want to eat. But this adds a layer of complication to getting fed at a catering hall.

Russians seem never to have heard of vegetarians. I've been told in some Russian catering halls that there is absolutely nothing available for me to eat. I find this shocking in the middle of New York City in the 21st century. Yet this dietary deafness exists.

It's a constant conversation that I am required to have with maître d's everywhere: "Excuse me, but when you feed the band if there is a vegetarian option available, I would be most grateful." This polite and nondemanding request is often met with civility and accommodation. But often it is not. It can be met with irritation, derision, and flat-out refusal.

Many catering managers conflate the concept of being vegetarian with also being on a diet. "Here's a salad."

"Thank you. I would like to live beyond the next five minutes that this salad will fill me up for. So what else do you have?"

Once at an old-school, now defunct Poconos vacation resort I was given a heaping plate of steamed carrots. Just carrots. "Enjoy."

I realize that my dietary choices are my own. I'm not trying to inflict my view on the world. I'm just trying to get through the gig without passing out from low blood sugar. To wit, I have been carrying protein bars in my bag as part of my standard gigging equipment for years.

Because of the abovementioned meal pricing structure, these catering halls will not give you food that they're otherwise throwing out. They waste mountains of food every day. As musicians we are not allowed to stand with a plate over the Dumpster when they're discarding the food because it would violate their ability to charge the clients for our board.

Furthermore, because I am required to perform these machinations requesting a vegetarian meal every time the band gets fed, and because I get a different plate of food from everyone else in the band, I am required to have some version of the same conversation I have had to endure for the past 30 years.

There is a cultural hysteria around vegetarianism that I just do not understand. The reason that I know it's cultural and that it's hysteria is that I get the exact same questions in almost the exact same order every … single … time:

"How long have you been a vegetarian?"

"Why did you become a vegetarian?"

"Is it for health or humanitarian reasons?"

"How do you get your protein?"

"Do you wear leather?"

I'm not suggesting, dear reader, that you have any of these questions circulating in the back of your mind. I'm just saying that everyone else does. I've heard them all before so many times in exactly that order that I'm no longer willing to have the same identical conversation any more. I just can't with this.

If you're really interested, there is a fine resource called Google that can tell you all you need to know about vegetarianism. But most people aren't really interested. They're just asking parroted questions that they don't even realize aren't theirs and reinforcing stereotypes they don't know they have.

This kind of cultural hysteria isn't limited to vegetarianism. There have been extensive articles written on these subjects. We are force-fed as kids a long litany of lies that we grow up accepting as facts that just aren't true. This misinformation gets imprinted on us very early in the "2+2=4" days. We have them on file in our brains as irrefutable facts. Unfortunately, even though they're a pack of lies, they're very difficult to revise in our crania and when challenged are often met with a virulent, "Nuh-uh!"

For instance, did you know that George Washington wasn't the first President of the United States? He was actually the 13th.

Did you know that Napoleon wasn't short? He was 5 ft. 6in., above average in his day.

Did you know that there weren't three wise men that traveled on camels from afar to visit the baby Jesus? The Bible never says exactly how many wise men there were, nor how they made their journey.

Did you know that lemmings don't blindly follow each other jumping off cliffs? That myth was created for a Disney movie.

I could go on. Most of what we've been taught is wrong.

Did you know that there is protein in broccoli? There are 4.2 grams per serving, to be precise. It has more protein per calorie than steak. But you have to eat a lot more broccoli to get the same number of calories as you do from a steak. And is this necessarily a good thing?

A cousin of mine sneered at me when I told her this. Her response was, "There's no protein in broccoli. I used to be a health teacher."

Congratulations! You've been poisoning the minds of the youth of America for decades. I didn't have the strength to fight it, to explain that the old official four food groups we were taught were the result of expensive government lobbying by the beef and dairy industries. It's all a lie. A deeply ingrained cultural hysteria based on a lie.

And I really don't care. I'm not here to get on a soapbox about it. All I want to do is get something to eat before the next set.

I have a few standard charming jokes I've come up with over the years to disarm and deflect the lies when people ask, "How long have you been a vegetarian?"

"Well, I'm just giving it a try to see if I like it." [Wait a beat.] If they don't automatically ask, I prompt them to inquire:

"So how long has it been?"

"Thirty years."

And the next inevitable question: "So is it for health or humanitarian reasons?"

To which I reply, "Oh, I'll kill them. I just won't eat them."

The next thing that the dudes in the band do is to start being "funny."

"Hey, man, why don't you eat a steak, hahaha!"

It's never funny. Furthermore, it's mean-spirited and illustrates that most people find the concept of vegetarianism threatening to them for some reason, like we're all claiming some higher moral ground because we're not carnivorous. As I've said before: you eat what you want to eat. Just leave me in peace.

After decades of this unwelcome scrutiny, even from fellow musicians, making me feel like an outsider among outsiders, when I do finally manage to get my special plate of non-meat whatever it is, I take it and walk away from the band (and everyone else) to be able to eat in peace.

Lest you think that it's only a personal quirk that I have developed about being made to feel that I'm less of a person in these wedding factory environments, I'll just mention a brief anecdote about my drummer pal, the late Crusher Green.

Crusher was an African-American gentleman with a lot of pride, which he well deserved. During the many years he was Wilson Pickett's drummer and music director, it was the Wicked Pickett himself who dubbed young Tyrone Green "Crusher." We didn't EVER call him Tyrone. He was a bad mother ("Shut your mouth!"). I'm just talking about Crusher! He was one of the baddest drummers you ever heard.

We were standing outside of some function hall somewhere either on a break or right after a Shirelles concert. We were in our tuxedos. Some band guys were smoking. Some guys were getting a breath of fresh air. Some guys were just hanging out. Here came White Dude out of the venue and handed Crusher his valet ticket for his car. Crusher held the ticket up, promptly made confetti out of it, dropped it on the guy's shoes, and walked off.

That's the cultural air of those establishments. And Crusher wasn't having it.

I played with disco diva Gloria Gaynor one time at Mar-a-Lago in Palm Beach, Florida. That's right, Donald Trump's dump. This was four or five years before he ever ran for whatever political office. To be fair, the event we played was a fund-raiser that had nothing to do with him. He wasn't there. We didn't meet him. He just owned the dump.

I think the management provided a green room for GG, as we called her, and the girls to change in before the show. But for the menfolk in the band there was nothing. We got to stand in the alleyway outdoors before the show drinking eight-ounce bottles of Trump water without a calorie to eat, a chair to sit down on, or even a pleasant hello.

But the kicker was this. Before we even arrived at the venue, we were informed that upon completion of our performance, we had exactly 15 minutes to exit the premises. You're done. Thank you very much. Get out.

This applied to Ms. Gaynor as well as to the rest of us working stiffs in the band. We all got in the passenger van together directly after the show and beat a hasty retreat past all of the Ferraris, Lamborghinis, and Rolls-Royces. Usually Ms. Gaynor tended to travel in her own SUV to and from these shows. But not at Mar-a-Lago.

Another time I was playing at a star-studded celebrity benefit show with a high-powered cast of famous millionaire session musicians in the house band. These are all heavy cats you probably know from seeing their credits on hundreds of recordings, or at least intimately know their work from hearing them on No. 1 hit records. The show was held in a large circus tent set up on the grounds of a resort hotel, which is a common venue for this type of event.

The event was for super high-roller billionaires and their ilk. When it came time to feed the band, the lowly millionaires (and I) were ushered out to a folding table and chairs in the open air behind the tent, out of sight of the bigwigs.

They did condescend to feed us what the main party was eating. They even went so far as to give us the same plates and silverware that the guests were enjoying. They just didn't extend floors, walls, ceilings, or climate control to us. I shall never forget dining al fresco under the stars with these famous musicians. I'm only glad it wasn't raining.

The point here is that no matter who you are or think that you are, there is someone who thinks they're better than you, richer than you, and more entitled than you. And they're right at least as far as the country club rules dictate.

Your job as the working-class musician is to play your songs at the appointed hour and the allowable volume; you're not to make eye contact with the guests, nor necessarily expect to be fed or hydrated. And you're to thank your gracious employers for the privilege at every turn. Often this is the game, as we all know. We accept it and show up for work knowing our "place" for the evening. But sometimes you get that extra stick in the eye to remind you just how worthless you really are.

Countless times, I've just poked my head in the front door or the kitchen of a catering hall and been yelled at unprovoked:

"You can't go there."

"You're not supposed to be there."

"Why are you here?"

"Can I help you?" Somehow this never comes off sounding as helpful as it probably should.

I remember pulling up beside a Dumpster at a country club in a gated community somewhere in Pennsylvania. The gates are always to keep the riffraff out, you know, like musicians. It's always another dance for me to try and figure out where the employee parking lot is (can't park your hooptie next to the Mercedei) and where the load-in door is when arriving at a new venue. Pulling up next to the Dumpster is always a good bet. It's usually right outside the kitchen door where they're going to allow you to load in.

This time was remarkable because I got yelled at before I even got out of the car. The head chef in his greasy kitchen whites was leaning against an old Jeep Cherokee dragging on a butt. He hollered, "You can't park there! What are you doing!?"

The guy who's not from around these parts with out-of-state plates, long hair, and wearing a tuxedo says the following painfully obvious things, "I'm in the band. I'm just going to load my equipment through here. Then I will move my car right away to whatever parking lot is cool."

"Oh, OK," he says before stubbing out his butt and returning to the salmonella factory that is his kitchen. What, and quit show business!?

So far the only time that this enter by the kitchen policy didn't feel like a complete "fuck you" was at a really old-school catering hall somewhere out in New Jersey. There are thousands of them, folks. I honestly don't remember most of them until I'm rolling up the driveway for maybe the dozenth time and start saying to myself, "Oh, yeah, this place looks familiar."

This particular one I remember for a couple of reasons. It's an old building, maybe 100 years, which is really old for New Jersey. The problem is that it's a faux Tudor-style mansion aping architecture from the 1500s. So it's a 100-year-old building masquerading as a 500-year-old building and not quite getting it right. It looks more like a set piece from a medieval-theme restaurant. "Roast turkey legs for everyone."

The other reason I remember it is the sign that marks the entrance for deliveries. Instead of saying: "vendors" or "deliveries" or "emotionally challenged," it says "Tradesmens Entrance."

What a refreshing sight that is. Instead of relegating us journeyman troubadours to the trash heap of humanity, the wording on that sign allows for the slight possibility that we might actually be craftspeople or artisans. This isn't even limited to musicians. It applies to all manner and nature of vendors who are visiting the site for the evening. It feels respectful on some level, even if they don't really mean it.

Of course, the last time I played that venue, the valet belligerently yelled at me and refused to allow me to even drive up to the Tradesmens Entrance to unload my car because it might be in view of the wedding ceremony. I understood his position, yet I still had a job that this wedding party emphatically wanted me to do.

Though I was being respectful yet resolute, bosses were radioed, managers were called, and quite a stir was created before I was finally allowed to disembark via another conveyance in order to schlep my amp to the bandstand. The happy couple and their lucky guests were thankfully able to dance into the night.

Tradesmens entrance

32 You Know Who You Look Like?

O h, boy, do I get this question a lot. Please allow me to save you some time and some inevitable well-deserved hatred. If you ever find yourself tempted to ask someone this question of anyone, or even if you have caught yourself too late and have already asked the question, stop yourself right there and just walk away. You're welcome.

Again, gentle reader, I'm not suggesting that you personally would ever be so crass as to commit such a faux pas. I'm just saying that an alarming number of people do it without realizing that they're being assholes.

It's never flattering. It's never funny, especially when the person thinks it is. It's never actually friendly. It never makes anyone want to have further conversation with the person. And trust me, whatever name you're about to say, unless it's Brad Pitt (and it never is for some reason), the person you're about to say it to has heard it a hundred times already. I can assure you that he or she hates hearing it every single time. Your brilliant, witty observation is the most tired trope imaginable.

Regularly, and I mean regularly, I hear all of the following comparisons, in no particular order:

- Gene Simmons, bassist/singer from KISS.
- "Weird Al" Yankovic, accordion wizard, often mispronounced "Yankovich."
- Dee Snider, singer from Twisted Sister.
- Geddy Lee, bassist/singer from Rush.
- John Kerry, former U.S. Secretary of State.
- Jay Leno, comedian/talk show host.
- Phil Lynott, bassist/lead singer of Thin Lizzy.
- Howard Stern, shock-jock radio host.
- Kenny G, smooth jazz saxophonist.
- Peter Mayhew, actor who played Chewbacca in *Star Wars*.

- Slash, guitarist from Guns N' Roses.
- Tiny Tim, ukulele and falsetto titan.

Show me the flattery of any of these comparisons. You can't. Because there is none. I sort of get it. Most of them are based on us both having long curly hair and/or a long face. But most of them are vague resemblances that constitute a stretch of the imagination. Sometimes it's an awkward attempt at starting a conversation or just having some interaction in a bus station men's room just in case I'm some minor celebrity.

One of my bosses, soul man Sam Moore, says repeatedly that I look like former Secretary of State John Kerry. He's said it so many times that I just roll my eyes now when he does. He does it just to annoy me.

A number of years ago, he did a gig at the White House where Secretary Kerry was present. I was not there that day. Sam told me that he went on and on to the Secretary about how his music director looks just like him. I'm sure the Secretary, who has never seen me and doesn't know who I am, was very polite about it.

I told Sam at the time that as an international touring musician, the last thing I want is for anyone at the U.S. State Department to know anything about who I am. All the Secretary would have had to do was to put out the word. I could envision being called into a special interview room the next time I tried to clear U.S. Customs. Thanks a lot, Sam.

Quite often I get approached by people who think I'm famous, though they don't know exactly why. I kind of get that, too. I'm always dressed like a rock star, or as I like to think of it: I'm always dressed the way I want to and not like an office-cubicle-inhabiting corporate zombie. I'm usually carrying a bass guitar in a gig bag on my back. This is a sure sign that I'm probably a musician. If you see someone of my advancing years carrying a musical instrument through an airport on a school day, it's a fair bet that he's a career musician rather than a weekend hobbyist.

Recently at LaGuardia Airport, a lady came up to me and said, "Are you in KISS?"

I said, "Those guys are in their 70s collecting Social Security, have had face-lifts, and have been in rehab for their hip replacements after wearing platform boots for 40 years. Do I look like I'm that old? Don't answer that."

While I'm no spring chicken myself, Gene Simmons is 15 years my senior. And I don't think I really look at all like him.

The lady at the airport scampered back to her traveling companion, saying in a loud Queens accent, "See? I told you he wasn't old enough!"

On a train trip down to Washington, D.C., to do a gig a few years back, the conductor came by to collect our tickets. I was traveling with the entire band of a certain disco diva. In the days since 9/11, Amtrak tickets are now required to have your legal name on them. A few minutes later, the conductor came back and said, "Hey, I hate to bother you, but could you autograph this ticket," you know, the one with my name on it.

He probably had time to Google me on his phone or whatever and felt that I was celebrated just enough to warrant a signed Amtrak ticket. Regardless, he was suffering under no delusions about who I actually was. It said my name right there.

Yet this sought autograph was overheard and witnessed by a woman and her son in the seat right in front of us. So now they wanted to get autographs and to take photos with me as well.

"I have all of your records," the lady said to me.

The band I was traveling with was in hysterics at this point because they knew exactly who I was: nobody! That particular short-haired band looked like a bunch of math teachers compared with me. So they weren't being sought out for autographs, just me.

Too late we realized that the only proper response to that false flattery from the lady should have been, "Oh, really? Which of my albums is your favorite?"

We never figured out exactly whose autograph or photo the lady and her son thought they got. Somewhere in the fray and the band's howls of laughter (mostly at me), the bandleader even said, "Who do you think he is?" This was directed out to the train car generally and not at the specific lady. So we never got an answer.

Many dozens of times I have been walking past an endless stream of people on crowded city streets only to notice that there is some bozo approaching me with his or her cell phone, photographing or filming me as I walk past. This is usually meant to appear to be either too subtle for me to notice or as a drive-by that's past me before I can protest. I never protest. I don't really care. If you think I'm that famous, you're more than welcome to have a souvenir photo. Just ask.

I find the attempted "stealth photo" to be kind of chicken shit on the part of the perpetrators. What do they think they have accomplished? And do they honestly think I don't notice that I'm being photographed without my permission?

It happens a lot. You would be surprised.

Another thing that happens equally often is that I will be legitimately recognized for something I have actually done. This delights me to no end and almost always follows the same script:

"Hey, man, I saw you play at, um, uh …"

"Where?" I say eagerly, hopefully. "Carnegie Hall? Conan O'Brien? The Kennedy Center? On Broadway?"

"No, no, it was at [insert name of biggest shithole nightclub imaginable] with [insert name of most embarrassingly awful singer-songwriter I've ever had the misfortune to accompany]."

To which I can only reply, "Oh, yeah, cool, thanks, man."

Other times I have been asked to take photos with random middle-aged German tourist ladies on the street on the off chance that I might be someone famous. I'm always too happy to oblige.

But the kicker occurs nearly as often when I'm asked if I wouldn't mind taking a photo.

"Of course," I always answer.

Then they hand me the camera. The photo they want taken isn't of me.

33 OH, YEAH, YOU BLEND

With apologies to Marisa Tomei, people seem to remember my face for some reason. I don't know why.

Perhaps it's because I'm very tall and have a lot of tattoos. Maybe it's just my winning personality. Whatever the reason, I seem to have a knack for sticking in people's minds. This is arguably a good thing for a performer.

Very often I get remembered by people that I don't remember at all. This is always strange when it happens. And it happens a lot. Often people have seen me on a stage or on social media and assume that because they have seen me I have also seen them. That is not necessarily true.

I also meet and play with a lot of people in my travels. A lot. If I did one blues gig with you at a bar in New Jersey 20 years ago, there is a slight possibility that I don't remember the gig or you. This is nothing personal. I repress a lot of stuff to keep from going crazy. And I have a bad memory anyway. A lot of it just blends together after a while.

As such, when I remeet famous people whom I was briefly introduced to once upon a time, I assume, usually correctly, that they don't remember me. I don't expect them to. How could they?

I have met Paul Shaffer, longtime music director for David Letterman, a bunch of different times over a long period of years. We have even had a few conversations. Yet each time I meet him, I'm convinced that for him it is the very first time. I may be misreading his vibe. But I don't think so. And that's fine.

There's absolutely no reason that he should know who I am, although I am impressed by his ability to put someone of my stunning good looks out of his memory so many times.

I have no sense of feeling entitled that people should necessarily remember me. But there were a few times with other "colleagues" when I was shocked not to have been remembered.

I mentioned earlier about the disco diva who fired me twice and didn't remember me at all the second time we met. I had even been her music director the first time around, not just another faceless sideman.

In her defense our meetings took place 15 years apart. I was only her music director for about three months the first time I worked for her, on the 10-day tour of Brazil and the one-nighter in Singapore. Also she was quite distracted with the personal family tragedy in her life unfolding while we were on tour in Brazil.

Still it was a little amazing to have conducted seven concerts for her and find out she had no memory of me when I reencountered her years later. During that second period of employment of two years, there could have been plenty of time to dust off old memories. None were unearthed.

Once while playing with Gloria Gaynor on a multi-act concert bill at Foxwoods Casino in Connecticut, I got called to also play a one-off opening set backing Sister Sledge. This version of Sister Sledge was the late Joni Sledge's band.

Of the four original Sledge sisters, I think three of them had rights to the name "Sister Sledge" and could tour under that banner anytime. Their youngest sister, Kathy, who sang lead on their biggest hits, tours separately and doesn't seem to be allowed to use "Sister" on her marquee. This may possibly be her choice. But I doubt it. I'm sure it's a very long story with a lot of lawyers involved. That, as they say, is showbiz.

Joni Sledge had a regular band based in Phoenix, Arizona. For some reason the bass player and the keyboard player were unable to make this particular gig in Connecticut. So the keyboard player in the diva's band and I were asked to cover the Sledge set as well.

Joni's band had no sheet music for us. All they had were some MP3s of live recordings. The keyboard player and I set about faithfully transcribing the parts on the original records verbatim and justifying the arrangements with the modern live versions.

I even went so far as to bring my Music Man bass to the gig since that was the brand of bass played on the group's original hits, which were produced by Nile Rodgers and Bernard Edwards from Chic.

Suffice to say, we did our homework. We did way more work than we were probably being paid for because we wanted to respect the great songs of the mighty Sister Sledge. "We Are Family" is an anthem for the ages. We wanted to do a good job.

And do a good job we did. We had a brief rehearsal at sound check that day. We nailed every song including all of their new arrangements. We killed on their show that night. We really felt good about it. We took pictures with them, got thanked profusely for our efforts, got paid, and went home. Mission accomplished.

Fast-forward a mere six months. That Connecticut show was in the summer. The following New Year's Eve we had another gig in Florida with the same stars on the bill. This time, however, the entire Sledge band was there. Our services weren't required, which was fine.

When we got to the venue, the Sledge band was sound checking. All the cats in the band who were on the summer show saw the keyboard player and me walk in and greeted us with joy and gusto. High fives all around, it's great to see you again, etc.

When the Sledge singers arrived to check their mics, Joni and the same two backing singers she had with her in Connecticut, I said to them, "Hey, it's really nice to see you again."

They just kind of blinked at me, obviously unaware of what the hell I was talking about.

So I prompted further, "Remember when we played for you last summer at Foxwoods?"

No, they didn't.

It was shocking. The whole band remembered us on sight. The singers had no clue who we were. We were all together on the same stage with band and singers for the same amount of time at the summer show. But there was some odd disconnect between the front and the back of the stage.

"But wait a minute," I hear you saying. "Maybe they were facing the audience as performers and not looking at the band."

That's a fair point. But that's not what happened.

We rehearsed their entire show with them at the sound check before the concert. They were looking straight at us all through rehearsal. And keep in mind that having a regular band as they did and not having sheet music to send out to subs on their show means that they never have subs. We saved their bacon back in Connecticut by pulling a rabbit out of our asses. That alone should have left an impression on them.

Apparently, it did not!

I had a regular gig playing with a blues and funk band in a bar in the West Village in New York City four nights a week, five hours a night, for five and a half years. I'm no mathematician, but that's a long time.

That gig alone covered probably over half of Malcolm Gladwell's 10,000 hours that one is supposed to spend practicing one's craft in order to become accomplished in one's field. Let's just say I played at that bar a lot.

It was a microscopically tiny stage with four or five people and their gear crammed onto it. We were surrounded on three sides by a bar with seated patrons right up in our faces. Fluids were exchanged every night just by nature of the extreme proximity.

It was hot, sweaty, and loud in there. We played three long sets every night and passed the tip jar compulsively since about two-thirds of our evening's income would be generated that way.

The club paid us weekly. Very weakly.

Before the New York City smoking ban went into effect, there was also a constant fog bank in there like trench warfare was being waged. It was a historically registered building. So no new ventilation could be added without authorization from the Pope, or something like that. Dive bars generally aren't known for expensive renovations beyond fashioning an upside-down umbrella to catch the ceiling leak before the water dripped on the patrons. This bar was no exception.

It was a shithole. But it was our shithole.

We had a lot of regular customers who were very colorful characters. There was a former burlesque star named Tanqueray, who had built a new business teaching straight dudes from the suburbs how to cross-dress. She would bring in a new gaggle of clients almost every weekend. Some of them looked like little more than football players who really hadn't extended themselves beyond lipstick and wigs. But they were a fun bunch.

There was also a predictable assortment of tourists, drunks, pimps, thieves, drug dealers, and hoi polloi who frequented the club.

One night a woman hurled a half-full beer bottle at my head, missing by inches and crashing on the rear wall of the club as she stormed out. It came at me as I was looking the other way. Had her aim been just a little better she would have creamed me. I can't imagine my bass playing offending someone that much. It seemed completely unprovoked. I hadn't made eye contact with her at any point in the evening. I wasn't even aware of her until I heard the crash and saw her storm out.

Chicken wire across the stage wouldn't have been completely out of character for that joint.

One of our favorite regulars was the late avant-garde jazz pianist Cecil Taylor. He would hold court in the basement of the club for hours with an omnipresent Brandy Alexander in hand. There was also occasional reaching for a house key to assist in dispensing minute quantities of Bolivian marching powder from a tiny Ziploc bag.

Cecil loved to get loaded and loved our funk band. He was at the club at least once a week for years. He loved our lead singer, the late Frankie Paris, who specialized in a very rhythmic style of blues and funk singing.

I always marveled at the dichotomy. Here was Cecil, a guy who was famous for helping to invent an entire genre of atonal, arrhythmic music. But he adored shaking his ass to the complete opposite of that: simplistically tonal, maniacally rhythmic music. Cecil was fun.

One week he was playing an engagement not far away at the Blue Note club in a duo format with drummer Elvin Jones. Our funk band all went down to see Cecil since he had seen us so many times. It was just the polite thing to do. Plus, we were interested to see what he really did for a living.

He and Elvin descended the staircase of the club, both dressed completely in white. Cecil put a manila folder down on the top of the piano and opened it to the first page. The folder was lying flat. We in the audience couldn't see what was on it. On some unspoken cue, he and Elvin launched into a tirade of sound that seemed to have no organization whatsoever. It was just an avalanche of apparently random notes.

Occasionally, in the middle of the cacophony, Cecil would reach up and turn the page in his folder and continue with his pianistic onslaught. There was one chord voicing I remember specifically since it involved him slamming both of his forearms down on the keyboard while simultaneously depressing every key in a 3-foot range. It was both beautiful and terrible to behold.

After 45 minutes of this nonstop performance, Cecil and Elvin both stopped at the same exact time without any visible cue. They stood up, took a bow, and left the stage. It was great.

I talked to Cecil about it the next time he was in the funk club. I asked him what was on his charts in the folder.

He said, "You know, some people think that I have a graph drawn on those pages. And I can assure you—it's not a graph."

He never said what it was. But I know it wasn't a graph. In pure Cecilian fashion, he was off onto the next topic of conversation.

He even propositioned me one night in the club while I was onstage playing. He said, "When am I going to taste those legs, boy?"

I explained that I was presently unavailable for such polygamy since I was spoken for, but thanks anyway.

No harm in asking.

I've told you all this merely to illustrate that Cecil and I were fully acquainted.

A few years after that regular nightclub gig ended, I happened to see Cecil holding court before a group of people at a restaurant with tables on the sidewalk on Second Avenue. They were dining alfresco, as New Yorkers are oft wont to do at the slightest provocation.

Since I was only feet away from him on the street, I took the liberty of saying hello to him.

He didn't remember who I was.

I was a little hurt by that, but not entirely shocked, I suppose. He was always loaded when he was hanging out with us at the club. He seemed no less loaded at the sidewalk café that night. I reminded him of my former boss, Frankie Paris.

He lucidly remembered, "Oh, yes, the maestro!" That's what he used to call Frankie.

He even remembered the keyboard player in the band, though not exactly by name. That made sense. They were both pianists. But my name and face seemed to be lost to history with him. I suppose he would have slept with me and then never called again. I'll never know.

Then there was the time I met blues guitar legend Robert Cray. I was playing in a band that was the opening act at a concert of his at a theatre in Connecticut. I was a fan and was excited to meet him.

After his sound check, I got the chance to say hello. I gave him one of my pink custom-printed guitar picks. I collect people's guitar picks whenever I can and give out mine, which have my website address printed on them.

When I was growing up, I always thought that custom guitar picks were some sort of mark of rock stardom. When I became a professional musician, it dawned on me that anyone could have custom guitar picks. All it required was calling up the company that made them and sending money. I had a little money, so I bought custom guitar picks for myself.

When I handed mine to Robert Cray, he said, "You already gave me one of these."

"Um, what? When?"

"In Berlin," he said.

"Oh, shit!" I said. I had completely forgotten.

The Sam Moore band had gone to see Eric Clapton play in Berlin on a night off one time a couple of years before. We got there after Eric's show had already started and had missed Robert's opening set, though he did sit in with Clapton during the night.

After the show, Clapton's people were doing a runner, which means getting into waiting vans and immediately exiting the grounds. There was no after-show meet-and-greet. It's that old trick: "Elvis has left the building." It's as much for crowd control as anything else. Plus that amphitheater in Berlin didn't have much of a backstage area.

As the band guys were leaving, we kind of gave them high fives like two sports teams congratulating each other after the match, even though we hadn't played that evening. Somewhere in that exchange, I had apparently handed Robert one of my picks. He had remembered. I hadn't.

I'm not sure which is the greater insult: being told that I look like someone that I don't resemble or not being remembered at all. If it is indeed the latter, I probably owe Robert Cray an apology.

34 I REMEMBER THIS ONE TIME …

I am including this, um, brief story because it is indicative of so many similar road experiences. Everything else about the gig was business as usual except for one glaring detail. For this one, I brought the receipts.

A live karaoke band I was playing with was staying at a nice three- or four-star major chain hotel in beautiful downtown Raleigh, North Carolina. While awaiting our 6:45 a.m. pickup to make a flight back home, we were treated to the spectacle of a gentleman striding calmly and confidently off the elevator, moving evenly with no sense of agitation or intrigue toward the front desk. He requested an additional room key and ambled coolly back to the elevator to return to his room. It was a nondescript scene that we have witnessed innumerable times.

The only thing that made this occasion at all notable was the fact that the gentleman was clad in nothing more than his tighty whitey underwear.

I don't care who you are or how little sleep you've gotten. That's an eye-opener.

On the man's way back to the elevator, our guitarist remarked to him, "I hope it was a big story."

To which the gentleman responded calmly, "Very big."

He seemed to still be quite intoxicated from the previous night. Since we had been hired that evening to assist a convention of about a thousand financial types in the art of partying like pretend rock stars, I had to assume that our work there was done.

In case you may doubt the veracity of my story, or feel I am somehow embellishing or employing poetic license in any way, I offer the following as exhibit A:

Tighty whiteys at the front desk, 6:45 a.m., Raleigh, North Carolina

35 Choose Your Words Carefully

Words matter. Words are important. The wrong words can hurt. Rather than pontificate on my theories of interpersonal communication, I will merely attempt to entertain you with some examples of fairly messed up stuff I have seen and heard as people have attempted to make their musical visions into reality.

This first illustration comes to us from the music book of an oldies act who shall remain nameless. It's not that I'm trying to protect the group's reputation. I honestly don't remember which group it was. All I remember is that I thought it was funny enough to take a picture of one of their charts with my phone.

It was on an all-day production schedule when we were rehearsing and then performing with half a dozen acts all on a single show. These types of days involve reams and reams of paper going by throughout the process. They also put your sight-reading ability invariably to the test, not only in terms of skill at reading properly written scores, but also, and maybe more importantly, your skill in interpreting what was actually meant from what the author wrote.

Many musical instructions and terms are in Italian. When the word forte appears, it means to play loudly. Fortissimo means play very loudly. Piano means softly. Pianississimo means so quiet that you could hear someone juggle cotton balls over the volume of the music. Stuff like that.

Ritardando is a common musical term, which translates into English as "slowing down" and indicates a gradual decrease in tempo. Typically, this might happen at the end of a song, for instance. Very often someone will abbreviate this in a musical score by writing: ritard.

I was reading one of these oldies charts in rehearsal when the following appeared:

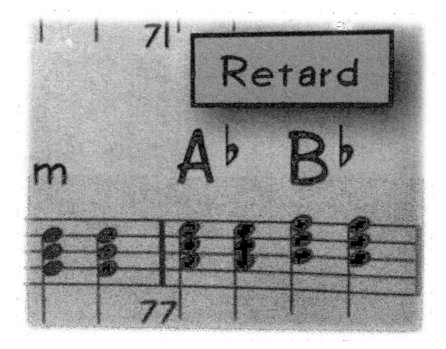

Whoa, what did he call me?

Swapping that one *i* for an *e* really changed the meaning of that instruction and became quite politically incorrect. I knew what the author meant. But it still made me giggle.

Another oldies act emailed me with a chart that was requesting a typical rock & roll ending for a particular song. This is sometimes called the "A-Train" ending since Duke Ellington used it so famously to end that song. Other people call it a "blues ending" because every blues song seems to terminate in that fashion. It's a familiar musical device and almost unnecessary to read or write. Almost everybody with any experience knows what to do when faced with that instruction.

As soon as I know this is going to be the ending to a song, I can take my eyes off the printed page and turn my attention to something more important like seeing what's happening on the TV screens over the bar, or possibly trying to imagine what misguided style magazines some of the people in the front row of the concert must be reading. You know, vital stuff like that.

The email from this act further stated that this was a revised version of an earlier chart because some mistakes had been found and corrected. I appreciate someone who checks his or her work and is constantly striving to make the music better.

As I was reading through the chart I came to the ending, which instructed me to do the following:

EOCK AND ROOL ENDING

There are a few problems here, not the least of which are the words that are supposed to be in English, "Eock and Rool Ending." I'm as guilty of typos as the next person. But remember that this is the "corrected" chart. The other problems should be clearly apparent to my musically literate brothers and sisters. The written pitches are correct. But the rhythms are all kinds of wrong.

Also, that little bird's-eye symbol written below the C9 chord is called a fermata. It indicates a pause in the music of unspecified length. It most commonly occurs over the last note of a song and means: you're done, finished. It's over. Get your paycheck. And go home.

It also definitely means to stop counting and keeping time. But notice that arc symbol, called a tie, linking that note to one in the next measure. This means definitely keep counting. So which is it, pal? Are we done or not?

Once again, I knew what the author meant. Apparently, the proofreading stopped right about the place where a skilled sight reader would lift his or her eyes from the page.

This next example comes not in the form of printed music but rather in a verbal instruction during a rehearsal that reduced the band to a group of giggling teenagers.

We were rehearsing a show with a disco diva who was demonstrating in both spoken word and body language a specific musical nuance that she wanted emphasized in a particular song.

She was a disco diva with a couple of monster crossover dance-pop hits from the '70s. We were huge fans of hers and wanted to do anything we could to cater to her wishes. This was also our first and only meeting with her. So we had no prior rapport or common language developed before this rehearsal.

What she was saying was that after every eight bars of a particular musical passage, she wanted us to emphasize an eighth-note anticipation of the next bar. If one was to count this type of phrase, one might say something like, "One, two, three, four-AND."

That's the music school version of what she wanted. We had a band full of music school nerds. In our minds, we were all saying "four-AND."

The disco diva chose instead to gyrate her body dramatically on the "AND" beat and said to us repeatedly, "You got to grab them snatches."

We were all adults and trained professionals. But every time a grown woman told us to "grab them snatches," we were reduced to being children on a playground hearing a word that we knew was naughty for the first time. It was all we could do to contain our laughter that was inspired by a word choice with such an unfortunate double entendre.

In the interest of full disclosure, this incident occurred a full seven years before a similar infamous utterance by a major-party political candidate.

Words can also be used to motivate and inspire. I did a recording a few years ago with a band called Eye to Eye. They made a couple of albums for Warner Bros. years before I met them in New York. I had heard of them, which was why I was thrilled to be asked to play on their next recording.

To my ears they sounded like a cross between Joni Mitchell and Steely Dan. It was very exciting music to play, super intelligent, expertly composed, and beautifully arranged. The whole process from rehearsals through the recording was amazing. It stands to this day as the recording I am most proud to have played on.

Part of what made it so great was the camaraderie. They were terrific people who were a lot of fun to be around.

Because the music was so specific, it was the type of gig where reading the charts was essential. I had to keep my eyes glued to the page throughout every song just to make sure I was in the right place and playing the right notes.

At the end of a couple of the charts, the keyboardist/arranger wrote the following instruction:

This was a fantastic way of letting us know that we had survived the entire chart and were now expected to keep playing the same section for as long as it took the recording engineer to fade the music out. Seeing an instruction like that coming from a friendly source automatically lightens the mood in the studio.

It also inspired us to improvise during the long fade-out, lifting the energy of the proceedings as the song rode off into the sunset.

36 SUMMERTIME IN THE PARK

T here was a period of time in the 1990s when I did a lot of free outdoor concerts in New York City parks with The Uptown Horns Revue. Many of these shows were way out in the badlands of Brooklyn amid housing projects and the destitution that comes from institutional financial disadvantage. Suffice to say many of them were tough neighborhoods. And we were clearly not from around there.

These were New York City Parks Department–sponsored concerts. They were held on outdoor mobile stages with hand-crank elevated lighting trusses the likes of which had fallen and broken the neck of Curtis Mayfield only a couple of years before, leaving him paralyzed for the rest of his life. We played on a bunch of these rigs in those parks.

One of these rigs was for a Percy Sledge gig. The stage was powered by a mobile diesel generator since hot-wiring a lamppost was out of the question for an officially sanctioned gig by the City of New York. It turned out that we might have been better off with the hot-wired rig.

The voltage coming out of the generator was slightly below the standard 120 volts and possibly also below the 60 cycles per second that comes out of a standard wall plug. The guitar amps seemed to work just fine. But the rented Hammond B3 organ was a "classic" instrument. The manufacturer stopped making them with the old tone wheel sound generators in the mid-1970s.

Getting Percy's classic FAME/Muscle Shoals B3 sound required using an instrument that was 20 to 30 years old. The wonky electricity from the generator rendered the organ about a quarter tone flat, give or take. I don't think the current or the pitch was anywhere near constant.

This meant that the sound the B3 generated was somewhere between the cracks of a standard piano. All of our electronic guitar tuners calibrated to a standard A = 440 hertz were rendered completely useless. We had to try to tune our instruments by ear to the slightly intoxicated sounding Hammond as best as we could.

I don't have perfect pitch by any means. I have pretty decent relative pitch. So if there is a defining tone from any source, I can play in tune with it fairly well, that is, if the reference pitch isn't also a moving target.

Percy, intoxicating soul singer that he was, tended to sing a hair sharp, above the pitch, bless his heart. The band was way below pitch. His vocals were somewhere above us. It made for an afternoon of what I call "charming" intonation. But we got through it.

He would exit the stage at the end of an already long version of his huge hit "When a Man Loves a Woman." We would be playing the chord progression over and over again, including the loudest sustained horn parts. Percy took his time leaving the stage in the fine fashion of old-school show business, blowing kisses to the audience, shaking hands with people in the front row, and taking extended bows.

I loved Percy. I thought he was fantastic. Our trumpet player needed to put ice on his face after playing that song for that length of time. He learned through negative reinforcement, like a puppy being hit with a rolled-up newspaper, that it was going to hurt. He didn't care for playing Percy's show at all.

At another one of those outdoor concerts, I was playing a fretless bass in direct sunlight. The intonation of that instrument was changing by the minute during the show. A different trumpet player was giving me some pained looks that day trying to stay in tune with me. I felt badly about it. It's hard to fight the sun, however.

Those shows in the parks found us backing Sam Moore, Martha Reeves & The Vandellas, Rufus Thomas, Carla Thomas, Eddie Floyd, Solomon Burke, and others. Thanks to my colleagues in The Uptown Horns I made some professional connections that have continued for decades like my longtime association with Sam Moore.

One of these shows nearly ended all future collaborations. We were hired to back up Chicago soul legend, Gene Chandler, the "Duke of Earl," on a double bill with Sam Moore. We had played with Sam before. But this was our first time with Mr. Chandler.

Through some comedy of errors, we weren't provided with any sheet music or reference recordings of Mr. Chandler's songs before the show. This wasn't an entirely unusual situation.

With Martha Reeves, for instance, she would bring folios of charts for each player on the day of the show. You would then read the charts down at rehearsal and perform the show that evening. It made it difficult to prepare for her gigs in advance. But it was a good test of your sight-reading ability.

I understand why she did this. Artists have to pay a lot of money to arrangers and copyists to write out their books. Many of them are reluctant to just give this work away to other musicians who might use the charts elsewhere.

That day Gene Chandler neither advanced us music, nor did he, as it turns out, bring anything with him to the gig for us to read. I have no idea how or why this happened. But there we were with the obligation to provide an hour's worth of quality entertainment as a nine-piece band with nothing more than our collective experience to guide us. We had almost no specific knowledge of his songs, keys, or arrangements.

We had to wing it.

We knew his biggest hit, "Duke of Earl," pretty well since it was really famous and mostly just a standard doo-wop chord progression. But Mr. Chandler had a lot of great hits throughout the '60s and '70s of which we knew little to nothing.

I've played with Mr. Chandler again recently in a much more prepared setting. His song "Groovy Situation" has one of the most psychotic bass lines in recorded soul music history. Even when I was given the chart in advance and had time to shed it, that song was a bit of a bear. Not having charts makes that song nearly impossible, without even considering the horn arrangements.

Back in the park, Mr. Chandler ended up dragging us through an improvised set of blues and really simple familiar R&B standards like "Stand by Me" to fill the time. He was quite "off book," as they say. But he got it done. One of his mechanisms to kill some time and to justify the looseness of the set was to explain to the audience that we, the band, hadn't prepared and didn't know his songs.

He basically publicly threw us under the bus for something that wasn't our fault. We were made the butt of his joke, which wasn't really funny. But, OK, "ha ha," we'll roll with it for the sake of the show. We were clearly struggling musically anyway.

This might have all been fine except for one detail. Our drummer, Crusher Green, was from Brooklyn, where we were playing. He took the attempted joke as a personal insult and complete disrespect in front of his hometown crowd. To an intensely proud man, the insult was severe indeed.

Crusher almost always had a fanny pack around his waist. He would keep his wallet and keys in there. The ritual I most often observed with the fanny pack occurred when he would sit at the drum kit preparing to play. Finger by finger he would remove his 10 ornate rings and place them in the fanny pack for safekeeping. At the end of the show, he would reverse the process finger by finger.

Also in the fanny pack was his pistol.

I wasn't present for the next few moments. But the scene has been recounted to me thusly. Crusher went into the dressing room after the show, which was just a utility shed at the outdoor park. His pistol was no longer stored in the fanny pack, but was in hand down by his side. He intended to right the wrong that was done to him publicly onstage.

He told Sam Moore and his wife, Joyce, that they needed to exit the premises forthwith because he intended to shoot Mr. Chandler. I'm not sure exactly how the shuttle diplomacy was conducted. Apparently, Crusher and Mr. Chandler were in separate rooms.

I was told that Mr. Chandler wasn't initially intimidated by the impending threat since he bragged that he was "from Chicago." Yet his better senses were prevailed upon when it was explained that Crusher was "from Brooklyn" and had a home-field advantage.

Eventually, diplomacy, cooler heads, and a waiting car service that provided a quick escape for Mr. Chandler carried the day. The two gentlemen never had a face-to-face confrontation. No shots were fired. We would mercifully all live to play soul music another day.

**Percy Sledge with The Uptown Horns band
L-R: Bob Funk, Crispin Cioe, Percy Sledge, Jon Paris,
and the bass player**

37 PHIL THE CAMEL

I did half a dozen performances subbing in the band at the Big Apple Circus a couple of years ago. Playing for the circus required a similar skill set and level of preparation necessary for subbing in a Broadway pit. It takes sight-reading skill and the ability to follow a conductor.

The main differences from performing over to the Broad Way are that you're playing outdoors in a (heated) tent in 20-degree weather and working for half the money. Also, you have the distinct impression that if you make a mistake, rather than that leading to an actor's potentially getting mad at you because you sabotaged his or her line, there is the very real possibility that a unitard-wearing Ukrainian dude could fall to his death.

It's a different level of responsibility.

When I first started working in theatrical situations, I was introduced to the concept of the "safety vamp." Occasionally you will see the word "safety" written over a one- or two-measure repeat sign in a musical score. This means keep playing those one or two measures for however long it takes the actor to speak his lines. The conductor will then wave her hand a little wider or higher indicating that it is time to continue reading on down the page. It is a common theatrical device for underscore music that is very effective.

This concept gets used by the circus to an extreme degree. Instead of possibly one or two safety vamps per musical number in a typical theatrical setting, during a circus act there might be as many as nine safeties in one song. I counted. Each safety is the setup for each trick in the act. If the juggler makes the catch, we go forward. If he drops his clubs, the conductor comes on the headset and says, "Back to measure 52!"

The band goes back into the vamp. The cat sets up the trick again and either makes it so that we get the cue to go on, or misses it another time. In that case, we will again hear in our headphones, "Back to measure 52!"

As a sub in the band not knowing the rhythm and flow of the show, not knowing how often certain acrobats tended to land or blow their tricks, and not being familiar enough with the next note one was expected to play, it was difficult to relax. These shows made for sitting in some tense postures. My eyes were constantly darting in rapid-fire fashion from the sheet music to the conductor's left hand, back to the music stand, and up to the conductor. It was an enjoyable challenge.

Walking backstage at these performances was just as colorful as you might imagine. Contortionists from former communist bloc countries would be warming up before their act. The ringmaster might be doing a quick change. Clowns were juggling to keep their blood flowing in the cold before they went on. There were rows and rows of motor homes where the performers and crew lived as they toured. And there were makeshift animal enclosures to house the various critters between performances.

My favorite animals backstage were the camels. They were in stables with barricades up to keep you a few feet from their doors and signs that said, "Warning, camels bite!" They spit, too. But I think these camels were fairly domesticated and not big spitters. Fortunately, the barricades helped keep us far enough away not to find out. I believed the biting sign because the first time I saw it, the camel was actively trying to chew up the metal sign. Point taken.

I don't know if the biting signs had been posted out of an abundance of caution or owing to hard-won experience. I can completely envision a child being given a backstage tour of the circus. What child could resist reaching out to pet the cute camel with a mitten that looked and smelled like the cotton candy the kid had just slobbered all over? Bang! Little Timmy loses a finger to a dromedary before he knows what hit him.

I'm a musician. I use my fingers to pay my rent. No, thank you.

There was a point in the show where we would play some vaguely Middle Eastern sounding music while an animal handler brought the camels out and made them do some kind of walking in formation routine. Unfortunately, where I was sitting on the bandstand, I couldn't see most of the circus ring. I also had my face buried in the music. So I knew the camels were on. But I didn't know exactly what they were up to.

Before my first show, I was told that though the camel routine was still in the show, Phil the camel, the biggest of all the camels, had been cut from the act.

What the hell? I had just seen Phil backstage. He was a big sucker. But he seemed super chill. Why did they cut him?

Apparently, the night before Phil went off script. He disobeyed his trainer, broke off from the pack and began running around the ring on his own. Reportedly, he also started enjoying some of the kids' popcorn in the front row. This was a little too close to the audience for the comfort of the circus management and their legal representatives. Phil was out.

There was a postulation floated to us band members about the reason for Phil's rebel nature. I have no independent scientific confirmation of this. But I like it anyway. So internally, it remains my official explanation.

Phil was castrated as many domesticated animals are. It is untoward for a camel to be thinking about humpin' (get it?) during a song-and-dance routine for small children. Their goolies are chopped off so that the animals have nothing better to do than to remember dance steps in an act that follows a literal "dog and pony" show. Seriously, a dog and a pony. It's the circus.

Anyhow, allegedly the vet performed the snippety-do-dah on Phil a little later in life than is optimal. Though he was now a gelding with no current hormonal temptations, apparently he still had some memories of better days. Everyone remembers the thrill of young love, right? Well, Phil was no exception. Even though he had been cut by the vet, he was now also cut from the show.

Sadly, someone also reported to us that at each performance when we began playing the music for Phil's act, he started becoming active in his stall, wondering why he wasn't going into the ring to thrill his fans.

Poor Phil. I don't know what became of him. Hopefully the circus folk found him a stall at Happy Camel Retirement Farms with all the desert grass he could ever want to eat.

Phil the Camel

38 TIME TO PAY THE PIPER

Said the elder bluesman to his protégé, "Always remember the three 'M's of the blues, son."

"What are those?" the novice asks.

The bluesman replies, "Number one: mmmoney. Number two: mmmusic. And number three: mmmmmmmpussy."

That's the joke version. The more serious breakdown that cats talk about all the time consists of: 1) the money, 2) the music, and 3) the hang.

Most gigs satisfy just one of these three. You should feel really fortunate when you find a gig that covers two of them. And you need to get down on your knees and thank your lucky stars and the eight-pound infant baby Jesus should you encounter a gig that regularly covers all three. They're quite rare.

In the joking and more serious versions, money is the first item on both lists. Getting compensated for your work allows you to be able to afford food and rent. Without those things covered it becomes much more difficult to continue to do more of the same kind of work.

I have been fortunate in my career to have been able to pay my rent as a full-time professional musician for 26 years now. As a freelance person, with each client you encounter, there is always the distinct possibility that after the work has been performed the payment may not be forthcoming in a timely manner. Very occasionally the money never shows up at all.

There was a bandleader who worked for a notorious star on the Chitlin' Circuit. Money hassles could be a nightly occurrence in that world. The bandleader would enter the dressing room after the show waving cash in the air that he had just extracted from their star. This was the band's salary for the evening. He would say to his compatriots, "Gentlemen, the gig has been confirmed."

The music business is so highly speculative that no booking is ever real until after the check clears. I'm lucky that I haven't had too much hassle in this regard in my travels. You know, except for those few times when I absolutely did.

I recognize that leading one's own band is a thankless money pit. It is an opportunity for an artist to realize his or her unique vision, which often requires the help of other people unless he or she is a one-person band.

Just looking at the simple economics of it, if someone starts a new band it is by definition an unknown entity with no marquee value. There is usually no way to compensate the band members without going into one's own pocket to do so. It's just the nature of the business. By default, all start-ups usually run a deficit. Everybody knows this.

While I have led bands of my own and am certainly sympathetic to the plight of the aspiring artist, when the gig is over, I want my damn money. If you can't afford me, perhaps you shouldn't hire me.

Almost always in my travels I am met at the end of an engagement with proper remuneration for my services. The previously agreed upon amount, whatever that is, usually shows up in my hand. For this I am thankful.

Occasionally the pay envelope is a little light, or there is some disagreement about the negotiated price. When this occurs, I am only too happy to open up the calendar on my phone and show the person who hired me that I always make a note of the hours of the engagement, the name of the artist I'm working for, the address of the venue, and the money they have agreed to pay me.

I. Write. Shit. Down.

This leaves little room for hemming and hawing and post-gig renegotiations.

A few times the artist has asked me to hold the slightly rubbery check he has written me for a couple of days until whatever money he's expecting to come in clears his account. That's fine. I don't live so hand-to-mouth that this is a problem.

Very occasionally, the check holding has extended for quite a lengthy amount of time. I had to chase the manager of a Grammy Award–winning platinum-selling soul star of yesteryear for months one time just to get paid $400 for a gig I had already played. This artist was a former member of a Motown supergroup, and is now deceased.

Demanding your pay is a difficult case to make to the manager because you've already done the work based on nothing more than a verbal agreement. The artist may never need your services again. So what is to prevent the management from just stiffing you completely?

In a situation like that managers tend to pay you only when they need you to do the next gig. Then you have to worry about getting paid for the second gig after that. The Grammy winner's manager finally cut me a new check months later and told me to discard the previous one. I still have the old one in a file somewhere, not worth the paper that it's written on.

Another of my more frequent bosses almost always paid me promptly for the gigs, but chronically left me holding receipts for travel expenses that needed to be reimbursed. Because I was the bandleader on those gigs, I would also often be required to rent the van with my personal credit card so that I could drive the musicians from the airport to the venue.

"I'll give you the money back," I was always told.

This was seldom the case. I would get my salary. The manager would ask me to send the receipts so that a check could be cut for me. I always sent the receipts within a couple of days. In nearly 30 years, I don't think I *ever* got a check in the mail.

The only way to get the money back was to get it at the next gig when the manager had just been paid, hopefully in cash at a casino gig. If there was money on the table, he or she would give me the outstanding balance. If he or she was paid with a check, I usually had to wait until the next gig where cash was involved. In one instance I was chasing a rental car reimbursement amount for an entire calendar year.

I was often told things like, "I paid you for that already."

"Um, no, you didn't." It was crazy making, but just par for the course with that artist.

In rare instances the payment for a gig just never comes. A singer-songwriter I did a few shows with was paying me more money than he probably should have for doing a set of original material at a nightclub in Manhattan. For a room that was charging a five-dollar cover at the door, economically it didn't make sense to pay me that much. It should probably have been a $100 gig at best. But be that as it may, he had agreed ahead of time to pay me $200 for a rehearsal plus the gig.

We did a couple of shows after which he promptly paid me the agreed upon amount. After the third or fourth show, he told me that he was a little short of money and asked if he could pay me later. Since he had been so generous in the past, I agreed to this. I thought that by the next gig we would surely settle up. The next gig never came and neither did my money. He neither paid me or tried to make arrangements to cover it, nor did he ever apologize for stiffing me.

What was so strange about the situation was that this cat was a heavy protest folk singer. He was super left wing and completely devoted to human rights causes. He was constantly campaigning for the voiceless, the downtrodden, the least of those among us. He was a hyper-political super-conscientious guy. I still get his email newsletter in which he talks about doing things like going to Afghanistan to lend his songwriter voice to the antiwar protests, and similar activist causes.

It just turned out that his regard for refugees didn't extend to bass players for whom he had made certain financial promises. It was fascinating to be robbed by such a self-proclaimed do-goodnik.

I had another dude pull a very similar type of scenario on me a few years back. It was even for the same amount of money. He was a cabaret performer who was into me for services for which he owed me $200. I knew he was short of money. I knew he was struggling financially and in over his head. And I also knew that he would continue to hire me for other things in the future.

I decided to take a calculated loss on the money. I figured that over time he would end up paying me more money than just the shortfall he owed me. I might have demanded and received the $200, but then never agreed to darken his door again. In my mind I just wrote it off for the potential big-picture gain.

But he surprised me. Every time I would see him after that incident he would say, "Oh, I know I still owe you money. Here's $20." Or he would give me a check for $50 or something. Over the course of about a year, the dude paid the bill in full. I was shocked.

He turned out to be one of the most honest and scrupulous people I have ever met in the music business or otherwise. His name is Daryl Glenn. I want you to know people like him exist in the world, who do what they say they're going to do, even if it takes them longer than they thought it would.

Thanks, Daryl, for reaffirming my faith in humanity. I need affirmation after some of the more painful financial lessons I have learned.

By far the worst of these was one of my earliest music business experiences at a restaurant start-up in London, after I had quit my record company gig, but before I ended up going back to music school. It seemed like a great fit for me musically as well as business-wise.

The owners of the restaurant hired me to book musical duos into the joint five or six nights a week, playing blues and jazz. The perk that I wrote into the deal for myself was that I was to be the house bass player in these duos every night. It was shaping up to be a great situation for me. They were also making noise about sponsoring me for a work visa so that I would be a documented alien. They were saying all the right things and were very charming about it.

I was there with them as they were constructing the place. I helped them with the sound system, auditioned musicians, and started filling up their entertainment calendar. I got to hire and then work with some incredibly talented people on this gig, some of whom have become lifelong friends. It was a great situation.

Until it wasn't.

The owners were high-minded dreamers. They seemed to be interested in surrounding themselves with all of the proper talent necessary to pull off something really nice. There were two problems. Number one was that this was their first venture into a restaurant. As everyone knows, it's a very difficult business to be successful in. They were certainly in over their heads.

The second problem was more subtle, but more insidious. The owners had met one another because they were all former members of a certain so-called religion famous for having a lot of big Hollywood actors as devotees. There have been numerous documentaries made about the alleged shady business dealings of this questionable church. I won't go into that here.

From what I was able to observe, this so-called church seemed to have taught these budding restaurateurs the life ethic that the ends justified the means. The atmosphere over there was Machiavellian. The owners were willing to say or do anything if they felt it furthered their agenda and personal interests.

This sounds like a potentially positive trait for a businessperson. The sharks are the ones who do best, right? But these guys went off the rails with this type of thinking especially when things started to go downhill for them. As the business was beginning to fail, and I'm being kind here because it never really had a chance, they started to become extremely unscrupulous.

They had no compunction whatsoever in telling you a complete lie right to your face. I don't even mean sugarcoating things or telling half-truths. They had the ability to propound an outright mendacity without batting an eyelash, with a huge smile on their faces.

I'll give you an example of what they did to me.

"Here is your paycheck," one of them said, with a warm handshake as he gave me a piece of scrap paper that looked like a check but in fact had zero value.

The owners had convinced me that it was typical in England for people to be paid monthly rather than weekly. So the check they gave me that bounced was for an entire month's wages. It took two more weeks of further broken promises and additional worthless checks before I finally had to walk away holding in my possession bounced checks for six weeks of wages totaling £1,400.

I took the owners to small claims court and got a judgment in my favor for the bounced checks, penalties, fees, and interest totaling £2,608.71. They admitted this debt to the court in writing and agreed to a payment plan of £200 per month until the debt was paid off.

For perspective, they owed me the equivalent of $2,691 in 1990 U.S. dollars for unpaid salary, and $5,014 for the eventual court judgment against them. It was not a small amount of money.

I received one check for £200 before the company declared bankruptcy. After that I got nothing else. Until the very end, they lied to the court by submitting a bogus repayment schedule that they never intended to keep. They were some pieces of work, these guys.

I ended up no longer being able to afford my cold-water flat. I moved into a spare bedroom at a pal's house as a lodger and tried to figure out my next move.

At least one of my musician friends, whom I had hired as an entertainer at the restaurant and accompanied as a bass player, also experienced some nonpayment of funds owed by these dudes. His outstanding balance was for a far smaller amount than what I had been owed.

In light of continuing lies and broken promises from the management, my friend wisely decided to settle the £100 he was owed by taking it in trade. A microphone on the restaurant stage retailed for just about £100. He pocketed it in a unilateral settlement of accounts. After my unsatisfactory experience with the management in court, I can unequivocally say that he did the right thing.

From my adventures in London, I decided that playing music was something I definitely wanted to pursue as a career. I realized also that because of this aspiration, I really needed to get some formal musical training if I was going to make a serious go of it.

Additionally, I decided that without a work permit, another broken promise from the restaurateurs, the U.K. was officially kicking my ass out. It reminded me of the idiotic hazing I used to get in high school: "If you don't like this country, why don't you just leave?" Usually punctuated with the word "faggot!"

Well, I can tell you this for a fact. It's not easy to leave. I tried. It's a myth. The rest of the world doesn't want you. You can't just pick up and move somewhere else.

At this point I decided: Goodbye, London, hello, Berklee College of Music. Next stop: Boston.

About 15 years after the London restaurant debacle, I ran into a random 20-something-year-old guy on a subway platform in Manhattan.

The kid recognized me by name and seemed shocked to run into me. He said he remembered me from the restaurant in London. This wasn't a total surprise to me since the owners had managed to hire a whole gaggle of American exchange students that summer as cheap labor to be their waitstaff. I didn't remember this kid's face at all, however. He never told me his name.

When I got home later that night, there was an email waiting for me from this kid's dad. As it turned out the dad was the lead manager/liar at the restaurant. The kid had been about 12 or 13 at the time when he was helping his dad out. I have to add that the kid was pretty lazy back then and really wasn't much help. I didn't recognize him as an adult.

The dad's email said how great it was that his kid had run into me, how great it was too for us to reconnect after all these years, and what a wonderful and small world it was. The email was all rainbows and unicorns.

I wrote back to him saying that I had traveled the world since our last meeting, that I had performed for millions of people since then, and that in all of my travels and all of my professional dealings, I had yet to encounter anyone on the planet as dishonest as he was. I told him I even had the court papers with the amount of money he still owed me, which I would be happy to show him if he liked.

He never responded.

London phone box

39 PUTTING ON THE BLAZER

There is a distinct difference between being in the backing band and being up front in the spotlight. In fact, this phenomenon was explored pretty faithfully in the 2013 movie *20 Feet from Stardom*.

Years ago, one of the three singers in The Tokens left the group. The Tokens had a huge hit in 1961 with "The Lion Sleeps Tonight." Lead singer, Jay Siegel, amazingly still does the falsetto part in the original key all these years later. Their stage costumes usually consist of three different yet brightly colored sports jackets. It is a smart, clean look that's easy to attain, maintain, and travels well.

A buddy of mine who normally played and sang backup in the band was in active negotiations at one point to, as he described it, "put on the blazer." Meaning he was going to move up front and become an official Token instead of a journeyman musician. That promotion never happened. But the image of it has stayed with me.

In recent years, I have found myself putting on the blazer with a classic rock act from the late 1960s/early 1970s. Only in this case, the blazer is a leather jacket. In very short order, I discovered what it meant to wear the blazer rather than being purely a hired gun.

People treat you differently. They have a fan energy about interacting with you. We sign autographs now and take photos with the fans. Music equipment manufacturers you may have known for decades are willing to work with you in a new and different way, adding you and your new "credit" to their website. Nothing fundamentally changed about who I am or what I do. But people look at me as if I have some newfound legitimacy.

Never mind that I am very much still a hired gun even with my leather jacket on. My employment with said act is just as tenuous as with any gig I've ever had, subject to the whims of bandleaders, market forces, and other players actively gunning for my job. Still, for now, I wear the blazer.

Let's explore a complicating factor in the modern music business when it comes to legacy acts such as the one I'm now in. Blood Sweat & Tears, Canned Heat, The Hollies, Iron Butterfly,

Little River Band, Quiet Riot, Thin Lizzy, Yes, Lynyrd Skynyrd, Foreigner, ELO, UFO; this is just a partial list of acts that share a common bond. They all have somewhere between zero and one original member left alive and actively touring with the group. At this point their trademark has become their thing. The marquee value is higher for ZZ Top with all original members (same three guys, same three chords). But these other acts are quite capable of still working and making a decent living.

The band I'm in now I'll call "Penitent Pastry" since it's an ongoing situation (albeit one suffering a pandemic hiatus as of this writing, as so many are). The fate of this current version of the band is still up in the air. I'm not even listed on the band's Wikipedia page. There is a bona fide trademark owned by their one surviving original member. But since that founding member doesn't feel healthy enough for the rigors of touring, he has decided to put together a great band to play the repertoire. He very closely monitors our creative output to maintain the high standards of the group's legacy. This is also done with the blessing of the families of the other deceased members of the band. It's the healthiest way I've ever seen a legacy act assembled or presented.

When I was first asked to join the band, I went online to search the original members of the group and was struck by photos of their original bass player. His main axe was a 1970s blonde-finish Fender Precision Bass. My first bass was a 1970s blonde Fender Precision. Clearly this was meant to be.

I changed my strings to vintage-style flatwounds to better capture the original sound of the band and stuffed some dampening foam under my strings near the bridge to further this vintage vibe. Magically my rig was transformed into nearly an exact replica of the original.

I spent many days transcribing and memorizing all of the original bass parts and background vocal parts of the band's current 90-minute show so I could hit the ground running. There was to be very little rehearsal time. I needed to be fully operational right out of the gate. At the first rehearsal, there were immediate smiles all around the room. I liked them. They liked me. My prep work had paid off.

When we started with this new version of the band, there hadn't been a Penitent Pastry tour in about 15 years. We were still in the process of discovering exactly what our marquee value currently was. We did a whole run of rock clubs where we managed to sell about half of the room in each market with no promotion or publicity. Everyone who came to see the band genuinely loved the show almost as much as we did playing onstage. The music was a joy to perform. The group was a pleasure to travel and work with. We were firing on all cylinders every night. It really was a dream come true.

That said, there are still business challenges the powers that be are facing in keeping the group rolling down the highway. While the marquee value of the group is still being re-established, it would probably benefit us to be on more "soft-ticket" shows, i.e., an opening spot on a big arena tour, festivals, casinos, and the like. But that's the job of the management and the booking agents. Our job as a band is to show up and rock. That's it. We do our job. And we do it well.

On our last swing through the Midwest, one afternoon I went to the back of the equipment truck to help with the gear load-in. Our road manager became quite grumpy with me when I tried to lift my amp and carry it into the club. "I don't want you lifting that. You play bass for a living," he told me.

I was taken aback. Never before in my career had anyone said something like that to me. I work for a living. I've been lifting amps my whole life. But I knew what he meant. And I appreciated that he was looking out for me. If I break a finger on a road case while moving gear, the road manager and the whole band would have a serious problem delivering the contracted show for the evening. He was protecting his own job by protecting mine. Now that's a great road manager.

There have always been naysayers in the world, sourpusses, curmudgeons. But in this digital age, there is a new breed of them in the form of internet trolls. Comedian Marc Maron calls them the Army of Unfuckable Hate Nerds. He's quite right.

We get a lot of vocal pushback about our lack of original members or the understandable absence of our deceased former lead singer from a small but rowdy minority of the trolls. Somebody who's dead is unlikely to make the gig tonight. But we promise to do a bang-up job if you'll just sit in the back of the theatre, shut up, and watch.

While our legacy is legitimate and our approach to the music is undeniable in its integrity, this negative chatter is hard to ignore. We as performing artists are constantly dealing with our own insecurities and trying our best to not suck in public. It's not always easy to ignore the Negative Nancys. Of course, that's exactly the attention they crave. And that's the very attention we cannot and should not give them.

Our job is to keep on keeping on, delivering a powerful and undeniable performance night after night. Then they can say whatever they like. We'll have enough friendly supporters who love the music as much as we do to keep the machine moving.

I take solace from the fact that I have even seen internet hate energy directed at solo artists whose marquee value is their own name. The Hate Nerds can't deny any connection to the band's trademark in those cases. But the haters are going to hate. So we have to keep on doing what we do and let them do what they do, sitting in their underwear behind their computers in their moms' basements trying to soothe their psychic pain by inflicting it on others.

Meanwhile, this band onstage is a snarling beast. There's absolutely no feeling quite like blasting pure musical energy right through the chest of every audience member and up into the rafters of the building. Cranking a power chord right down the gullet of everyone in the front row is a truly exciting and fun thing to do. Our music is loud, powerful, and deeply soulful. All of the cats in the band are seasoned, experienced, and seriously on their game. It's definitely a situation where the whole is greater than the sum of its parts.

When we hit the stage blasting, we love the audience. They love us. We all love the music. A transcendent evening is upon us all. It's a special privilege indeed, which I feel very lucky to be a part of. Long live The Pastry!

1978 Fender Precision Bass with new flatwound strings

40 CLIMBING THE SAME MOUNTAIN EVERY DAY

The summary of my life looks something like the instructions on the back of a shampoo bottle: procrastinate, work, sleep, repeat (ad infinitum).

It's the curse of Sisyphus in a way. For all my self-aggrandizing aspirations to be in show business, I am forced to climb the same mountain every single day. And though I may be able to roll the boulder quite far up the hill some days, less far other days, the next morning I have to start from base camp yet again. There is no summit. Even if there is a high peak, it does little more than afford me a view of the taller mountains around me.

I enjoy my work. I like playing the bass. I love playing music. I dig what I do. But it can feel like a thankless job sometimes. Every day when I wake up, the hardest part is taking the first step. The distance to cover seems immense and undoable. Even though I know intellectually that the way to climb mountains is one step at a time, taking that first step feels like digging out of quicksand.

Once I'm up and walking, everything is cool. I like working hard. I like accomplishing things. I like going places and seeing stuff. It's just that there's a cumulative aftereffect of those first painful steps.

Some days after an exhausting stretch of rushing to gig after gig, traveling mile after mile of endless road, hoping against hope that I have shown up at the right gig on the right day with the right bass, the right charts, the right shirt, the right attitude, I just have to crash. I'll spend a day staring at a wall or a TV and doing nothing but scratching myself. Then I'll inevitably feel bad about accomplishing nothing even though I know that recharging the batteries is part of the process.

Here is a summertime social media post I wrote a little while ago, "I'll be in seclusion today since I just finished a run of 15 gigs in 16 days with 10 different acts in 4 states (NY, NJ, RI & NC) including live band rock & roll karaoke, multiple private party/wedding bands (American, Russian, and otherwise), a New

Orleans piano band, a 14-year-old Broadway performer's showcase, a funk band, a blues band, and a Motown tribute act. Make hay while the hot sun is shining. One must save up some nuts for the long winter's hibernation."

I also find that I work better with deadlines. When I need to have something done by tomorrow, it gets done. When I need to have something done somewhere between six months from now and never, it might never get done.

Writing this book is a prime example. Since I did it on my own without a deadline, it took forever. Sitting down to generate a couple of paragraphs on any given day felt like a giant hurdle to get over. There are nagging questions in the back of my head. Why am I writing this book? Who's going to read it? Who cares about any of this stuff? I don't have the answers. These fears are paralyzing. Believe me.

As he mentioned in the foreword to this book, I have explained to Stanley Clarke about my constant fear that I'll never work again, about how sitting still bothers me because I'm convinced the jig is up. They're finally onto me. I've been fooling them all these years and managed to somehow make a living at it.

Stanley has told me that I do more gigs than anyone he knows. He says that there is a name for my fear of the phone not ringing. It's called "mental disease."

He's right.

I've talked to and worked with people at various levels of fame and obscurity throughout the industry. We all seem to have a tendency to be worried about what's next rather than focused on what we've just done. The money from the last gig has been spent already.

Similarly, whatever bump up in self-esteem we get from the shows has also been spent already. Playing a prestigious or high-profile gig can give you good mental go-go juice for a couple of weeks. But if that next couple of weeks is spent sitting on the recliner at home, the esteem fades to black very quickly.

The mountain has to be climbed again the very next day. There's no choice. A shark has to constantly keep swimming to keep from drowning. So must I continue to do whatever it is that I do or surely perish.

Since this planet is only really on temporary loan to us humans from the cockroaches and the slime molds, we must beat back the encroaching weeds every day just to keep our tiny part of the forest clear. Some days it's a joy. Other days it feels like a real chore.

These existential dilemmas are fairly universal. But they can feel extremely localized to my psyche when I'm out on the road by myself staring at the ceiling of yet another in the long line of countless Bates motels.

Even just getting myself up when I'm home, going for a run, and making some breakfast so that I can get started practicing or transcribing music for an upcoming gig feels daunting.

The beneficial results of practicing a musical instrument manifest themselves very slowly over a long period of time. It's unusual to notice any improvement day-to-day. But after six months, you'll realize that certain things are easier than they once were. It's hard to keep that big picture view in focus all the time. Often it feels like two steps forward, one step back.

I'm a better player than I was 5 or 10 years ago even though I was a competent player back then. It's all part of the journey. Hopefully the journey itself is enjoyable for its own sake.

I had an ex who was focused on the eventualities of her life and never on the current reality. She would always talk about how if she accomplished X, then she would be happy. If she could only go to destination Y, then she would be happy. She never really got to X or Y. Surprise, surprise, she never really seemed happy or content.

Because of her negative example, I have tried to learn to enjoy the ride. It turns out that the journey really is the whole thing. The destination is nothing more than a turnaround point to head back home again.

There's an old quote that people try to attribute to Confucius. But I'm pretty sure it's from the 1984 movie *Buckaroo Banzai*: "Remember, no matter where you go, there you are."

To me this simply means that there is no escape from one's inner demons. No change of venue can alter how you feel about yourself. Fame isn't contentment, fulfillment, or happiness. Fame is just notoriety and everything that comes with it, most of which is just a pain in the ass.

Rolling the boulder up the hill is what it's all about. I have tried to pick out a nice rock I truly like and to put my shoulder into it.

41 MIDNIGHT TRAIN TO NYC

O n January 20, 2009, Sam Moore got called to perform at an Inaugural ball for President Obama thrown by the Creative Coalition, a supposedly nonpartisan group of Hollywood stars turned political activists. It was to be an A-list bunch of attendees, including but not limited to: Anne Hathaway, Susan Sarandon, Ron Howard, Spike Lee, Kerry Washington, Alfre Woodard, Maggie Gyllenhaal, Peter Sarsgaard, Wendie Malick, Matthew Modine, Alan Cumming, and Ellen Burstyn. And those are just the ones that I had heard of.

Incidentally, though I performed for these folks, I didn't meet any of them over the course of the following events. I only know they were there having read the scant press accounts of the night that barely even acknowledged the musical performance, which was the centerpiece of the event. Press reports were scant because there was a bigger headliner in town that night. I don't know if you heard.

Film director Barry Levinson made a documentary about the Creative Coalition and the involvement of Hollywood in the election cycle that year called *Poliwood*. The Inaugural ball features prominently in the film. You can see me on-screen a couple of times, if you don't blink.

The mission we chose to accept that cold January day was to perform as the Sam Moore band with a 13-piece combo and to back up Sam's special guests for the evening, Rock & Roll Hall of Famers Elvis Costello and Mr. Sting. I was to be the music director, band contractor, arranger, and road manager. But at least I didn't get paid any extra money for wearing all of those hats. So that's cool.

That was the good news. The bad news was that, owing to the historic event, Washington, D.C., was completely booked up that night. There were no accommodations to be had within a 100-mile radius. There was literally no room at the inn. We were therefore booked on a round-trip Amtrak ticket with a 3 a.m. return train to New York, not actually the "midnight train." This fact wasn't enough to deter anyone from taking the gig, however.

When we pulled into Washington Union Station around midday, the air in the city was electric. People who had never thought about attending an Inauguration flocked to town. The Park Service estimates approximately 1.8 million people decided to witness history that day. The place was super crowded and also locked down tighter than it had ever been before. The security was enormous. The parade route and the National Mall were cordoned off by a tightly controlled perimeter, more than likely with sharpshooters on every rooftop.

We noticed upon arrival that there was no one there to pick us up and transport us from the train station to the venue. Trying to be resourceful, a quick check on Google Maps revealed that the concert hall was only a little under a mile away. I suggested to the band that we walk. They all agreed. We had a very pleasant stroll through ebullient crowds and thousands of vendors selling bootleg swag. I think we each bought at least one souvenir T-shirt. It was that kind of occasion.

Unfortunately, the most direct route suggested by Google Maps wasn't available to us because of the security perimeter. We had to circumnavigate the roadblocks and find our way to the theatre by trial and error. The route we took was certainly a longer distance. But it was still fun just to be in the festive atmosphere of it all, even though we were hand-carrying our instruments the entire way. For the singers, this wasn't a problem. For the baritone sax and trombone players, it was a little more arduous.

Finally, we rounded a corner and saw an entrance to the theatre. Yet we were still about 100 yards away and facing yet another roadblock. The officer manning the post asked us for our credentials. We had none. We had been provided with none. It had never occurred to us to ask for any. We were musicians on a mission from God. We don't need no stinkin' badges! That is, except for this day, which was the most secured event in the nation's history. It was a problem.

The officer sighed and pointed the way to the next checkpoint, which was at the parking lot gate for the theatre. Apparently, we weren't the first people that day to have the same problem. Our musical army was allowed to advance to the next barricade.

Upon arrival at this blockade, the officer asked us for our credentials. We explained again that we didn't have any, but that we were performing for the event in the hall that evening. We were met with another heavy sigh from law enforcement and told to proceed to the stage door of the theatre for the next checkpoint.

At the stage door, we were once again asked for our credentials. But this time it wasn't by a D.C. city cop or a Virginia State Trooper on temporary assignment. This time it was the Secret Service. These guys were not amused by our plight and not about to entertain our sad story without some verification. We were told to stand to the side of the hallway that contained airport-style metal detectors and wait while people were called.

The Secret Service detail all looked huge and were undoubtedly packing lethal force. While we were waiting to learn our fate, we got to watch them prosecute their duties. A pushcart full of food was being brought in by the caterers. We watched a gargantuan agent the size of a side of beef diligently search through the salads. These guys were not messing around, nor were they to be trifled with. We kept our mouths shut and waited.

As we were waiting, an old Berklee classmate of mine coincidentally walked in. My pal, Tariqh Akoni, lives in Los Angeles and is music director for Josh Groban. It was a happy reunion but an unlikely place to meet. Tariqh said he was playing with Josh there that night. That's great, I thought. I had no idea we were on the same bill.

We then heard a band onstage sound checking. They played a Smokey Robinson song that we loved. Then they played another Smokey Robinson song. Then another Smokey Robinson song. Clearly, the artist sound checking at that moment was … Smokey Robinson.

My thoughts in rapid succession were: "Wow, what an incredible night of music," and "Hey, we're not on the same show with Smokey Robinson or Josh Groban. We're in the wrong place!"

We were in the wrong place.

There were so many full-production shows in Washington that night that we had seen all the trucks parked outside and mistakenly assumed that was our gig.

Generally, we had been successful with this game. Whenever you pull into a new town, you always look for evidence of a gig: a theatre, PA speakers, outdoor staging, lighting rigs, and equipment trucks. This makes it easy to deduce where you need to be for work that day.

After a further conference with the Secret Service, we determined that our gig was really two blocks away. But, again, we couldn't walk the two blocks directly because of the perimeter. So it was two blocks up, two blocks over, and two blocks back down again.

When we finally arrived at the Harman Center, our actual home for the evening, we were greeted at the front door by a very nice woman sitting behind a folding card table who said, "Name, please?" Instantly it dawned on us. The President wasn't attending our function. It turned out that even with all of the celebrity firepower in attendance, this was still an unofficial Inaugural function.

Once finally on the correct site, another potential hardship we faced was that we only had a partial list of songs that our special guests were to perform and no specific keys in which to play them. The reasons for this are a little complicated.

Typically, managers tightly control access to their artists. It's part of their job to protect their clients from the daily onslaught of people from all levels of the industry and the fans in general who crave direct access to the artists. Managers will communicate with other managers but are loath to hand off direct access to their bass players, for instance. This is understandable. On more than one occasion, I have demonstrated that I cannot and should not be trusted to fully and accurately represent the interests of my employers when speaking on my own to other rock stars. That is why I'm not a manager, I suppose.

There is also a general lack of understanding that businesspeople seem to have about the mechanics of what it takes to get a 13-piece ensemble performing at the highest level. There are a lot of moving parts involved. This made my job as music arranger for the evening quite difficult. I felt like I was literally herding cats. I've heard a saying that seems to apply to situations like these: "I'm solving problems you don't know you have in ways you can't understand."

For example, Elvis Costello & The Attractions famously covered a Sam & Dave song in 1980 called "I Can't Stand Up for

Falling Down." It was the lead track on their album *Get Happy!!* Sam & Dave originally recorded this song in 1967 in the key of F as a 12/8 ballad. The Attractions recorded it in the key of C as an up-tempo punkish rocker. The two versions are in no way compatible for a live medley. They're two quite different readings of the song. I was told that we would perform it Sam & Dave–style first with Elvis as a duet partner, then immediately again, but Elvis Costello–style.

I was also told by management that we were to keep Elvis's version in Sam's key since Elvis was our guest. This would have gone very badly for Elvis. I didn't want to see that happen because, ironically, the first time I had heard that song growing up was from Elvis, not Sam.

As a side note, I had a similar experience with first hearing the song "I Thank You" from ZZ Top instead of Sam & Dave. What can I say? I grew up in the burbs. But I quickly learned the error of my ways and got educated.

We had a great horn section in our band that Elvis Costello didn't have on his version, which was recorded with just a rock quartet. I wanted to use our Uptown Horns since we had them that night. With the help of baritone sax player Dan Cipriano, who had some music notation software on his laptop, I finished an Otis Redding–style horn arrangement for Elvis's version of "I Can't Stand Up" on the train on the way to D.C.

In Elvis's key of C.

This was me opting not to follow orders and potentially jeopardizing my job in the process. My plan was to pull Elvis aside at rehearsal and tell him that when we got to The Attractions' version of the song that he was to absolutely take the helm. Sam wouldn't know Elvis's arrangement. It would be in the wrong key for Sam. It was imperative that Elvis step up. It was a foolproof plan. No one would ever know.

But Elvis never came to the rehearsal. I never got a chance to meet him before, during, or after the show. The only person I had access to was Milo, his road manager. I had the discussion with Milo that I had intended for Elvis. I tried to urge him to impart all of this information to his boss so that when we were onstage it wouldn't all go pear-shaped. I had no way of knowing that the information got successfully passed along until we stormed into the song during the show. Elvis took the mic and sang lead like a boss. It was a great moment. I heaved a sigh of relief.

I was excited to play with Elvis Costello, a childhood hero of mine. I have audience photos and camera-phone clips from the evening that I found online. Our band is even featured in the Barry Levinson documentary backing him. But I never got to meet Elvis.

Mr. Sting, however, did come to rehearsal. As I wrote earlier, we had worked with him and Sam before. We had been told that we were backing him only for "Every Breath You Take" and that he was going to perform "Message in a Bottle" solo as he famously had at *The Secret Policeman's Other Ball* in 1981. Fine. I was a little heartbroken about that because I had played "Message" at my first-ever high school talent show, my first time onstage as a musician. But I was happy to get to play with him at all.

I did something else in preparation for Mr. Sting's set that I knew would be me basically taking my life into my own hands (again). I wrote a very gentle horn arrangement for "Every Breath You Take." Nothing grandstanding or showy, just a way to include these instruments in the performance. I knew it was potentially bad form to rewrite rock & roll history without permission when backing the original artist and songwriter. I decided to roll the dice anyway. It was Sam's band after all, with Mr. Sting as special guest.

In preparation I told the horn players that they were not to mention under any circumstances that they had a chart for "Every Breath." I further told them not to be standing at their microphones looking like they were ready to play on the song. I asked them to say and do nothing to betray the fact that they were about to chime in.

When we played the song in the rehearsal with Mr. Sting, at the first bridge the horns just gently came in with a whole-note voicing that I had written out for them. The instant the first molecule of spit hit a trumpet valve, his head shot around like lightning toward the horn players. My entire career instantly flashed before my eyes.

But … he was smiling.

I heaved another sigh of relief. There would be many such sighs over the course of that evening. He liked the horn arrangement and went on to use it on at least two other occasions that I know about for sure.

He was so pleased at how "Every Breath" went that I decided to ask him if he wanted us to also back him on "Message in a Bottle."

He asked, "Do you know it?"

"In C sharp?" I confirmed. Of course, I knew it. It was one of the first songs I ever learned to play.

"Right," he said, but quickly added to our amazing drummer, Tony Lewis, "but I don't want a Stewart Copeland type of thing."

Mr. Sting had just finished the Police reunion tour the year before and had enough of that style of drumming, apparently. No worries. We got you, man. We gave him the soul version.

It was a life full circle moment for me. Twenty-seven years after my high school debut performance, I was getting to play "Message" again, this time onstage with the man himself.

Furthermore, it turned out Mr. Sting was planning to perform his song "Brand New Day" solo that night with a prerecorded backing track. Once again, I offered our services to accompany him and the track. And once again, he accepted. However, this was going to require that his aide-de-camp email me a copy of the track, which I would have to transcribe off of my phone backstage with a pencil. No pressure. I did just that, found a production office with a Xerox machine, and distributed copies to the band while everyone else was enjoying a dinner break. No rest for the bass player.

At the show that evening, Sam and the band were on fire. Our special guests were stellar. The audience was enraptured by the performance and giddy from the day's political events. It was a career high, a once-in-a-lifetime event. At the end of the night, we were all spent but exhilarated.

I had complained earlier in the day to the organizers that we hadn't been met at the train station on our arrival. I was assured that three town cars had been arranged to get us back in time for our overnight train to New York.

At the end of the night, the stars, their managers, and all the organizers disappeared to whatever after-parties they went to. We exited the theatre to find only two town cars waiting, certainly not three. The drivers informed us that it would be $50 in cash for each car for a one-mile ride back to the train station. Inaugural price gouging was in full effect.

OF COURSE, nobody from the event had bothered to prepay our transportation. I knew enough from dealing with these situations in the past that getting reimbursed for expenses that hadn't been explicitly agreed upon beforehand was nearly impossible. I wasn't willing to lay out the cash myself and was unwilling to ask the band to pay for it. So I suggested once again that we walk.

It was just a final little "F.U." The band had performed miraculously under difficult circumstances and made our bosses comfortable enough to be able to sing their hearts out. It was one of the greatest nights of our lives. Yet we still had to walk a mile back to the train station at 1 a.m. in freezing 20-degree weather, drenched in sweat and hand-carrying our instruments.

We made our 3 a.m. train with time to spare. The entire band was sound asleep as soon as we pulled out of the station bound for our 6 a.m. arrival back in New York City. Everyone, that is, except for me. I was so wound up from the adrenaline and stress of the day that I didn't, couldn't sleep a wink the whole ride. I stared out the window at the nighttime rushing by and tried to process what had just happened to us.

All in all, we had many more successes than failures on this grand adventure. My sole regret was not being able to get a photo with Elvis Costello on the "suspicious" occasion of our first working together. I already had a photo with Mr. Sting from a previous gig.

Ten years later, Blondie played at Forest Hills Stadium, about four blocks from my apartment in Queens. I have some really great friends in that band. Every time I'm near a show of theirs, I like to try to see if I can sneak in and get backstage without any valid credentials. Usually I have good luck. But I knew the security at Forest Hills Stadium might be a little tough. My strategy was to go around sound check time in the afternoon and to hang any random couple of laminate passes from unrelated past gigs around my neck so I would look like maybe I should be there.

It worked. I walked through the vendor's gate and right up onstage during Blondie's sound check. When I accomplish these security breaches, my pal Tommy Kessler, who plays guitar for the band, always says to me, "How did you get back here?"

"I just walked in, man."

Once inside, Tommy is always kind enough to get me an official laminate for the show so I can stay back there for the rest of the evening without worry. I even got to enjoy the backstage catering that day, which was very kind of them.

In the catering tent, I noticed a gentleman standing near the ice cream freezer. After a brief internal pep talk, I decided to approach him and introduce myself.

Blondie's co-headliner for the evening was Elvis Costello. I reminded him of our previous adventure in Washington, D.C. He remembered. Ten short years later, I finally got to take a photo with him.

Elvis Costello – 2019

42 EPILOGUE – I THINK WE'VE ALL LEARNED SOMETHING HERE TODAY

There's an old joke that goes: I didn't get into show business for the money. And so far, it's working out.

Clearly if just making money were my focus, I would have gone into finance or lawyering, doctoring, or some such. A life in the arts can be a wonderful way to achieve self-expression. But it's a tough row to hoe. You have to really want it.

You almost have to feel the way I did when I quit my lucrative burgeoning record company career. I felt I had no choice, that there was nothing else in life I really wanted to do. I felt that somehow whatever the sacrifices were going to be, anything would be better than rotting behind a desk trying to sell someone else's dreams to people who weren't in the market for them.

In a very real sense, my deciding to play music for a living was basically chasing the applause I heard at the talent show in that high school gymnasium for the rest of my life. It's a search for acceptance.

In my case it doesn't feel like a continual search for rabid adulation or complete idol worship. It's a much milder pursuit for me. It's more like just trying to find a place where I am merely tolerated and allowed to be myself. I enjoy when people appreciate my work. But at this point if I get a compliment for 1 out of 10 gigs, I feel I'm doing pretty good.

Most gigs we do are just working for a living, punching the clock, "dance, monkey, dance." There are many more of those type of gigs than the rock star stuff, which is fine. That's how it's supposed to work. It takes thousands of hours of preparation to get ready for those three minutes on TV. It takes about 10 years to become an overnight sensation.

I've been playing the bass for nearly 40 years. That means that either I've become an overnight sensation three and a half times or I'm doing something wrong.

Of course, it means nothing of the kind. Fame is down to luck, maybe even more than ability or native talent. Fame is relative. Fame is fleeting. Fame is selective. The real question is, Am I enjoying the journey?

I am.

I have played with famous people. I have had my name in magazines, on theatre marquees, and on album covers. I've done a lot of famousy stuff. But I'm quite sure that I am by no means truly famous, even if I might be well-known among New York City bartenders, for example.

It comes down to a decision about how you want to live your life. Do you want to spend your time doing something you enjoy or something you hate that might (or might not) pay you more money?

I've had office jobs. I've had music industry jobs. But I kind of hit the wall with all of that. I realized there was nothing else I really wanted to do other than play the dang bass for a living. It was a jarring and terrible revelation when it finally came to me.

The odds of being able to even pay your rent, much less be famous while doing it, are pretty small. It's an uphill battle every day trying to keep focused on music and creativity while also making sure you're able to pay the light bill.

When people ask me for advice about getting into the industry or becoming a professional musician, I invariably advise them to do *anything* else if they possibly can. Between the successes, there is almost too much heartache and self-degradation to have made it all worthwhile. There are so many other easier paths to choose in life.

Life on the road is also a very lonely existence. I was a lonely kid growing up mostly without friends until maybe my senior year of high school when I found friendship with my fellow drama nerds and the dudes in that first talent show band.

There are a lot of hard miles spent by yourself on planes and buses going to unknown destinations to meet up with strangers. Even when traveling with groups, I'm often a substitute player in the band. So they aren't truly my companions.

I have a lot of professional colleagues these days. I have very few friends. Being a freelance mercenary requires that level of independence. I guess I was groomed for it by never having much of a social network to count on when I was a kid.

If people asking my advice are resolute in their desire to pursue music the way I was all those years ago, I tell them that they need to work hard, show up on time, be a nice person, and hope for those rare lucky breaks. That's the only way. One cannot plan for fame. But one can aspire to be a solid working craftsperson if that is the intent.

A career never goes the way you think it's going to go. You can dream about it and work toward goals all you want. It's just going to come out differently from what you originally thought it would be, guaranteed. You can only go through the doors that are open. Sure, you can knock. But if they still don't open, you're going to have to choose another path. Sometimes the reality you end up with is better than what you could have imagined. But it's always different from what you envisioned.

I have been a full-time professional musician for 26 years. I've been semipro for closer to 29 years. And I have had a bass guitar in my hand in some fashion for nearly 40 years now. I guess it's working out. I would play music anyway even if it didn't pay my rent or afford me these brief glimpses into the lifestyles of the rich and famous.

What would my being rich or famous fix? That's the big question, the core issue. It would fix nothing. I've seen it up close. The richest dude I ever hung out with was also the most miserable person I ever met. He drank himself to death on more than a fifth of vodka a day.

The most famous people I've ever met don't seem particularly well-adjusted to me. They seem more preoccupied with staying famous than with creating the art that made them famous. Being a superstar seems to require the desire to become famous by crushing everyone else around you, as in, "This town ain't big enough for the two of us." That's an exhausting way to live.

It sure is lucky I don't have any of that cursed money or any of that awful fame to drag me down. Now I can continue to concentrate on playing Motown cover tunes and getting on with my life of being the envy of everyone in the catering hall at the wedding.

The only problem is that my self-esteem seems directly tied to my immediate employment. I don't sit still well or take time off comfortably. That nagging voice is in the back of my head saying, "You ain't shit." I know it's not real. I know it's a vestigial echo from the distant past. But it's still there. It has grown fainter over time, for sure.

I was carrying my bass on my back and my amp on a luggage cart in the subway one day a couple of years ago, as I so often do. That day I got randomly approached to be photographed and featured on the website *Humans of New York.*

The caption under my photo, which was based on what I told the photographer in our three-minute discussion, was: "I find it really hard to feel a sense of accomplishment in retrospect. No matter what I achieve, my self-worth always seems to be tied to the next booking."

There is just some crater in my personality that craves acceptance, craves love. The crater is probably from the meteor that hit me sometime around my parents' divorce. But there was an asteroid shower of damaging hits that came from so many quarters during my formative years. It's impossible to pin it all on a single event like that.

Acceptance feels like it can come from roomfuls of complete strangers standing and applauding. It gives an instant replay of the initial endorphin rush of that gymnasium full of classmates who actively hated me screaming with approval, though it was only temporary. The kids at school went right back to hazing me the very next morning.

Being a descendant of the narcissistic maternal line of my family with the instantaneous and constantly changing judgments, this felt normal in a way. Having acceptance thrust upon me and then almost instantly removed again was par for the course.

Fortunately, the crater in my soul isn't as deep these days as it once was. Years of therapy helped fill it in quite a bit. Having a loving partner for the past seven years has been amazing too. Eventually I hope to come to the internal conclusion that just being me is a good enough thing to be. All of the applause or all of the money in the world won't really make me feel better about myself.

Some days I'm closer to this state of mind than others. It's gotten a lot better later in my life than when I was an angry young man. Now I'm just a mildly perturbed middle-aged dude with nothing really left to prove.

Three years ago, I even managed to buy a New York City apartment with nickels and dimes I had saved up from over two decades of wedding gigs. How many, you ask? I estimate that my apartment cost exactly 1,053 Russian wedding gigs or 1,843 oldies gigs or 1,340 Broadway performances. My actual career has been a mix of everything. Let's just say that it took a while. All this was made possible by buying that $425 bass with my summer dishwashing money. I still have that bass.

At the end of it all, at the core, I really like to play the Fender bass. In fact, the only place I believe I have a shot at feeling comfortable is on a stage with a bass guitar in my hands.

There are no guarantees of this happiness, of course. There are so many factors that can put a damper on an evening like a bandleader throwing a tantrum, a drunk girl screaming at the top of her lungs two feet away from my head all night thinking she was "singing," an idiot blowing with all of his might into a harmonica in the wrong key in the front row and who refused to take it out of his piehole all stinking night. All that happened just last Thursday, my friend.

Because being onstage is the only time I have a shot at being at ease with myself, it is also one of the only places I get emotional. Onstage is also the only place where I lose my temper.

If someone is being careless with the music that I so dearly love, it can make me see red. It's disrespectful to the audience, to the artist that we're backing, to everyone in the band, and to the music itself. The only time I ever physically pushed a dude was when a drummer was fucking up the groove thinking that he was telling some kind of musical joke. It sent me into a rage.

But I'm a dyed-in-the-wool pacifist. Besides that one palm to the drummer's chest, I've never laid a hand on another human being in anger. He might have had it coming, however. But he knew me, knew my personality, and knew what a pushover I was. He just laughed when I pushed him.

That's exactly what he should have done. My "rage" was comic in how misplaced it was. I got more offended by someone intentionally misplacing an eighth note than I would have if they had axe-murdered my family.

Perspective, folks. I apologized to him. He and I are still friends.

Meanwhile I continue to ride down the highway in my used Hyundai Elantra that I am prouder of than any possible fancy car anyone else owns. I don't covet expensive automobiles. I do value my freedom, which owning a car in New York City signifies. It also demonstrates my ability to be self-motivated and to get to the gig on time.

I've long maintained that what the successful New York City wedding band musician most needs is a tuxedo and a car. It's not the Jersey Turnpike itself that keeps me going, nor are tollbooths where I aspire to be. But I like driving my own car.

Many years ago, I was wondering out loud to a blind date whom I had just met and who had come to see me at a gig. I said I didn't feel that playing in the house band at a blues jam session in a bar at 3 a.m. for drunks seemed like a lofty pursuit or an even remotely artistic one.

She quickly corrected me by saying that music unites people in a very special way. Even for a short time, a roomful of strangers can be bound together in a common experience through sound and through participating in a live performance just by listening and reacting. It was a kind of hippie-dippie way of looking at what I do. She also reeked of patchouli oil. So I shouldn't have been surprised. But she had a point.

Though the blind date didn't work out, that conversation has stayed with me for decades. I hear it echoing around in the back of my head often. I constantly remind myself of those very kind words from that stranger.

All I do is not for naught. Even if one person finds enjoyment or solace from listening to me play, that's a good day. If I can accomplish that for my annual average of 228 gigs a calendar year, I will officially have had more good days than bad. And that's worth something, isn't it?

Apartment purchased with proceeds earned from a $425 used Fender bass

PHOTOS

Mr. Sting

"Bongo" from U2

Kevin Bacon & Charlie Giordano

Jennifer Hudson

Jack Black

Bill Cosby (you never know whom you'll meet)

Sam Moore & Shirley Alston Reeves (my surrogate road parents)

Wynonna Judd & my dad

Darlene Love

Gloria Gaynor

Felipe Rose (Village People)

Dee Snider (Twisted Sister)

Nicko McBrain (Iron Maiden)

Ben E. King

Martha Reeves & The Vandellas

Rufus Thomas

Stanley Clarke

Fabian

Memories from my record company days

Clockwise from top left: Gregg Allman, Sheila E., Sade, Charlie Daniels, Rick Nielsen (Cheap Trick), Stanley Clarke

Gregg Allman photo: Greg Allen

Clockwise from top left: Cyndi Lauper, Stevie Ray Vaughan, Alice Cooper & Vernon Reid (Living Colour), Gene Simmons (KISS), James Brown

SRV photo: Greg Allen

Clockwise from top: Meat Loaf & Jennifer Rush, Ozzy Osbourne, Living Colour, Melissa Etheridge & Indigo Girls.

Ozzy Osbourne photo: Greg Allen

APPENDIX – MY RÉSUMÉ

W hen I first got to New York City, I temped for three years. I was typing résumés for the people that the phone company was laying off. It was a good karma job. One thing I learned well on that job was how to write a résumé. I know how. And apparently, I choose not to do it that way.

What follows is my ludicrously long curriculum vitae. It rambles on for an unconscionable 10 full pages in this book. In my defense, I have never sent it out to anyone. All this information is up on my website, however. I keep it up there to give my two stalkers something to read late at night.

This is all stuff that I actually did, including the many people you've never heard of. While I do seem to lack a filter, there's no extra padding here that so many people feel the need to have. It's real stuff and fair game. I mentioned before that I keep the full list of credits because it's impossible to know which one out of the 165 or so names a reader will identify with.

I do have an edited one-page biography that I send out occasionally. That's a much more palatable, easily digested document.

Way more than you ever wanted to know about me is also available at my website: www.funkboy.net.

ivan "funkboy" bodley
electric & acoustic bass
www.funkboy.net

SUMMARY

Performed with 50 Rock & Roll Hall of Fame inductees and in 12 Broadway shows. Magna cum laude Berklee College of Music graduate with diverse music industry experience. New York Blues Hall of Fame Inductee. Creative and versatile bassist, performer, producer, music director, composer, arranger, vocalist, and instructor. Acoustic, electric, fretted, fretless, four-string, and five-string basses. Solid professional experience in diverse musical genres from hip-hop to bebop. Ivan uses Fender, Moxy, Warrior, and Gretsch basses, Hartke amplification, DR strings, PRA Audio wireless, and Tech 21, Digitech and Line 6 signal processors.

RRHF Indicates Rock & Roll Hall of Fame Inductee.

MUSIC DIRECTION/CONDUCTING

- Eric Bazilian (Hooters)
- CHIC & Nile Rodgers **RRHF**
- The Chiffons
- The Chi-Lites
- John Ford Coley (England Dan)
- The Crystals
- *Emeril Live* (Food Network)
- Eye to Eye
- Gloria Gaynor
- Jazz/Funk Unit
- Garland Jeffreys
- Andy Kim
- The Limelites
- AJ Loria

- The Marvelettes
- Jo Dee Messina
- Sam Moore (Sam & Dave) **RRHF**, with special guests Sting **RRHF**, Elvis Costello **RRHF**, Wynonna Judd, Travis Tritt, Paul Rodgers, Lorrie Morgan, Jo Dee Messina, David Foster
- Lorrie Morgan
- Maxine Nightingale

- Ola Onabule
- Frankie Paris & Cold Sweat
- The Platters **RRHF**
- Martha Reeves & The Vandellas **RRHF**
- Merrilee Rush
- The Shirelles **RRHF**
- Terry Sylvester (Hollies) **RRHF**
- A Taste of Honey
- Howard Tate
- Charlie Thomas (Drifters) **RRHF**

- Timothea
- The Tokens

- Mary Wilson
  (Supremes)
  RRHF

ROCK & ROLL HALL OF FAMERS (50)

- Rosalind Ashford (Vandellas)
- Jeff "Skunk" Baxter (Doobie Bros.)
- Hal Blaine (Wrecking Crew)
- Jackson Browne
- King Solomon Burke
- Fred Cash (Impressions)
- Felix Cavaliere (Rascals)
- The Coasters
- Clarence Collins (Imperials)
- Gene Cornish (Rascals)
- Elvis Costello
- Joe D'Ambrosio (Comets)
- Bo Diddley
- Lamont Dozier (Holland-Dozier-Holland)
- The Edge (U2)
- Greg Errico (Family Stone)
- Ahmet Ertegun

- Harvey Fuqua (Moonglows)
- Sam Gooden (Impressions)
- Little Anthony Gourdine
- Doris Jackson (Shirelles)
- Terry "Buzzy" Johnson (Flamingos)
- Ben E. King (Drifters)
- The Limelites
- Darlene Love
- Barry Mann
- Jerry Martini (Family Stone)
- Bill Medley (Righteous Bros.)
- Jimmy Merchant (Teenagers)
- Sam Moore (Sam & Dave)
- The Orioles
- The Platters
- Noel Redding (Jimi Hendrix)
- Martha Reeves (Vandellas)

- Lois Reeves (Vandellas)
- Shirley Alston Reeves (Shirelles)
- Dick Richards (Comets)
- Nile Rodgers (CHIC)
- Carlos Santana
- Herman Santiago (Teenagers)
- Pete Seeger
- Percy Sledge
- Annette Beard Sterling (Vandellas)
- Sting
- Richard Street (Temptations)
- Terry Sylvester (Hollies)
- Charlie Thomas (Drifters)
- Mary Wilson (Supremes)
- Ernest Wright (Imperials)
- Vince Welnick (Grateful Dead)

PERFORMANCES

- Alive 'n' Kickin'
- Lee Andrews & The Hearts
- The Angels
- Ankara State Symphony Orchestra, Turkey
- Kenny Aronoff
- Teodross Avery
- Bacon Brothers
- Jeff "Skunk" Baxter **RRHF**
- Eric Bazilian (Hooters)
- Big Apple Circus
- Jack Black
- The Blue Note House Band
- Gary U.S. Bonds
- Bowzer (Sha Na Na)
- Bridgeport, CT Symphony Orchestra
- Jackson Browne **RRHF**
- Don Bryant
- Massimo Bubola (WEA/Italy)
- King Solomon Burke **RRHF**
- Billy Burnette
- Bursa State Symphony

- Orchestra, Turkey
- Freddy "Boom Boom" Cannon
- The Capris
- Felix Cavaliere (Rascals) **RRHF**
- Michael Cerveris
- Lester Chambers (Chambers Bros.)
- Larry Chance & The Earls
- Gene Chandler
- The Chantels
- The Chiffons
- The Chi-Lites
- Darren Criss
- Lou Christie
- The Coasters **RRHF**
- Marc Cohn
- John Ford Coley (England Dan)
- The Comets **RRHF**
- Harry Connick, Jr.
- Johnny Contardo (Sha Na Na)
- Johnny Copeland
- Elvis Costello **RRHF**
- Darren Criss
- The Crests with Tommy Mara

- The Crystals
- Bob D'Andrea (Knockouts)
- Dash Rip Rock
- Debbie Davies
- Spencer Davis
- Joey Dee (Starliters)
- Bo Diddley **RRHF**
- Taye Diggs
- Lamont Dozier **RRHF**
- The Drifters **RRHF**
- The Dubs
- The Edge **RRHF**
- Greg Errico (Family Stone) **RRHF**
- Eskisehir State Symphony Orchestra, Turkey
- Eye to Eye
- Fabian
- Jimmy Fallon
- Johnny Farina (Santo & Johnny)
- The Flamingos **RRHF**
- Eddie Floyd
- Frankie Ford
- David Foster

- Bernard Fowler (Rolling Stones)
- Micki Free
- Jay Jay French (Twisted Sister)
- Harvey Fuqua & The Moonglows **RRHF**
- Gloria Gaynor
- Sonny Geraci (Outsiders, Climax)
- Corey Glover (Living Colour)
- Jeff Golub
- Lena Hall
- The Mighty Hannibal
- The Happenings
- Barbara Harris (Toys)
- Eddie Holman
- Gov. Mike Huckabee
- Jennifer Hudson
- Humble Pie
- Brian Hyland
- Israel Symphony Orchestra, Rishon LeZion
- Istanbul State Symphony Orchestra, Turkey
- Izmir State Symphony

Orchestra, Turkey
- J. (Polydor)
- Jay & The Americans
- Jazz/Funk Unit
- Chuck Jackson
- Garland Jeffreys
- David Johansen
- Wynonna Judd
- Andy Kim
- Ben E. King **RRHF**
- Earl King
- Al Kooper
- Jane Krakowski
- Albert Lee
- Dickey Lee
- Phoebe Legere
- The Limelites
- Little Anthony & The Imperials **RRHF**
- Darlene Love **RRHF**
- Stephen Lynch
- Barry Mann **RRHF**
- Jerry Martini (Family Stone) **RRHF**
- King Nino & The Slave Girls
- Rick Margitza
- Alexander Markov

- Constantine Maroulis
- The Marvelettes
- Midtown Men
- Nicko McBrain (Iron Maiden)
- Mighty Sam McClain
- Jo Dee Messina
- John Cameron Mitchell
- Monterrey, Mexico Symphony Orchestra
- Rudy Ray Moore (Dolemite)
- Moses Mo
- Sam Moore **RRHF**
- Lorrie Morgan
- Bob Neuwirth
- Maxine Nightingale
- Willie Nile
- Peter Noone (Herman's Hermits)
- Ola Onabule
- The Orioles **RRHF**
- The Orlons
- Frankie Paris & Cold Sweat
- Freda Payne
- Ann Peebles

- Vito Picone (Elegants)
- The Platters **RRHF**
- Buster Poindexter
- Popa Chubby
- Billy Porter
- Finley Quaye (550/Epic)
- The Quotations
- Brenda Russell
- Radical Shiite God Squad
- Martha Reeves & The Vandellas **RRHF**
- Vernon Reid (Living Colour)
- Paul Rodgers (Bad Co./Free)
- Merrilee Rush
- Brenda Russell
- Bobby Rydell
- St. Louis Symphony Orchestra

- Shades of Blue
- The Shangri-Las
- Ryan Shaw
- The Shirelles **RRHF**
- Sister Sledge
- Muzz Skillings (Living Colour)
- The Skyliners
- Percy Sledge **RRHF**
- Dee Snider (Twisted Sister)
- The Solitaires
- David Somerville (Diamonds)
- Soul Survivors
- Sting **RRHF**
- Richard Street (Temptations '71-'95) **RRHF**
- Emil Stucchio & The Classics
- Terry Sylvester (Hollies) **RRHF**

- A Taste of Honey
- Howard Tate
- The Teenagers **RRHF**
- Carla Thomas
- Rufus Thomas
- Timothea
- The Tokens
- Travis Tritt
- The Uptown Horns
- Jimmy Vivino
- Joe Louis Walker
- Andre Williams
- Mary Wilson (Supremes) **RRHF**
- Peter Wolf
- World Peace Orchestra
- Bill Wyman's Rhythm Kings
- Dennis Yost (Classics IV)
- Zucchero

RECORDINGS
- Eric Bazilian (Hooters)
- BC Fox (Technotronic)
- *Berklee Studio Projects*
- Berman Brothers

- *Broadway's Carols for a Cure*, Vols. 13, 14, 15, 17, 19 & 21 with casts of *Rock of Ages, Phantom of the Opera, Lion*

King, Ain't Too Proud, Charlie & The Chocolate Factory, and *Amazing Grace*
- *Burnzy's Last Call* (soundtrack)

- Chocolate Genius
- Lisa J. Cornelio
- Cracked Ice
- Raphael Cruz - **Grammy Nominated**
- Dash Riprock
- Rhett Davies
- Don Dixon
- Julia Douglass
- Lauren Echo
- Eye to Eye
- Tom Gavornik
- Ruth Gerson
- Corey Glover
- Sophie B. Hawkins
- Rupert Holmes
- Intro (Atlantic)
- Jazz/Funk Unit
- Ben Jelen (Maverick Records)
- David Johansen
- Killer Joe & The Lido Soul Revue
- Lady Miss Kier (Deee-Lite)
- AJ Loria/King Nino
- Stephen Lynch
- Tom "Bones" Malone
- Justin Marcus
- Constantine Maroulis
- Mighty Sam McClain
- Mercy Beat
- Moses Mo (Mother's Finest)
- Sam Moore **RRHF**
- Frankie Paris & Cold Sweat
- Meredith Patterson
- Pipes & Drums of The NYPD Emerald Society
- Bernard "Pretty" Purdie
- Finley Quaye (550/Epic)
- Julianne Richards (Geffen)
- Santana **RRHF**
- Marlon Saunders
- Pete Seeger **RRHF - Grammy Nominated**
- Nicky Siano
- Cody Simpson
- 22 Brides
- Uncle Carl
- The Uptown Horns
- Ben Vereen
- Kathy Zimmer

PRODUCER

- Ivan "Funkboy" Bodley, *Look at That Cookie, Pigs Feet & Potted Meat, & iBOD*
- Raphael Cruz, *A Mano*
- Matthew Curran, *Star Spangled Banner/Voodoo Chile*
- Tom Gavornik, *Acceleration*
- Jazz/Funk Unit, *Jazz/Funk Unit*
- AJ Loria, *King Nino: Louisiana Lounge Lizard*
- Pack of Wolves, *Dress Full of Soul*
- Stephen Lynch, *A Little Bit Special*
- Sherryl Marshall, *Black Cohosh*
- Kathy Zimmer, *Spare Key, Dreamin'*

FILM & TV

- ABC, BBC, CBS, CNN, CNBC, MSNBC, NBC, NHK, PBS
- *America After Hours* (CNBC)
- *Break a Leg* (CNBC)
- *Burnzy's Last Call* (feature sdtk.)
- *Charlie Rose Show* (PBS)
- *City Arts* (WNET, NYC)
- *Cook'n Music Show,* France
- Cyprus TV
- *The Deli* (feature sdtk.)
- *Emeril Live* (Food Network)
- *Fox & Friends* (Fox News Channel)
- Fuji TV (Japan)
- *Howard Tate: Soul Man* (documentary)
- *Imus In The Morning* (MSNBC)
- Israeli TV
- Italian TV
- *Kennedy Center Mark Twain Prize* honoring George Carlin (2009), Tina Fey (2010), and Will Ferrell (2011) (PBS)
- *Late Late Show with Craig Ferguson* (CBS)
- *Late Night with Conan O'Brien* (NBC)
- *Law & Order* (Pierced Man)
- *Live! With Regis & Kelly* (ABC)
- *Love Walked In* (feature sdtk.)
- *Lowball* (actor, sdtk., feature film)
- *Northfork* (feature sdtk. w/Nick Nolte)
- *N.O.TV* (host/producer)
- *Only The Strong Survive* (DVD bonus features)
- *Restaurant* (actor, sdtk., feature film w/Adrien Brody)
- *Revenge of The Not Goods* (actor, sdtk., short feature)
- *Sam & Dave: The Original Soul Men* (2008 DVD)
- Singapore TV
- *Soul Britannia* (BBC)
- Swedish TV
- Swiss TV
- *TODAY Show* (NBC)
- *Today in New York* (WNBC)
- Turkish TV
- *UCP Telethon* (WWOR, NYC)

THEATRE/BROADWAY (12)

- *Ain't Too Proud*
- *Amazing Grace*
- *Escape to Margaritaville*
- *Fun Home*
- *Hedwig & The Angry Inch*
- *Kinky Boots*

- *Once on This Island*
- *The Prom*
- *Rock of Ages* (Broadway, Off-Broadway & Singapore)
- *Spider-Man, Turn Off the Dark*
- *SpongeBob SquarePants – The Musical*
- *Summer – The Donna Summer Musical*
- *Chix 6* (Off-Broadway)
- *For Colored Girls Who Have Considered Suicide/When the Rainbow Is Enuf* (Off-Broadway – Public Theater)
- *This Ain't No Disco* (Off-Broadway – Atlantic Theatre)

JINGLES/COMMERCIALS
- Del Taco
- Lancombe
- Listerine
- NBA
- Popeye's
- Texaco

JAM SESSIONS
- Joe Bataan
- Madeline Bell
- Bo Bice
- Hal Blaine **RRHF**
- Joe Bonamassa
- Chris Botti
- Maxine Brown
- Hiram Bullock
- Eric Burdon
- Will Calhoun (Living Colour)
- Dana Carvey
- Roseanne Cash
- Stanley Clarke
- Gene Cornish (Rascals) **RRHF**
- Cowboy Mouth
- Gavin DeGraw
- Rick Derringer
- Ahmet Ertegun **RRHF**
- Kathie Lee Gifford
- Roy Hargrove
- Nona Hendryx
- Peter Himmelman
- The Impressions **RRHF**
- Wyclef Jean
- Stanley Jordan
- Will Lee
- John Leventhal
- Johnny Maestro & The Brooklyn Bridge
- "Blue Lou" Marini
- Vince Martell (Vanilla Fudge)
- Sid McGuiness
- Bill Medley (Righteous Brothers) **RRHF**
- Raul Midon
- Buddy Miles
- Modern English
- The Naked Cowboy
- Cyril Neville (Neville Bros.)
- George Porter, Jr. (Meters)
- Noel Redding (Jimi Hendrix) **RRHF**
- The Roots
- Sam the Sham
- Valerie Simpson
- Southside Johnny

- Jordin Sparks
- BJ Thomas
- Pat Travers

- Chris Tucker
- Geno Washington

- Vince Welnick (Grateful Dead) **RRHF**

NOTABLE PERFORMANCES

- Ahmet Ertegun Tribute, Led Zeppelin Reunion Concert after-party, O2 Arena, London
- Avery Fisher Hall, Lincoln Center, NYC
- Big Apple Circus, Lincoln Center
- Carnegie Hall (featured soloist)
- Celebrate Brooklyn, NY, Prospect Park
- Creative Coalition, Obama Inaugural Ball
- Hatch Band Shell, Boston, MA
- Jazz Festivals, JVC, NYC; Nice, France; New Orleans Jazz & Heritage; Newport at Saratoga, NY; Pitea Dansar Och Ler Festival, Sweden; Pori, Finland; Tokyo, Japan
- *Kennedy Center Mark Twain Prize*, celebrating George Carlin (2009), Tina Fey (2010), and Will Ferrell (2011)

- Meadowlands Stadium, NY Jets halftime, 82,566 fans
- New Jersey Performing Arts Center
- New York Blues Hall of Fame Inductee
- PNC Bank/Garden State Arts Arena, NJ
- Rock & Roll Hall of Fame Museum
- *Rock of Ages* (Broadway, Off-Broadway & Singapore)
- Ryman Auditorium, historic Grand Ole Opry
- Summer Stage, Central Park, NYC
- Symphony Orchestras, Ankara, Turkey; Bridgeport, CT; Bursa, Turkey; Eskisihir, Turkey; Istanbul, Turkey; Izmir, Turkey; Monterrey, Mexico; Rishon LeZion, Israel; St. Louis, MO, Tupelo, MS
- Town Hall, NYC

COUNTRIES VISITED/PERFORMED IN (29)

- Aruba
- Austria
- Bermuda
- Brazil

- Canada
- Cyprus
- Dominican Republic

- England
- Finland
- France
- Germany

- Greece
- Honduras
- Hong Kong
- India
- Israel
- Italy

- Japan
- Mexico
- Peru
- St. Croix
- St. Maarten
- Scotland

- Singapore
- Spain
- Sweden
- Switzerland
- Turkey
- USA (44 States)

GIGS I _DIDN'T_ GET (and why)
See Chapter 27

EARLY JOBS

- Dishwasher at a Dude Ranch
- Envelope Stuffer
- Oldies Nightclub DJ
- College Radio DJ/Music Director
- Record Label Promotions College Rep/Intern

- Record Label Publicist
- Record Label Publicity Assistant
- Record Store Clerk
- Security Guard
- Temp Secretary

ACKNOWLEDGMENTS

I owe tremendous thanks to all of my family and friends who have assisted or encouraged me along the way. I probably owe equal thanks to those who tried to discourage me in my life and ended up motivating me more in the process. I am indebted to a long list of people that includes but is not limited to the following lovely individuals:

Dr. Terry Stoller for invaluable copyediting, Susan Stoller, Florence Stoller, Julie McBride, Andrew Bodley, Lesley Bodley, Isabelle Bodley, Rooker Bodley, Tucker Bodley, Bowman Bodley, Stanley Clarke, "Killer Joe" Ferraro, Jaime Babbitt, Dr. Karen Davis, Cassie J. Sneider, Dr. Jeffrey DeMouy, Neal Coomer, Riq Lazarus, Ed Huey, Fred Mollin, Sam and Joyce Moore, Shirley Alston Reeves – Original Lead Singer of The World-Famous Shirelles, Martha Reeves & The Vandellas, Dee Dee Kenniebrew & The Crystals, Jay Siegel & The Tokens, Jon "Bowzer" Bauman, Gloria Gaynor, The Uptown Horns, Aaron Neville, Don Dixon, Marti Jones, Charlie Giordano, Chris Frantz and Tina Weymouth, Mike Visceglia, Will Lee, Winston Roye, Cynthia Burstein Waldman, and Lee Popa.

There are far too many others to mention, including extended family, friends, and so many professional colleagues along the road. Hopefully y'all know who y'all are.

I want to send an extra special shout-out to my fallen comrades in the trenches. Some I knew well and loved dearly. Some I encountered only briefly. Others I came close to working with but never quite made it to the finish line. All of them touched my journey in some way. All of them have gone on home:

Don Bodley, Judy Stoller, Bob Stoller, King Solomon Burke, Percy Sledge, Ben E. King, Bo Diddley, Mary Wilson, Earl King, Frankie Ford, Bobby Vee, "Diamond David" Somerville, "Mighty Sam" McClain, Tyrone "Crusher" Green, Ronnie Evans, Mr. Bill Sims, Jr., Ben Delgadillo, Wally "Gator" Watson, Tommy Mara, Don Prager, Andrew Frawley, Eugene Record, Rufus Thomas, Harvey Fuqua, Howard Tate, Jerry Ragovoy, Timothea Beckerman,

Frankie Paris, Mic Gillette, Michael Tait, Johnny "Tasty" Parker, Eric Udel, Nick Cordero, Doris Jackson, Ahmet Ertegun, Noel Redding, Pete Seeger, Richard Street, Pepe Cardona, Vince Welnick, Lee Andrews, Rudy Ray Moore aka Dolemite, Cecil Taylor, The Mighty Hannibal, Hiram Bullock, Johnny Maestro, Buddy Miles, Ernie K-Doe, Allen Toussaint, Little Eva, Wilson Pickett, Jimmy Beaumont, Hubert Sumlin, Johnny Winter, Sharon Jones, Andre Williams, Dave Finley, Kenny Gorka, Kenneth Kelly, Redell Reeves, Derrill Bodley, Deora Bodley, Charlie Daniels, James Brown, Gregg Allman, Stevie Ray Vaughan.

INDEX

Rock & Roll Hall of Fame 1, 14, 32, 43, 65, 114, 142, 160, 243, 272, 273, 280
Rock of Ages 104, 276, 279, 280
Rodgers, Paul......... 22, 272, 276
Rolling Stones 22, 97, 116, 117, 275
Rush, Jennifer...................... 270
Sade 268
Sam & Dave 218, 246, 247, 272, 273, 278
Santana 151
Sha Na Na................ 32, 34, 274
Shaffer, Paul 202
Shea Stadium............... 117, 118
Shirelles, The 32, 114, 115, 116, 117, 135, 138, 139, 140, 163, 164, 193, 272, 273, 276, 282
Simmons, Gene .. 140, 149, 198, 200, 269
Sister Sledge........ 203, 204, 276
Sledge, Joni 203
Sledge, Percy 21, 117, 217, 221, 273, 276, 282
Sly & The Family Stone... 5, 11, 12, 28
Snider, Dee 198, 264, 276
Spector, Ronnie 153, 154
Spider-Man Turn Off the Dark 2, 279
Stewart, Rod 154

Sting 8, 243, 248, 249, 250, 259, 272, 273, 276
Sumlin, Hubert 153, 283
Tate, Howard...... 117, 272, 276, 278, 282
Taylor, Cecil................ 206, 283
Tex & The Horseheads.......... 41
This Is Spinal Tap.... 32, 91, 146
Thomas, Carla 117, 218, 276
Thomas, Rufus ... 117, 218, 266, 276, 282
Tokens, Jay Siegel & The .. 234, 273, 276, 282
Tokyo Jazz Festival..5, 7, 11, 13
Tony Awards........................... 3
Tower of Power................... 158
Travers, Pat 158, 280
Tulane........................... 39, 166
Uptown Horns 14, 15, 116, 117, 153, 162, 217, 218, 221, 247, 276, 277, 282
Vaughan, Stevie Ray... 269, 283
Village People 174, 264
Warrior Instruments ... 111, 112, 113, 272
Wavelength Magazine 47
Winter, Johnny 158, 283
Wolf, Peter 117, 276
WTUL 39, 40, 47, 159
Wyman, Bill 21, 22, 24, 276
Yankovic, "Weird Al"... 61, 198